Between
Past & Presence

A Spiritual View of the Moon & Sun

Eric Meyers, M.A.

Astrology Sight Publishing

Between Past & Presence
A Spiritual View of the Moon & Sun

Published by ASP:

Astrology Sight Publishing
4401 Redmond Dr.
#22–105
Longmont, CO 80503
(303) 684-8264

ISBN Number: 0-9747766-1-0

Printed in the United States of America

Cover Art by Evelyn Terranova
www.moonbeamgallery.com

Order online at:
www.AstrologySight.com
info@AstrologySight.com

Also by the author:
The Arrow's Ascent
Astrology & The Quest for Meaning

Dedicated to Josh Levin:
Torchbearer of the Unconscious

"If the Moon represents the "past," the Sun stands for the "present" – simply because it provides the power to exist as a living organism here and now."

Dane Rudhyar, *The Planetary and Lunar Nodes*

Contents

Milk of the Moon

Seasons of the Sun

Patterns of Light

Introduction

A child throws a temper tantrum because the teacher didn't call on him. For no apparent reason, a woman suspects her companion is cheating on her. A tired gentleman yells at a harmless telemarketer, and a couch potato slowly lifts another chip to her mouth, completely unaware she's eaten the entire bag.

There are countless stories of how we behave unconsciously. Stuck on autopilot, we act instinctually or strategize for survival. Tethered to our past, we continually bump into our edges, our lessons, and reflections of ourselves in disguise. All of us have overreacted on occasion, letting what was previously submerged surface. In a moment of awareness, we understand how distanced we've become from what is actually occurring in the present moment.

Habitual and instinctual behaviors originate in the well of the unconscious. Like sponges, we absorb all of life—the good, the bad and, yes, some of the ugly. This material is assimilated and influences who and what we are. A whole catalogue of instinct, expectations, reactions and roles await our activation. Like faithful script readers, we play the parts. It has been said, "You may be done with the past, but the past isn't done with you."

Sometimes we respond to life in fresh and creative ways. The option is always available, but the entrance fee is acknowledgement of the unconscious using awareness and intention. When we do stretch ourselves into novel response-abilities, a whole set of potentials is opened. In order to move forward, we must arise from darkness and begin to take conscious steps. This is part of the bargain of the human condition—bridging the past with the present.

From Darkness to Light

The Moon reveals the hidden places in the soul, the whispers of ancient memories. She compels the desire for peaceful connection—great Luna speaks to our tenderness. In all her beautiful vulnerability, she sustains the purity of the heart. Concealed within a reservoir of drama, we gradually understand her depth. Encircling the Earth, she's a traveling companion as we emerge from unconsciousness.

The blazing fireball in the sky and commanding center of the solar system, the Sun's massive power is apparent to all. The radiant energy provides the light of awareness, the heat of vitality. We are emboldened by its strength, continually learning to fulfill its resplendent promise as we grow toward spiritual illumination.

Much has been written about the Moon and Sun, but still they remain mysterious. In the following pages we will explore the luminaries in a spiritual context which assumes we attain soul growth by learning lessons in successive lifetimes. To evolve is to simply grow out of the limitations of our earlier versions. The language of reincarnation is used here, but readers uncomfortable with this philosophy may substitute a genealogical, developmental or other understanding.

This perspective focuses on *why* we have the charts we do. It suggests that there are meaningful reasons based on the history of the soul. Astrology is commonly seen as a descriptive tool like a personality inventory. A soul-focused astrology reaches further back to reveal past life influences within a thematic context, thereby providing a lens through which to view the current lifetime.

An "evolutionary" or soul growth paradigm is relatively new to astrological thinking in the Western world. Billions of people on the planet believe in, have some personal experience of, or are philosophically open to the idea of reincarnation. However, Western astrology has tended to focus on personality and psychology while negating the transpersonal because it's seen as speculative territory. We are now integrating astrology further into a more inclusive and accessible understanding of soul development.

The opening chapter, *Spiritual Photosynthesis*, will describe the framework of the luminaries being presented. The Moon concerns the past: instinctual, protective, and largely unconscious needs and strategies designed for survival. The soul brings this well of emotional material to each successive lifetime. Spiritual growth concerns the integration of unconscious patterns through sharpened awareness. The Sun involves a process of *becoming*, which is contingent upon healing limiting tendencies. Successful development gives greater access to the love reposing in the lunar well, but concealed by our emotional coping patterns and scars.

Milk of the Moon covers chapters 2 through 5. Chapters 2 and 3 address the Moon itself—with an emphasis on understanding how a soul *feels*. Luna will be explored in each of the 12 signs. Discussion of house placement and aspects will be included along with general interpretive guidelines. Chapters 4 and 5 will be a discussion of the Nodes of the Moon, which chronicle the central *lessons* regarding the soul's past brought into the present for attention. The Lunar Nodes are often considered as being apart from the Moon itself. These chapters will bring the soul's innate feeling (Moon) into closer alignment with the central work or lessons (Lunar Nodes) being managed.

Chapters 6 through 8 comprise *Seasons of the Sun*. Chapters 6 and 7 discuss the Sun in a natal chart as the primary energy a soul intends to develop and radiate now. The Sun is a conscious, integrative principle that provides nurturing light and heat to the ancient spiritual history. The solar function is readily accessible, but mastery of its promise is a lifelong proposition. Here, we'll address the main variables regarding the Sun: sign, house, aspects. The connection between the Sun and spiritual growth will be further addressed in Chapter 8. The link between personal awareness (Sun) and the greater embrace of Spirit will be featured, as well as how the Sun's awareness teams with the Moon to develop consciousness.

The final 3 chapters fall under the heading *Patterns of Light* and will further unite the luminaries. These chapters address the dynamic interplay of the past (Moon) weaving around the energy of the present (Sun). Chapter 9 describes the lunar cycle, and Chapter 10 addresses eclipses. Chapter 11 brings all the information presented together in the analysis of several celebrity charts. Applying this method of chart analysis brings not only greater clarity to our interpretations, but also frames the chart in terms of spiritual growth.

Chapter 1
Spiritual Photosynthesis

A plant begins as seed potential in the soil. Like the Moon, it is hidden and vulnerable. As water nurtures its growth, a stem gradually surfaces and begins to branch out in several directions. The organism is sustained by the light and heat of the Sun. Flowers blossom and the seed grows into its fullness.

There is a developmental progression—from what the plant was, to what it is becoming. A plant emerges into the world, growing upward and outward, increasing in color and complexity. Water is the primary ingredient for what the plant was in its seed state (yin: receptive, inward), and this liquid nourishment is necessary throughout its life. The plant becomes rooted and strong with an underground system reaching up to deliver nourishment throughout the organism.

The Sun strengthens what a plant is becoming as it unfolds (yang: active, outward). Plants will not thrive where it is dark and cold. The Sun's light and heat are necessary for growth and expansion. Photosynthesis is the process that converts the energy in sunlight into chemical forms of energy that can be used by biological systems.

This biological process of photosynthesis has spiritual correlates. The spiritual parallel to light is awareness. When we "shed some light" on an issue, we become alert and responsive to it. People who display a healthy sense of awareness are considered bright. We all know the famous depiction of the light bulb over the head that signifies the "a ha" moment. Spiritual practitioners seek en**light**enment—to maximize awareness.

The Sun also radiates heat, which correlates to vitality—being alive, having presence. Humans flourish at around 98.6 degrees Fahrenheit. Becoming radiant is life affirming and engaging. We're "on fire" when we enthusiastically respond to those things in life that "turn us on" such as a hobby or passion.

In our soul development, we are performing *spiritual* photosynthesis. The biological parallels are light and heat, but the goal is not to become brighter and warmer in a literal sense. Rather, the blossoming of soul potential is catalyzed when we integrate awareness (light) and vitality (heat). This is done by being awake and present to life.

The Moon indicates what we essentially are in the seed state, while the Sun indicates the potential flowering. This doesn't mean that the Moon is "bad" while the Sun is "good"—in fact, the Moon holds our beauty while the Sun is, at least initially, merely a good intention. Better words would be "old" and "new." Just like plants continually need water, we do not leave the Moon behind. Rather, we assist it in *maturing*, for Moon seeds sprout into Sun flowers.

It is our Moons that enable us to survive in what often seems a hostile and unwelcoming world. However, survival often means contraction. We are learning to release the restrictive qualities of the Moon and expand. Picture the Moon as a gemstone with soot on it. The Sun is like a laser that can blast this soot away with its piercing light and heat. After issues are worked through and resolved, the Moon is better able to connect with others more openly. As we emerge from unconsciousness, we explore new frontiers of potential while also illuminating the hidden gifts of the heart. The Moon and Sun forge an alliance and complement each other—they are, in fact, partners.

Psychological & Spiritual Levels to the Luminaries

At the psychological level, the Sun and Moon are associated with gender—the Sun is a "masculine" function while the Moon is more classically "feminine". Many astrologers look at the Sun and Moon to get information about the chart owner's father and mother. Men are encouraged to get in touch with the softer side of the Moon, while women are directed to the take-charge and get-noticed qualities of the Sun.

The great achievement of 20th century astrology is a more structured and fruitful merging with psychology. This integration has increased our understanding of the planets at the psychological level, but it has at the same time minimized spiritual possibilities that are also relevant. The theoretical position of this work is not to suggest that we need to grow out of our primary feminine function (Moon) in order to be more masculine (Sun). Rather, there are spiritual dimensions to the luminaries that are completely gender neutral. It is possible to see the overarching movement from seed (Moon) to flower (Sun) while also noticing that we have yin (feminine) and yang (masculine) functions that respectively contract energy in or propel it out. In the busyness of everyday life, we are more attuned to the psychological level. With a broader view, we can see the spiritual unfolding.

At the spiritual level, the Moon is what a soul feels like: how the soul journey has been absorbed, the emotional memory bank, and what unconscious tendencies have been cultivated to survive. We are receptive to life—this is *lunar*, not exclusively feminine. We are learning to engage more radiantly in life by increasing our vitality and awareness. This is *solar*, not merely masculine.

Seen through a spiritual lens, the luminaries are connected to heart (Moon) and soul intention (Sun). The heart is personal and embodied. The soul intention is to creatively use the limitless potentials of energy which connect us with our spiritual source.

Everything in the universe is energy. Let's consider that this dynamic state of transformative energy relates to the astrological element of fire. So, all of the various pieces of energy in our world are like individual flames in a larger fire. Indeed, it's common to compare one's essence or soul to fire. Souls are independent, but connected to Spirit—our personal energy (Sun, fire) is simultaneously autonomous but also a part of the universe.

Through the *development* of awareness and the ability to be present, our solar function consciously realizes Spirit. The strength and luminosity of the Sun may intensify. Imagine the brightness of a bulb increasing in wattage: 60, 100, 1000, all the way to 10,000 and beyond. Similarly, the development of the Sun operates in this manner. We are becoming increasingly more aligned with the spiritual energy that envelops us. The solar function is not the soul, but *has access to soul realization* by turning up the wattage of awareness and presence—truly embracing life.

Since the Sun is energetic potential and the Moon is physical, the luminaries must work together. We are continually assimilating spiritual essence (photosynthesis) into the depths of the self. Integrating Sun into Moon furthers soul growth as well as potentially connecting us with Spirit.

So here we are at the crossroads of self and Spirit, autonomy and universality, unconsciousness and awareness, dimness and vitality, heart and soul, past and presence. We are here to resolve (Moon) and evolve (Sun).

Resolution and Evolution

The Moon anchors us in our emotional well of experience. Absorbing life and building an inner fortress, the Moon endures and protects its preservation. In the best of all possible worlds, the lunar unconscious is filled with love and emotional reserves of strength and security. A more realistic appraisal is that most, if not all, of us are here to grow out of emotional limitations and restrictive coping patterns.

The reason why we can universalize this process is that we have all incarnated to evolve spiritually. Something in us needs greater resolution. Since the Moon concerns the past, and no one's past is perfect, it holds on to remnants of our spiritual history that promoted survival, but at the cost of contraction. Consider that the emotional Moon (past) orbits around the Earth (sphere of incarnation) and is our closest companion. All of us have "enrolled" in this emotional school to find greater resolution

14

in some way. Just as children grow into adults, we are similarly maturing.

Contraction and expansion, regression and advancement, the luminaries are a pairing of energetic motion that some would call negative and positive. These terms are not value judgments, but indicate the direction of movement. As seen in the metaphor of seeds blossoming into flowers, the negative pull of the Moon inhibits positive expansion when it becomes too contracted. Therefore, it is essential that the Moon learn to relax its regressive pull for growth to advance.

Those who refuse to release restrictive emotional patterns are living in the past. The reasons for such coping measures may no longer be relevant in the present lifetime—what's done is done. The best method for performing an emotional release is to allow protected feelings to be actually experienced—truly connecting with our vulnerability. Directing *energy* in an inward *motion* elicits *emotion*.

The Sun is our energy. As the agent of awareness and presence, it illuminates the contents of the unconscious, our authentic foundation of being. When activated, emotional imprints can be brought to the present through conscious acknowledgment. We can grant their usefulness and their limitations. Exposing painful feeling may also trigger the familiar self-protective measures again. Either way, the past is brought into the present. We can either renew or break through our patterns.

In contrast to the regressive pull of the Moon, the Sun's nature is expansive and positive. When resolution gathers momentum, new possibilities for soul evolution are accessed. The Sun is a statement of what is possible if we are in the present. It is a lifelong proposition to actualize this focal soul intention. An aware Sun shines brightly and becomes one's center. This is in stark contrast to the condition at birth, when we incarnate (Earth) and our past (Moon) orbits around us.

The Message of Polarities

The Moon rules Cancer, and Saturn rules the opposite sign Capricorn. The Sun holds rulership of Leo, while Uranus rules Aquarius. The association of the Moon with the past and the Sun with the present can be seen through these astrological polarities.

The relationship between Cancer and Capricorn is a pairing that concerns *emotional maturation*. More than the other planets, the Moon and Saturn concern the past and its resolution. Saturn is known as the "lord of karma," of working through the consequences of prior action. It is associated with tradition, preservation and what is old. By respecting Saturn, we become mature and wise. The Moon is commonly associated with unconscious emotional patterns that are a result of childhood conditioning. By balancing instinctual defenses and emotional coping strategies (Moon, Cancer) with a disciplined program of growth and mastery (Saturn, Capricorn), we can grow out of the restrictive and protective lunar function into a greater sense of solidity and integrity.

In contrast, the Sun and Uranus form a dyad that involves the process of *self-realization*—the development of one's unique talents and an alignment with one's individuality. Just as children grow into more evolved versions of themselves as they age, similarly we learn to direct the life force through greater awareness. We are not born radiating the clarity of our Sun signs; rather there is a process of becoming. Uranus (Aquarius) is the energy of bringing in the future, and the polarity with the Sun (Leo) illustrates how we are continually being drawn into greater energetic embodiment of spiritual progress.

Another quality of this Sun/Uranus dynamic is the bridging of the personal (Sun) and the transpersonal (Uranus). By developing both awareness and the ability to be fully present in life (Sun), we may connect to our authentic spiritual promise (Uranus), sometimes called the "higher self." We become divine instruments furthering evolution, embodying the Uranian impetus for creative change that connects to a larger design.

Both the Sun and Uranus involve awakening. Ideally, the solar function becomes less about the ego as we learn to identify more with the workings of Spirit's intelligence and ally with it. The Sun can serve an active role in collective evolution (Uranus). Sign rulership polarities reveal how the Moon concerns the past and the Sun is about claiming present and future potentials.

Celestial Interplay

We are stationed here on Earth. When we look at an astrology chart, we do not see the Earth indicated because everything is oriented from the perspective on this planet. The Ascendant is where the Sun rises as viewed from a particular vantage point. Just as life is experienced by a person at some relative position on the planet, all astrological events impact us (stationed on the Earth) from this point in the solar system. The Earth represents the sphere of incarnation, our embodied entrance into the life within this incredible solar system.

The Moon orbits around the Earth, symbolizing how the past is continually surrounding us and influencing our instinctual behaviors. The Sun sits at the center of the system, signifying its importance. The Earth (incarnation) revolves around the present reality (Sun) and is bathed in light (awareness) and heat (vitality) from the radiant fire-sphere. The Earth pulls the Moon (past) along as it learns lessons applicable to the present incarnation. The Sun is far grander than the Moon in scope and power within this system—and we too are *becoming* the greater.

The Moon has a secure position in the solar system because of the Sun. The Moon (autonomous consciousness rooted to the physical body) needs the Sun, but the Sun (spiritual essence) doesn't need the Moon. The light of awareness and universal vitality in the universe does not need individual consciousness for it to exist, but individuals need to have a vessel of body and consciousness to contain or accommodate spiritual essence.

From our perspective on Earth, the Moon is always seen in one of its changing phases. The Moon reflects, rather than gives, light so we only understand and perceive it in relation to its solar partner. Our view of the past continually changes as we grow in the present. In a complete lunar cycle, the Moon (embodied unconsciousness) ventures out into life before returning back to the Sun. This is analogous to how individuals enter the world to attain experience before returning to the spiritual source. The end of incarnated life is mirrored in the waning crescent lunar phase—when embodiment releases and consciousness merges with the unified spiritual essence. The amount of awareness and vitality achieved and integrated during the lifetime is consolidated and carried forth into future incarnations.

The Lunar Nodes indicate where the Moon (past) intersects with the Earth's orbit (incarnation) as it revolves around the Sun (present reality). The South Node is the point where the Moon travels from above to below the Earth's ecliptic, and the North Node illustrates the intersection from below to above. Here's a reflection of the theme of reaching down (South), as in exhuming from the past, to rising up (North) into new and creative uses.

An analogy may be helpful to conceptualize the Nodes. Picture a jogger who circles through a neighborhood. The local commuter bus also has a route through the same town. At a bus station the jogger's route and the bus route intersect. Two separate paths come together at a single point—jogger and bus meet at the station.

The Nodes are sites of intersection like the bus station. The jogger is like the Moon, traveling about with his own needs. The bus is like the Earth, the vehicle that hosts incarnation. The bus route symbolizes the revolving path around the Sun, called the ecliptic. The bus is headed for a tour around the entire country, to experience a wider reality. The familiar bus stop where a jogger initially boards is analogous to the South Node, and its polar opposite, the North Node, is on the map as a destination to get to.

There are many different bus stops throughout the country. Indeed, the Nodes can be at any of the 360 degrees of the zodiac. The enormous array of possibilities is narrowed down to a specific route in a natal chart. The South Node is extremely relevant as it's located at the intersection between past and present soul intentions. It conveys the nature of the transfer, the *conditions* that bring the soul into this life.

Since the Moon holds the memories of countless stories, it would be impossible to have a strategic plan to resolve its entire voluminous scope in any one lifetime. The Nodes *of the Moon* tells us what is intersecting from the lunar unconscious to the present incarnation for greater resolution and integration. Like the bus stop, they portray a particular scene. Some have a wild ambiance and others have a more proper décor. Some bus stops are the meeting places for drug deals and others sit quaintly beside a rural garden.

The South Node portrays the familiar scene when a soul boards the bus, which includes both strengths and challenges. The evolutionary level a soul has attained cannot be deduced from the chart—therefore, it's prudent to view the South Node as holding great resources for the soul, but also holding repetitive responses that may contribute to stagnation. The South Node illustrates the psychological factors at play and situational determinants that helped shape the lunar unconscious. It is useful to interpret them as thematic stories providing a detailed account of what actually went on in the past. Specific past life details will always remain elusive—astrology functions in a far more general way. The North Node points to what is unfamiliar—to complement what is already established and known by the soul with new attributes and suggested areas of exploration.

The Nodes are connected into the entire astrology chart. They occupy signs, which provide information about the character of the bus stops. They are located in houses, each with its own meaning. The Nodes are points that may make aspects to planets anywhere in the chart. Planets are the energy in the system and activate the themes that the Nodes convey—those that touch the Nodal axis by aspect and rulership serve as catalysts to the Nodal storyline.

Let's say that at a particular bus stop sits a grizzly bear or maybe a golden retriever—those energies are brought to the story. Pluto is like the bear and we may think of Venus as the golden retriever. All planets have a specific nature to their energy, and when making strong aspects to the Nodal axis, they play integral roles in conveying the kind of work or lessons that the unconscious is resolving. We mustn't forget the jogger. All of the Nodal scenery relates back to the Moon, which is discovering how to resolve its lessons and move into the present. Joggers interested in growing want to settle the conditions at the bus stop and see more of the country.

The themes the Nodes communicate are incredibly valuable and have been used effectively by many astrologers. The proof of Nodal efficacy is verified by clients who report strong resonance with these themes. In fact, it is usually the most emotional part of an evolutionary (soul growth) astrology consultation. This is consistent with the Nodes as they relate to the Moon itself, the feeling component within the body-mind. When something hits home and touches us deeply, we tread upon sensitive ground and find rich territory for spiritual progress.

The Nodes and the Luminaries

The essential difference between the Lunar Nodes and the Moon itself is that the Nodes indicate lessons—how a soul habitually approaches the world and what forces have caused crisis and challenge. They also illustrate past strengths and successes. The Nodes are points, and they point to what we're working on, and what is familiar. The Moon is embodied, the eternal heart maturing in the spiritual journey.

Every soul is steeped in drama (Nodal story) and has submerged whatever emotions are connected with that drama into the unconscious (Moon). Bringing greater awareness and vitality (Sun) into the unconscious (Moon) passes through the gateway of the Nodes—which are positioned at the intersection between past and present (as noted, this is symbolically replicated by the spatial relations of the Earth, Sun and Moon).

If spiritual growth proceeds optimally, a person becomes increasingly more aware (Sun) of the lessons (Nodes) and how they have impacted the emotional body (Moon). By taking conscious steps, the habitual and reflexive behaviors (Moon) gradually lose their grip and open to newer ways of operating. The gifts within the South Node are acknowledged and its challenges are respected. The North Node is championed and ardently worked upon and a soul reaches a new state of potential. The Sun increases in luminosity, flowering into a present and aware disposition that is healthy, strong and clear.

If a path of growth is not pursued, the story changes quite a bit. Unbeknownst to the person, behavior remains motivated by the unconscious (Moon) stemming from ancient patterns and/or struggles. There is little awareness or creativity in the personality (Sun). Rather, the lunar autopilot is frantically trying to get its needs met, while the less evolved facets of the Sun will unfortunately manifest. Meanwhile, the events of the biographical life will thematically present the lessons depicted by the Nodes. The soul in question will retreat to familiar and instinctual ways of handling the situation(s), thereby replicating or renewing the crisis in the present life. This strategy will not succeed and advancement toward the North Node will not gather momentum.

Awareness, being present and acting with clarity can reverse a downward spiral at any point in the soul's journey. It is never too late to grow. The possibility of spiritual advancement is offered in every lifetime—indeed, in every moment.

Milk of the Moon

Chapter 2
Moon Seeds: Inheriting the Heart

In the psychological view of astrology, ideas of reincarnation are generally not part of the scope. The prevailing thought is to address what we know for sure. With the insistence on pragmatics, the baby is thrown out with the bath water. Let's take a closer look at the baby, for we are not blank slates at birth. When a child is born, she has an innate temperament—a specific orientation to her body and its needs.

Behavior at birth is classically lunar with its unconsciousness, urgency of needs and easily provoked emotional displays. As is commonly stated in astrological literature, the Moon relates to the past, but a newborn infant doesn't have a past. When does the Moon *start*? How should we account for a particular lunar profile at the moment of birth, when no experience in the present life has been gained?

The psychological paradigm would ascribe hereditary factors to explain variations in disposition witnessed in infants. Additionally, there is a biological connection to the mother in the womb, and a baby is a product of its environment. So, the Moon is strongly linked to the mother in Western astrology. From this perspective, the Moon would start upon conception and would develop in utero. Thus, the regressive and infantile components of the Moon are traced back before birth. When a baby is born, the Moon gradually develops as experience is absorbed.

It is commonly agreed that the Moon concerns contraction, a regressive pull to the past. Therefore, at the moment of birth, a child's behavior is either influenced solely by genetics and the gestation period, or by these factors as well as influences from past lives. Is it possible there is a spiritual dimension that impacts more tangible levels of reality? Since the vast majority of all religious and spiritual systems proclaim there are transcendent levels of consciousness, this is certainly a possibility. The concept of a soul is a widespread and universal concept.

The spiritual view presented here releases the imprinting of the Moon from the confines of the womb and hereditary factors, and allows it to have a timeless reach. When does the Moon *start*? It's been in a process of evolving indefinitely. The Moon absorbs and consolidates experience into the emotional unconscious. This reservoir of experience is brought to successive lifetimes as a foundation to build upon, but also to mend and resolve any leftover emotional work that needs attendance.

The Moon's feeling nature endures and becomes unconscious just like the memories of youth. In childhood we're like saplings, replicating the drama of our spiritual legacies in the conditions of our early home life. In a sense, we play out the basic emotional state of the soul. Past life and childhood influences are quite strong, but we can mature from our habitual patterns and learn to tap the Moon's enormous resources.

The lunar function is geared for survival and the meeting of our most primal needs including safety, touch and nurturance. Traditionally associated with the urges of the infant, the Moon is impulsive and unrefined. Lunar behavior is primitive and tenacious, indicating the ways in which we have been nurtured, what is experienced as nurturing, and what is needed to feel secure.

Emotions are visceral, connected to bodily processes. Therefore, the historical emotional journey of the soul becomes contained throughout the cellular memory in the body. The posture, gait, constitution and overall heath of the body result from the experiences we encounter and how those experiences become assimilated. The Moon is receptive—a repository of all the anger, joy, fear, love and sadness we have accumulated. By examining the lunar profile described in a chart, we get a sense of the fundamental disposition of the soul.

We are all here to achieve some form of emotional healing. Even the most "healthy" among us have certainly experienced anguish and hurt—and there is nothing shameful about it. We can become intentionally conscious of it, or it will come to our attention through the consequences of unconscious behavior.

Interpreting the Moon

The prime variable in understanding a natal chart is the level of consciousness (or evolutionary/spiritual condition) that the chart owner has attained in the soul's journey. Consciousness brings the potential witnessed on the 2-dimensional chart into the vibrancy of life. This presents quite a dilemma because we cannot determine how conscious or evolved a soul is by glancing at the paper. We are also limited by a tendency to view others through our own perceptual filters and from our own level of spiritual growth. In short, we are subject to personal bias.

Although this is a formidable challenge, we may still usefully interpret a chart by adopting a few principles. 1) The recognition that no one is perfect. All of us can become more conscious. 2) Most of us fall somewhere in the middle on a spectrum of spiritual development. There are few who arrive with outstanding wisdom, and few who behave completely without awareness and accountability. The vast majority of souls have made some progress, but still, there is significant work. 3) Due to the reality that there is unfinished work to address, we may acknowledge both strengths and challenges, with an eye toward possible improvement. It is not harsh or critical to discuss the average spiritual condition as unfinished—in fact, it would be irresponsible to do otherwise.

The Moon in particular concerns unconsciousness. It is appropriate to examine the lunar profile with the knowledge that every soul incarnates to grow out of the habitual tendencies that served survival in the past, to be strong and potent in the present.

25

Therefore, it is prudent to view the Moon in accordance with its defensive and protective inclinations and discuss how it sees to its preservation. The first piece to consider is the Moon sign. We approach this by addressing how the style and processes of a sign assisted the soul during its most vulnerable stages.

The Moon through the Signs

The following paragraphs about Moon signs are intentionally general. They aim to give a flavor of each of the styles and processes. The best way to understand the Moon is to *feel* it—and these paragraphs are written with that goal in mind.

Following each description of the Moon in a sign will be a celebrity chart example that illustrates how a Moon sign manifests in real people, including the central aspects the Moon makes with other planets. Following sections will address other interpretive variables more thoroughly, but we will begin to link the Moon into the chart through the examples given.

Aries Moon

The sign of the Ram is active, fiery, aligned with the power of will and eager to meet life. The spectrum of the Aries archetype goes from courage, exercise of the will, leadership qualities and power, on the one hand, to aggression and violence, anti-social behaviors, impulsivity and abrasiveness on the other. This cardinal fire sign is concerned with how the self establishes its own sense of autonomy and efficacy.

How does an Aries Moon feel? It is reasonable to presume that the survival instincts of the Moon have been activated. In the spiritual history, this Moon has likely met conflict, and the temperament is more ready to fight than in any other placement. The soul has absorbed much intensity and, as a result, it has adopted a fierce, battle-ready disposition.

An Aries Moon may be competitive, uncompromisingly selfish, burning with anger or emotionally frustrated. It may also be passionately motivated to pursue its needs, driven to correct a perceived injustice or willing to fight to protect its kin. The ferocity of the mother grizzly bear safeguarding her cubs is an illustration of the strength of this Moon placement.

There is some incompatibility between planet and sign here. The Moon is perhaps the softest and most fragile of the planets, while Aries is the most forceful and aggressive of the signs. It's almost like taking a kitten and throwing her into a pack of rabid hyenas—the guard is most certainly up. When some kind of emotional threat is perceived, the tension between planet (Moon) and sign (Aries) becomes exaggerated. Reacting unconsciously, an Aries Moon may behave in the "heat of the moment" and make newspaper headlines. It is nearly impossible to defeat or placate this Moon when it becomes emotionally charged and loses control.

During more routine moments, the Aries Moon temperament may show its hardy engagement with life—a disposition tending toward extraversion and openness. When not emotionally shaken, these people are naturally lively with infectious energy. The martial arts or athletics or the achievement of set goals are some ways this energy is best channeled.

These people benefit from some form of emotional management technique. In order to reach a greater sense of equilibrium, Aries Moons are learning to transform the intensity into more judicious uses. Achieving a level of peace and gracefulness in the disposition complements the fiery moods, and connecting harmoniously with others becomes more likely.

The movie *Braveheart* illustrates the psychic drama of this strong placement. Brave (Aries) heart (Moon) is the warrior, and the essence of his passion is succinctly expressed in his words, "every man dies, but not every man *really* lives." Much of the healing method here requires decisive action in order to reach a point of inner strength. By so doing, the Aries Moon calms the fire and reaches the lunar goal of peaceful self-love.

Angelina Jolie

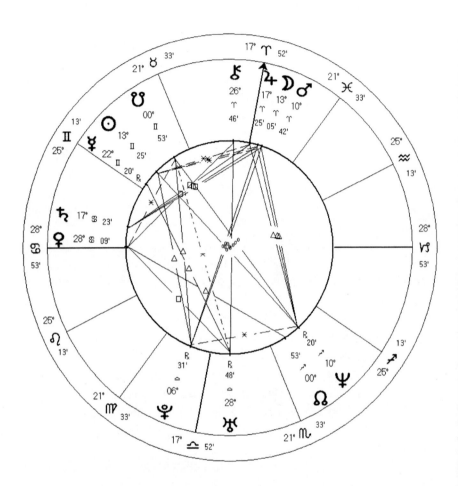

Actress Angelina Jolie may be the epitome of an Aries Moon. Underneath her Hollywood glamour is a fierce warrior. She simmers with intensity, almost begging others to test her. Jolie has starred in several action films and is famous for performing many of her own stunts. Her reputation is of a femme fatale, the beautiful but dangerous vixen.

Her biography details a series of conflicts. From her public feuding with her father (Jon Voigt), through her turbulent marriage with Billy Bob Thornton, to her relationship with a barely divorced Brad Pitt, Jolie seems to revel in excessive displays of emotional passion. We can feel in her a palpable need for excitement, battle and power.

Her Aries Moon is conjunct Mars, which is unrestrained in its home sign. This brings an even more pronounced forcefulness and channels her need for power in an aggressive or sexual direction. She is clearly someone who gets what she wants! The Moon is also conjunct Jupiter in Aries further amplifying her risk-taking and adventuresome demeanor. There is an exaggerated need to align action (Aries) with a sense of direction (Jupiter). Indeed, Jolie is a spirited crusader for the causes she believes in.

Her Moon resides in the 9th House, the realm of distances, travel and philosophy. Jolie has chosen to nurture (Moon) children from foreign nations (9th). She is clearly motivated by a sense of purpose and conviction, and is not deterred by any potential complications such a pursuit risks. In fact, it seems like she *needs* to take charge with this issue and serve as an example for others. Her Moon is also trine Neptune in Sagittarius in the 5th House—a consistent statement about idealism (Neptune) regarding foreign (Sagittarius) children (5th).

We may speculate that part of her karmic difficulty (Saturn) involves loss (12th) around nurturing issues (Cancer). This Saturn is square her Moon, bringing urgency to the need to realize a more solid and healthy parent/child bond. This may be applied, and played out, in both directions for Angelina—as a child and as a parent.

Her Moon is also opposed Pluto, bringing even greater psychological power and determination to her spirited demeanor. This further emphasizes the need to make an impact on others and to potentially enter crisis situations. The lesson for her is to finally arrive at peace (Pluto in Libra) within her emotional interactions.

The Sun is sextile the Moon. It sits in the 11th House in Gemini—stating the soul's intention to communicate (Gemini) her spirited needs (Moon) to the world (11th) in the present life.

She is to use her driven (Mars) and purposeful nature (Jupiter) to educate (Gemini) and build bridges among humanity (11th).

Taurus Moon

Taurus the Bull is peaceful, secure, natural and sensuous. It may also become headstrong, inert, gluttonous, over-concerned with safety and simple-minded. The Moon is considered well-placed (traditionally "exalted") in Taurus, as the serenity of the sign provides comfort and security, exactly what the Moon longs for.

The Moon generally feels content in the fixed earth sign of Taurus. Although this temperament may be preferred, there are also some drawbacks. Contentment often leads to indolence—the Moon's strategy here is not to risk or venture away from sources of stability. This aversion to risk limits progress, so the Taurus Moon may sometimes indicate spiritual stagnation.

Another possibility within the soul history could be an over-reliance on the self for nurturance. This may lead to disconnecting with others, sabotaging the attachments the Moon craves. A Taurus Moon may also indicate an over-inflated need to attain security through money, "comfort" foods, possessions and the resources of the material world. Underneath the fortification of accumulated resources is a soul that may be avoiding the root issues that compel the materialist tendencies.

Indeed, when this Moon feels its sensitivity, the tendency is to placate and soothe. In contrast, when the Taurus Moon feels threatened, the more protective side of its animal nature emerges. The Bull likes to be left alone, but when provoked, it is a most worthy adversary. Armed with horns and an ample frame, Taurus simply bruises and squashes its foe—then quietly returns to his patch of grass. Those with this Moon placement are not looking to start conflict, but are not looking to be messed with either.

Taurus likes to take it easy, but getting in touch with psychological complexity and intensity may be rich soil for new ways to connect. Taurus benefits by learning to risk more by revealing itself to others honestly and directly. This helps to correct the natural inclination towards indolence.

Much of the work for a Taurus Moon is to release its clinging to safety, its tendency for fortification and its exaggerated self-reliance. Learning to be more active and enthusiastic, to become stimulated by new experiences, propels the soul from its earthy fortress. Undoubtedly, the soul yearns for something exciting.

Bob Dylan

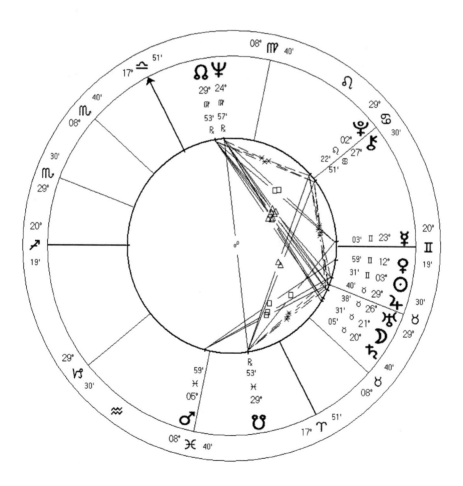

31

Bob Dylan's Taurus Moon seeks peacefulness, an earthy engagement with the goodness of life (5th House). There is simplicity, naturalness and ease to his basic temperament. His attraction to folk music fits nicely since the genre often extols the virtues of living off the land and being connected to the richness it promises.

Dylan (and folk music in general) channels the need for attaining earthy harmony through raising social conscience. He has the Moon conjunct Saturn, Uranus and Jupiter—planets involved in sociology, institutional structures and their changes. Dylan has a need (Moon) to have stability (Saturn) and peace (Taurus). Though this combination typically speaks of emotional heaviness, even to the point of fear, the other planets involved modify his yearnings toward societal change.

Moon conjunct Uranus indicates a deep-seated need to upset the status quo, to revolutionize his own emotional nature and that of the world he inhabits. There is likely some degree of shock or surprise in his spiritual biography. This awakens the need to be a catalyst for what he perceives as necessary changes in the world.

Jupiter's connection to the stellium directs his need for change into workable (Taurus) philosophical (Jupiter) frameworks. Having all of these planets in an earth sign gives the impetus to sculpt a body of work geared toward a purpose. Moon conjunct Jupiter is the mark of the optimist—though Dylan is balanced with realism (Saturn) about his desires.

The emotional yearning for collective change is yet even more emphasized by the trine from the Moon to Neptune. Neptune in the 9th House (spiritual direction, meaning) brings to mind the soul of the visionary. Neptune's residence in Virgo signals a practical vision.

The Sun appears in early Gemini, kind of jumping on the interconnected railroad cars of the lunar stellium. The lunar resources he has are best channeled toward developing (6th House) his voice (Gemini)—to be the storyteller, with a large body of work.

Interestingly, both Dylan and Jolie have a Gemini Sun. We notice a similar busyness and even brilliance in their personalities, but Dylan is clearly more settled, folksy and secure in himself. Jolie feels like a warrior (Aries), while Dylan has the feel of contentment (Taurus).

Gemini Moon

The range of the mutable air sign Gemini goes from the articulate, witty, intelligent and flexible-minded student of life to the scattered, rushed, emotionally immature and deflective young upstart. The Moon is soft, vulnerable and tender. Putting it in this sign conjures up a striking image. Imagine a beating heart in all of its pulpy glory being dissected by a bunch of scientists and mathematicians. Sure, we'll learn about the valve operations and pulse rates, but are we in *touch* with it?

There is a major disparity between the Moon's *feeling* and Gemini's *thinking*. Why would a soul be in such a situation? There are several reasons to consider. First, this may be a protective function—to rationalize emotions to avoid feeling them. Another possibility is that the soul itself is youthful and is in the process of attaining more experience. Perhaps it hasn't been through enough to have the heaviness that normally is part of the lunar experience. A third example may be that a sense of direction is lacking—the eternal student, questioner or Peter Pan refusing to face reality. In all of these circumstances, a Gemini Moon points to some degree of emotional disorganization or naiveté.

A Gemini Moon is learning about emotional maturation. Within the spiritual history could be the condition of youthful indiscretion—behaving foolishly by simply not knowing better. When faced with lessons of maturation, the defensive strategy is to keep the messages of evolution within the brain rather than allowing them to sink down into the heart and body. When deepening can be accomplished, Gemini is able to direct behavior more purposefully from a place of emotional conviction.

A major avenue of growth for the Gemini Moon is to channel the curious disposition into emotional scenarios. This Moon is eager to learn and extremely energetic. With the right "teacher," or set of circumstances, the necessary deepening may occur. For this to unfold, the Gemini Moon must learn to settle down. Therefore, spiritual growth is a see-saw process between actively learning and engaging and more quietly integrating and assimilating. It would greatly benefit Gemini Moon people to find a program or develop the skills to go within: anything from breathing techniques, yoga and meditation to more direct clinical or therapeutic tools designed to foster introspection.

There is a clear schism between rational and emotional functions evident in the Gemini Moon, but with successful integration, there can be balance and emotional clarity. The Gemini Moon's greatest strength is its willingness to increase its knowledge. Ultimately, greater emotional intelligence is developed.

John Kerry

Former Presidential candidate and current senator, John Kerry's Gemini Moon is in the 7th House. This indicates a need for communication and stimulation in partnerships. The type of "emotional disorganization" in the 7th may show he doesn't know what he needs or who he is in relation to others. Indeed, the dominant criticism of Kerry in the 2004 election was that he was a "flip-flopper," someone who lacks convictions (Gemini) and just wants to please (7th House).

The Moon is conjunct Saturn, which brings gravity and perhaps even stiffness to his emotional body. Residing in Gemini, this conveys an intellectual seriousness in his soul, which has calcified the naturalness of his demeanor. This is the soul of a serious thinker motivated to have loving connections (7th) with others, which has been a karmic Achilles heel (Saturn).

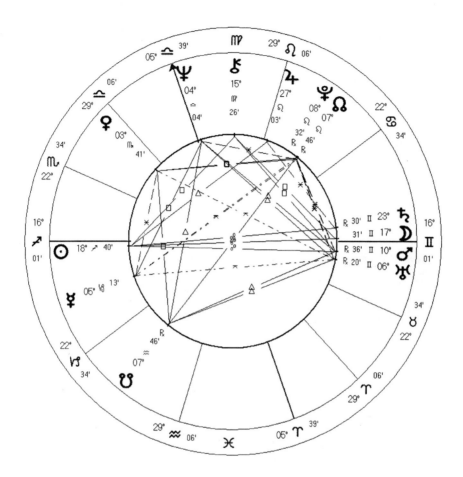

Another major component is the Moon's conjunction with Mars, which is in the 6th House. This Mars in Gemini is a savvy intellectual warrior, a most prepared (6th) and diligent one. This is a classic signature of a debater. Connected with the Moon, there is forceful urgency to make his point, stemming from the soul's familiarity with needing to prove itself. Mars, in turn, is conjunct Uranus, only adding explosiveness or turbulence to this fighting spirit. This soul has absorbed some shock or defeat and is restless and thorough about settling the score.

The Moon is square Chiron in Virgo in the 9th House, indicating some struggle in grounding (Virgo) his philosophy (9th), and contributing something meaningful to the world. This

35

square may also suggest some wounding (Chiron) from organized philosophical institutions (including religion), or in overseas travel. Kerry's soul may have received messages (9th House) of shame (Virgo), or been made to feel not good enough. His soul is not at peace with his religious views and has moved in the direction of intellectual (Gemini) fortification to feel secure (Moon).

This issue looms large enough to warrant major attention in the present life. With a Sagittarius Sun in the 1st House tightly opposed the Gemini Moon, the soul is interested in embodying (Sun) and actively behaving (1st House) from a place of philosophical conviction (Sagittarius). Kerry is learning to have a mission. A career in politics is one ideal manifestation as he can use the ample intellectual resources in his soul for this purpose.

The Full Moon will highlight his emotional tendencies and allow him to use this awareness to more strongly take charge. With successful resolution of his Lunar challenge, he is ready to assume the single-minded focus of his Sun.

Cancer Moon

The Moon's home is naturally in the cardinal water sign of Cancer, so the feeling component is quite strong. However, this emotional strength is still located somewhere on a spectrum of spiritual growth. The range of Cancer extends from heart-centered, emotionally intelligent, empathic and loving to defensive, hurt, protective, lonely and crabby. A Cancer Moon is vulnerable, capable of tremendous love and most likely introverted and parental.

Cancer Moons seek attachment and connection. They may well be clingy, and some people find them too needy. We can surmise that they feel natural with home, clan, family and their roots. Caretaking comes easily to them, so the instinct is to settle down and nurture. Experiencing the beautiful bond between parent and child may have deepened the heart center, but a challenge is to break free from the metaphorical womb of a safe home.

36

It may also be the case that the primal parent/child connection was not fully actualized in a healthy way and the soul is yearning for it. Instead of defending against this by being self-reliant or intellectual, a Cancer Moon has allowed itself to feel its vulnerability. The gift is that the person is able to really love and establish connections. The struggle could be a more palpable sense of upset and hurt when others are unable to reciprocate healthy attachment behaviors.

The theme of retreat is part of this Moon. A soul that carries this placement is more content at home than in the busyness of the world. Some examples would be the stay-at-home mother, the chronically depressed, or the shy, protective loner. People with this placement are becoming more adept at adding greater self-expression and more worldly ambition to their established emotional orientation. Their growth involves the development of greater toughness. Sometimes it's important to blockade the emotional floodgates and become more productive.

Cancer Moons have nurtured their feelings. Now comes the season of greater expansion. Learning to bring the inner gifts into the world allows connections to be made earnestly. These souls are to be treasured—it's up to them not to be buried.

Franklin Roosevelt

President Roosevelt's Cancer Moon is in the 10th House. He has the need to be seen as authoritative (10th) but nurturing (Cancer). This Moon feels responsible and concerned about public issues as well as interested in self-promotion. Serving at a time of despair (Great Depression), Roosevelt was able to comfort and provide hope for the nation.

His Moon is tightly sextile Saturn in Taurus in the 8th House. This emphasizes emotional sturdiness and highlights his ambitious nature. Residing in the 8th House, this Saturn is concerned with power. Saturn's location in Taurus indicates an interest in ownership and endurance (he held his office longer than any other President).

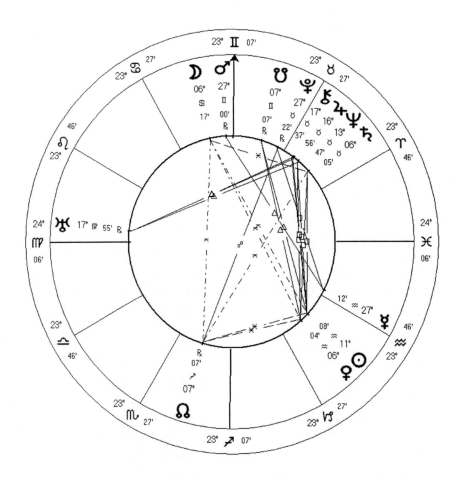

The Moon is loosely conjunct Mars in Gemini. This teams his nurturing nature with a far more spirited need for intellectual assertion. Roosevelt is eager to take on fights, to show (10th) his leadership, particularly through the use of arguments (Gemini). In fact, the quincunx from the Moon to the 3rd House Sagittarian North Node shows that greater spiritual growth is achieved by following through with his commitment to stand firm with his intellectual (3rd House) convictions (Sagittarius).

Venus in Aquarius in the 5th House forms a close quincunx with the Moon. This indicates a desire to express (5th) humanitarian (Aquarius) ideals of connection (Venus) and community. The New Deal was designed with this objective. The Sun is also close to Venus. The soul intention is to personally embody this ideal and to somehow figure out how to connect it (quincunx) to the lunar need for leadership.

Leo Moon

The Moon and the fixed fire sign Leo tend to be self-absorbed. Here we have a Moon that feels happy, but not necessarily humble or broad-minded. The range of Leo extends from charismatic, creative, noble and colorfully self-expressive to egocentric, entitled, boasting and childish. There is an emotional need for affection, to feel thought of with appreciation.

What can we deduce about the spiritual history? Perhaps this is a soul that feels special for some reason. Certainly there are many figures throughout history that have had rewards bestowed on them. This lionization doesn't necessarily have to be on a large scale—every family or group has some form of "favorite" no matter how unspoken it may be. Another possibility is that the soul has not been thought of well by others, and the emotional life revolves around that goal. Additionally, some of these people have a lot of experience identifying emotionally with children, entertainment or feeling innocent and open in some way. Leo trusts life and can be gullible. Some souls with this placement refuse to grow up.

One major defensive strategy often used by a Leo Moon is to ignore difficult emotions. Whereas the Gemini Moon may intellectualize emotions, here they are plainly rejected or minimized. The tendency to look at the bright side of life has made these souls unrealistic or unsympathetic about the true struggles that exist in the world, and in themselves.

Like all Moons, the goal is to mature out of limiting emotional habits. With Leo, it is important to have a greater sense of perspective—to not continually project self-needs into their surroundings. A Leo Moon may falsely interpret a news story, a conversation among other people or an innocuous message as being personally relevant. Much of the spiritual development involves the ability to be satisfied within—not subject to the approval of others. A greater sense of self-alignment readies them to contribute to the wider world family instead of just focusing on their immediate concerns.

Leo Moons are generally likeable and happy people. They are learning to be more involved in the world and less in themselves. Emotional management includes the process of detachment when appropriate. With a more detached style, they can truly shine their gifts into the world from a place of inner strength rather than seek validation. Leo Moons develop by taking a humble and realistic look at the self and by making concerted efforts to improve.

Julia Roberts

Oscar-winning actress Julia Roberts has a Leo Moon in the 2nd House—the need to perform and receive adulation (Leo) to bolster a sense of self-worth (2nd). Her soul's resource (2nd) is a need for the limelight, as that was likely a way she could feel potent. There is an underlying charisma with this Moon, but placed in the 2nd House it is pragmatic and results-oriented.

The Moon is conjunct Jupiter in Virgo. This slants the need for attention even more in the direction of earthy (Virgo) benefit (Jupiter). Jupiter in Virgo is a hard-worker who is willing to take on great effort in order to bring about concrete results. This is an industrious (Virgo) entertainer (Leo Moon) with big (Jupiter) dreams.

The Moon is square Neptune in the 5th House in Scorpio. There is an inherent conflict between her Leonine need, and the realization of the dream (Neptune), to perform (5th House). Neptune's residence in Scorpio may indicate that the aspiration results from unresolved wounding, perhaps in receiving attention. Moon contacts with Neptune show an emotional yearning, and here it concerns self-expression and artistry. When integrated successfully, this pairing positions Julia to make a compelling impact on others.

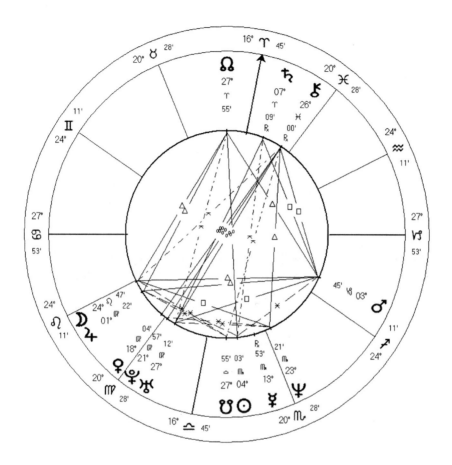

Her Moon is sextile a Libra South Node in the 4th House and trine the Aries North Node in the 10th. In a karmic sense, her talent was instrumental in bringing emotional sustenance to a family system (4th House South Node). Her role is of peacemaker (Libra South Node), and the ability to perform and work diligently as a bread-winner brought greater harmony. We can surmise that her true art (5th House Neptune) could not be utilized in order to satisfy familial obligation (4th House South Node). The Moon's trine to the North Node suggests that growth is furthered by aligning with her will (Aries) to fashion a career (10th House) of her design.

The Moon is quincunx the 9th House Chiron in Pisces. Her heart (Moon) has unfinished work around resolving a wound (Chiron) about longing (Pisces) for a more meaningful (9th House) existence. It would make sense that in previous incarnations she was not free to do as she pleased. Reconciliation involves taking measures to heal (Pisces) her relationship with her world-views (9th), to surrender (Pisces) to her mission (9th House).

Virgo Moon

The mutable earth sign Virgo is frequently stereotyped as critical, anxious, obsessive, worn-out or repressed. The higher manifestation includes satisfied, professional, competent, precise and a master-craftsman. This is the sign of self-improvement and hard work—doing a task well and feeling good about the effort extended. A Virgo theme is modesty and humility, feeling small in a great big world. Many with this Moon placement are truly well-intentioned souls who want to make a contribution to the world.

With the Moon in Virgo, the emotional nature tends to be self-critical—the "I can do better" mentality. This may lead to feelings of inferiority or subservience. The spiritual history of a soul with this Moon may be tied to feelings of service or being industrious. The emotional survival method was to stay focused and not complain too loudly.

Many followers of rigid paths incarnate with this Moon placement. Virgo has a connection with chastity and "doing the right thing." These souls have learned not to rock the boat, but to fix it when needed. The emotional nature is controlled. Virgo is an earth sign, and like Taurus, there is a sense of continuity with the status quo. Further evolutionary steps require the release of tight-fisted control and the welcoming of grace.

Another possibility is a soul who feels guilt, shame, remorse or the need to atone for something. This is a confessional and humble disposition that wants to patch things up. Carrying the baggage of feeling "bad" may be severely limiting and anxiety producing. The spiritual cleansing process requires letting this go and taking measures to incorporate new behavior patterns.

The emotional need to "be better" may limit the attainment of equal partnerships. Virgo Moons are working on attaining balance or parity with other people. When they are able to receive as much as they give, they have access to a new set of emotional skills that includes interdependence and mutual appreciation.

Virgo Moons benefit by just letting loose. The restricted emotional nature, and sometimes body posture, may become more free through delving into edgy experiences, travels within consciousness and imagination, or whatever other "peak experiences" they feel calling. Virgo Moons have earned the right to engage more passionately with life. There is substantial license to become more light and lofty with one's aims. This can happen if they only let it.

The Dalai Lama

His Holiness The Dalai Lama has a Virgo Moon in the 3rd House. His mindset (3rd) is full of loving (Moon) humility and service (Virgo). His perceptual faculties are highly attuned to satisfying his needs for modest assistance to the world. He is looking for opportunities to help make reparations (Virgo).

The Moon is conjunct Neptune, bringing this need to a more collective and transpersonal scope. This is the soul of a visionary (Neptune) but one who is most interested in making pragmatic (Virgo) improvements. There is a well of compassion (Moon conjunct Neptune) in his soul.

The Moon is opposed by Saturn in Pisces in the 9th House. This Saturn speaks of spiritual leadership and positions of authority. His need for compassionate service is given greater breadth and focus as a spiritual leader. The opposition serves as a connecting link between Moon and Saturn, but it does suggest some tension. Perhaps his more meditative (Neptune) needs are continually interrupted by the demands of his worldly position.

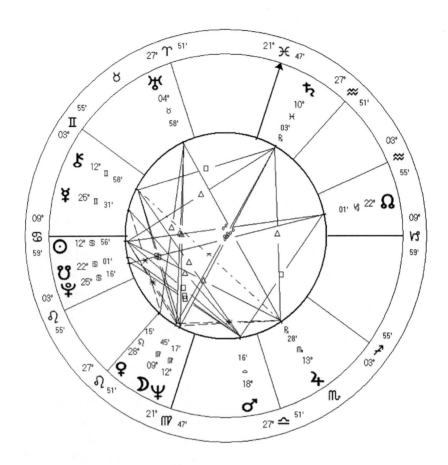

Chiron in Gemini in the 12th House squares the Moon. His emotional nature is wounded (Chiron) by the calls (Gemini) from the collective consciousness (12th). He hears the voices (Gemini) of the suffering (12th) and wants to be of help (Virgo Moon). The square suggests that these calls do not stop and that there is only so much one man can do.

Jupiter in Scorpio forms a sextile to the Moon. The Dalai Lama is expressive (5th House) about his religious (Jupiter) passion (Scorpio). He is not shy at all about giving voice to the compassionate yearnings of his Moon through religious teachings (5th House Jupiter). He delivers his message in the most honest and straightforward manner, stemming from his own depths (Scorpio).

The Moon is also trine Uranus in Taurus in the 11th House. There is a need to find a breakthrough (Uranus) toward peace (Taurus) for his people (11th House). Uranus trine Moon shows emotional brilliance, truly aligning the heart with a global or universal perspective. Here, it is specifically involved in bringing greater stability (Taurus) to a community (11th House).

Finally, the Moon is sextile the 1st House Cancer Sun. The present incarnation involves being an emotional (Cancer) leader (1st House). The emotional basin of the past is linked right in with this statement of continuing to act in accordance with his heart. The waxing sextile does suggest an active surge of energy to perform this task.

Libra Moon

Like Taurus, the cardinal air sign Libra is ruled by Venus and at its best feels good. The Moon and Libra share a natural affinity for peaceful connection, forming attachments and having a sense of pleasantness. Since we are discussing the Moon, we must look to where the emotional needs are. With a Libra Moon, the soul needs other people, harmony and the reassurance that "everything will be ok." Since the world can't give that reassurance, a Libra Moon needs to face the difficult truths.

The evasion of the more unseemly aspects of human nature serves a protective function. Not letting in the horrors of war, genocide or abuse allows someone to trust the world more openly, but it's important sometimes *not* to trust. As an air sign, Libra has romantic expectations of humanity. With the Moon, this is applied to personal associations and more specifically to marriage or other long-term commitments.

The soul may have absorbed the feeling component of civility, aesthetics, proper manners, refinement and a taste for culture. There may be a need for sophistication or pleasantness—when extreme it's perceived as "snobbishness" by others. A Libra

Moon takes cues from external factors in arriving at inner satisfaction.

There is the need to check in with others to reach a place of self-assurance. In some cases this leads to co-dependence instead of interdependence, which would be healthier. One major possibility of the soul history is the familiarity with partnerships—being considerate of others' feelings and wanting to nurture a pair bond. Since this is such an instinctual pull, a Libra Moon may unwittingly lose a sense of self-orientation.

Part of the Libra Moon's development is to find emotional nourishment from within, from Spirit or from sources that are not directly related only to friendships or romantic bonds. Becoming more bold or risky may help a Libra Moon learn about the complexity of life, and through that process, attain more courage and feelings of power.

Libra Moons have enormous gifts to share with others. They help bring about cooperation, diplomacy and common ground. They have a need for what is just and fair. Upon successful development, they will find that life is just as rewarding in the more charged and edgy moments of the human experiences. A Libra Moon doesn't have to play second fiddle to anyone, unless of course they choose to.

Tori Amos

Known for her extraordinary musical talent, gracefulness and popularity, it is no surprise that musician Tori Amos has a Libra Moon in the 11th House. Ruled by Venus, Libra has associations with refinement—it is pleasing and aims to secure flowing connections. Located in the 11th, this Moon is particularly invested in forging an alliance with an audience. In particular, Libra involves the arts.

A Libra Moon *needs* others. Although Tori is admired by millions, she maintains, even *nurtures*, a relationship (Libra) with her group (11th). She is comfortable representing the ideal of a strong feminine presence (Moon), an advocate for beauty and a giver (Libra) of her exceptional gift.

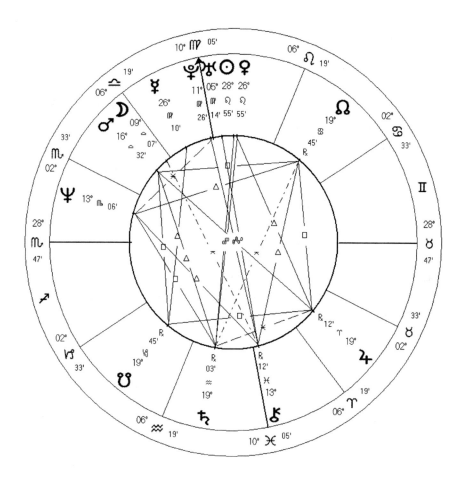

This Libra Moon is conjunct Mars. The lunar need is driven and takes on more leadership potentials with the go-getter quality of the red planet. She is emotionally aligned (Moon) with a powerful desire (Mars) to please (Libra). Mars provides some of the edge to her character and her willingness to take musical risks. Tori is also a vocal advocate for female empowerment issues including support for rape victims. She represents the combination of feminine beauty (Libra) mixed with toughness (Mars). The Moon/Mars conjunction is opposed by Jupiter in Aries in the 5th House. This Jupiter finds meaning by becoming a leader (Aries) in realms of performance (5th). She realizes that the aims of her Moon only become satisfied by taking risks and making her passion (Aries) a spiritual path (Jupiter).

As Jupiter squares the Nodal axis, we can conclude that exercising this right is spiritual work seeking greater resolution. The Cancer North Node has the Moon as its ruler. This brings the drama of her lunar profile squarely into the main lessons of the lifetime. Her work involves assuming emotional power (Cancer North Node in the 8th) by becoming a representation of graceful feminine strength.

The Moon is quincunx Chiron in Pisces in the 4th. Deep within her being (4th House) is a longing (Pisces) that was somehow wounded (Chiron) in her spiritual past. She likely had many visions (Pisces) of sharing her talent which were not fully actualized. The family system (4th) likely plays an inhibiting role in her development. Tori is learning to find her own direction and supportive community.

Scorpio Moon

The Moon is traditionally considered in its "fall" in Scorpio because this fixed water sign deals with interpersonal wounding, intensity and darkness. The Moon wants a hug or bowl of chicken soup, while Scorpio wants the truth as it prepares its stinger. The range of Scorpio extends from purposeful intensity, determination, psychological complexity and spiritual and/or sexual intimacy down to all types of abuse, betrayals, manipulations, and vengeful behaviors. This sign is passionately charged and relentless.

We bond with others at all levels: physically, emotionally, intellectually and spiritually. A Scorpio Moon seeks interpenetration at any and all of these levels. In contrast to the Pollyanna style of Libra, the Scorpio Moon has a deep reservoir of life experiences that has led to greater psychological realism. The struggle may be a deep-rooted paranoia in regard to the motives of others.

A quick glance at history reminds us that there has been massive psychological wounding in all places, in all time periods.

Those with this Moon placement have likely experienced a piece of it more so than others. Whether through perpetration or being a victim, or even probing and studying issues of death, catastrophe or sin, these souls are at the edge that separates light from dark and they know how delicate the divide really is.

We do not absorb intensity and darkness without being intimately impacted. There are reasons why a soul develops emotional force and a need for confrontation. The soul history may include emotional, physical or sexual violations which have caused the soul to assume a suspicious mentality. Scorpio is an interpersonal sign—how we are emotionally affected by others.

When a Scorpio Moon acts unconsciously and lashes out, mice scatter into their holes and children cover their eyes. It is time for truth—what is *really* going on, usually in the form of altercation. Scorpio Moons have a natural ability to sense other people's motives and know what they are capable of—making them outstanding therapists.

What is often lacking is a feeling of comfort and inner security. To attain that level of peace, it is necessary to heal—and most anyone with this Moon placement needs to make disturbing psychic material more conscious and integrated. If this can be successfully accomplished, access to the higher qualities of the sign becomes possible. These people may potentially become our great psychic detectives and healers, shamans, risk-takers and revolutionaries. They develop an uncanny sense of mission—a more resolute attitude toward their goals.

Bruce Lee

Marital arts specialist and entertainer Bruce Lee has a Scorpio Moon in the 12th House. He is learning to resolve (12th) a tremendous spiritual legacy of conflict and brutality (Scorpio). There is great loss and sorrow (12th) in his biography, which calls for cleansing and renewal.

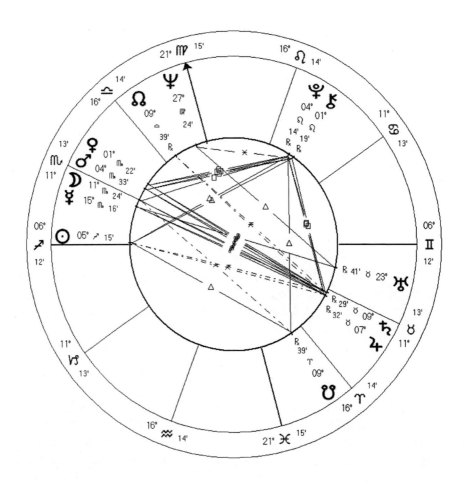

This Scorpio Moon is conjunct Mars and Venus, both also in the searing sign of Scorpio. There is a marked need for violence, to passionately clash with others. His emotional intensity (Scorpio Moon) joins with physical expressions (Mars) of force as a way of connecting with others (Venus). He works out his emotions through aggressive confrontation. Mars and Venus are in the 11th House, bringing his lunar need to a visible arena—an audience and group of like-minded warriors.

The Moon opposes a Jupiter/Saturn conjunction in Taurus in the 5th House. The opposition sets up the "I–Thou" relationship, while Jupiter and Saturn indicate institutions or social structures he is up against. Indeed, there is the theme of having to topple some form of oppressive empire in many of his movies. Bruce is at odds with the establishment, and evokes the archetype of spiritual warrior or savior.

Another angle is to see this opposition in terms of his own ambition (Saturn) and life direction (Jupiter). These two planets combine in Taurus to yield a business and entrepreneurial focus. He may bring his need for Martial conflict into realms of performance (5th House) for capital gain (Taurus). This transforms the source of his antagonism (Jupiter/Saturn) into a solid career foundation.

The Scorpio Moon is also conjunct Mercury in the 12th House. In his past, his voice similarly met defeat and he is highly charged to speak out. Part of the healing is to speak with piercing honesty toward those who have hurt him. There is an emotional need (Moon) to spread a message (Mercury).

The Moon is square the Pluto/Chiron conjunction in the 8th House in Leo. This aspect is brought to even tighter connection through the involvement with Mars and Venus, which square Pluto/Chiron more precisely. This contact provides several exclamation marks to the notion that he will fight to the death. Here, Leo's association with joy boils in the cauldrons of conflict (8th House)—this Pluto/Chiron square to the Moon shows a marked wounding in his ability to trust life. Much of the spiritual work is to perform the necessary transformation to have access to joy again. Leo, like the 5th House, correlates to performance. Channeling his personal drama into entertainment would be quite natural.

Bruce Lee did eventually die prematurely, and went down fighting 'til the end…entertaining millions and earning probably the same.

Sagittarius Moon

Like all signs, Sagittarius ranges from light to dark. The brighter side includes the philosopher, traveler and politician while the darker side includes the fanatic, dogmatist, know-it-all and even the cult leader. The Moon in Sagittarius has a need to be right and do what it wants. Whether this translates to a life lived with moral clarity or the gross manipulation of others to get them to adhere to specific rules and behaviors depends on the consciousness of the owner.

Sagittarius includes, but is not limited to, religious thinking. Any belief system that is strong qualifies, so uncompromising atheism fits under the umbrella of this mutable fire sign. Many with the Moon in Sagittarius have a spiritual legacy that includes solid convictions about how to approach life, which often leads to narrowness of perspective and inflexibility. Alternative viewpoints, mixing with a diversity of people and expanding the knowledge base into new frontiers may chip away at the emotional need to make the world neat and tidy and fit squarely into their chosen path.

The Moon here may also suggest a soul of a wanderer or explorer. There may be a lack of feeling rooted and sheltered, which are of prime concern to the Moon. The soul may be used to moving and needing to adjust to new experiences. When faced with opportunities to have greater stability, this may be unconsciously sabotaged. Ultimately, it serves the growth of Sagittarius to become more committed and grounded within reliable structures.

Indeed, some with a Sagittarius Moon are used to freedom—an expansive, carefree existence devoid of responsibility. Here, we see the disposition of, "Don't tell me what to do. I know what I want and how to live my life." In contrast to the youthful, even naïve Gemini, this Moon is more seasoned and feels it has a "right" to enjoy its liberties and openness. Whereas Gemini is curious, Sagittarius is entitled and filled with bravado.

A Sagittarius Moon may have a buoyant and grand spirit. Ruled by broad-minded and expansive Jupiter, some with this lunar placement carry the emotional need for adventure and to claim the riches that life has to offer. Those further along on the evolutionary road have used this inner need for boundary-expanding experiences as rocket fuel for living large. This can be a most magnanimous temperament.

Being a mutable sign and fiery, Sagittarius is not grounded. With the Moon here, the emotional life may be unsettled or prone to deflecting heavier feelings. Sometimes it's appropriate to feel sadness or vulnerability—even melancholia serves an important function. Instead of welcoming these internal states, there is a tendency to flee. A Sagittarius Moon may feign invincibility while the whole act may be avoidance and a lack of accountability.

Maturation through acceptance of all emotions enables the Sagittarius Moon to attain greater wisdom—the true goal of the sign. By accepting greater responsibility and choosing to make a concerted effort toward one's goals, these people become our teachers and sources of inspiration. They give the gift of clarity, the example of humane morality and the ability to make sound choices.

Albert Einstein

Physicist, philosopher and genius—Einstein is perhaps the embodiment of Man's eternal quest for meaning and answers. He has a Sagittarius Moon in the 6th House—a clear statement of an emotional need (Moon) to work hard (6th House) to discover larger truths (Sagittarius). Instead of the usual rigidity or dogmatism Sagittarius is prone to, the residence in the 6th shows humility, questioning and a safeguard from complacency. Einstein is motivated by an authentic pursuit to understand (Sagittarius) the universe.

His Moon is trine Venus in Aries in the 10th House. This aspect connects the lunar need to a more public and visible area, mainly the career. Venus is interested in collaboration, though in Aries it secures Einstein the position of a trailblazer. Its residence in the 10th House, where Mercury and Saturn also reside, does suggest intellectual authority. Moon trine Venus shows a willingness to form public connections, a smooth touch with others. However, it stems from purpose (Sagittarius Moon) and is motivated by self-interest (Venus in Aries).

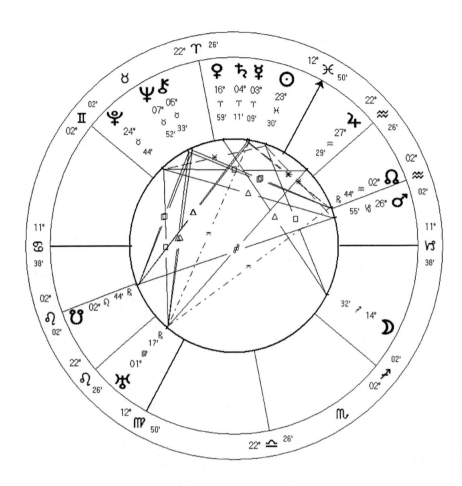

The Moon is square the 10th House Pisces Sun. The philosophical lunar need connects to the solar intention to assume a commanding role (10th House) as a visionary (Pisces). The square suggests a challenge in bringing his thoroughness (6th House) and speculations into greater expertise (10th House) as an inspiring presence (Pisces Sun). The orb for this aspect is 9 degrees, but considering that both luminaries are involved, there is license to make this connection. Moon/Sun connections directly bridge past with present. Although every chart contains both of these planets, some people are working and building from the spiritual history in more concrete ways than others. The gifts that Einstein has previously developed in his soulful musings on the cosmos are ripe for greater public dispersal.

It is also noteworthy that Einstein's Moon rules the Cancer Ascendant, so it influences and colors his approach to life. Much of his natural behavior and orientation is toward his philosophical, some would even say religious (Sagittarius), need to understand the ineffable.

Capricorn Moon

The Moon is considered in its "detriment" in Capricorn since its natural home is the opposing sign Cancer. There is a fundamental incompatibility between the softness of the Moon and the toughness of Capricorn. This cardinal earth sign ranges from being powerful, enduring, reliable, dignified and wise, down to uncaring, obsessed with control, afraid, shut-down and domineering. The Moon in this sign is facing lessons of greater fortitude and strength while moving away from the tendency to repress or restrict feelings.

A Capricorn Moon needs to feel in charge and on top of the emotional nature—a refusal to be seen as weak or vulnerable. Capricorn is publicly focused and is concerned with issues of status and reputation. This Moon placement has felt the weight of responsibility and chosen to concentrate and rise to the challenges at hand. Being an earth sign, Capricorn is industrious and managerial. Along the way, sensitivity may have been sacrificed in favor of results.

The parent/child bond is ideally one of unconditional love and nurturance. The style of a Capricorn Moon is more of tough love and delivering lessons. A soul with this placement may be familiar with issues of dominance or great expectations from parental figures or have that predisposition within the self.

In order to reach the goal of increased fortitude, a Capricorn Moon is learning to welcome and be with all emotional states. There is likely a component of fear that needs to be overcome. If not, there may be a temperament of stoicism designed to conceal any inner trembling. By moving inward and learning to relax into the tenderness the Moon thrives in, a Capricorn Moon strongly reemerges. The integration produces greater wisdom—the power is fueled by the heart instead of blind ambition.

Another lesson for the Capricorn Moon is to be absolutely true to its aspirations, not just seeing that the bills are paid. This Moon can be so caught up in appearances that power is sought for the sake of power, disregarding any humanitarian or global concerns. An orientation process back to what is really important in life assists the Capricorn Moon in loosening its grip and finding new ways to operate. They are becoming more individuated and able to care about the world.

We need Capricorn Moons to be our elders, those that have a sturdy hand on the wheel. It is most comforting when they lead by looking not only forward, but also inward. For when they touch their own hearts, they may then truly change and better this world.

Cher

Singer, actress and celebrity personality Cher has a driven Capricorn Moon in the 7th House. There is a need (Moon) to form business (Capricorn) partnerships (7th House). Indeed, she teamed with Sonny Bono as a teenager when he was in his thirties. This enabled her to springboard to the levels of success and visibility she craves. She apparently was focused on this goal from a very early age; she practiced signing her autograph as an adolescent.

When the Moon makes contact with Saturn, the softer facets of the inner life are buried under the weight of assuming great responsibility. Cher not only has her Capricorn Moon in opposition to Saturn; these planets are angular and in mutual reception. Her 1st House Saturn in Cancer indicates that she plays the part of the durable and determined leader. This is in opposition to her authentic need for strong partners. The potential for conflict is likely. Cher's involvement with prominent men and the resulting challenges of these relationships is testament to the centrality of this opposition in her life.

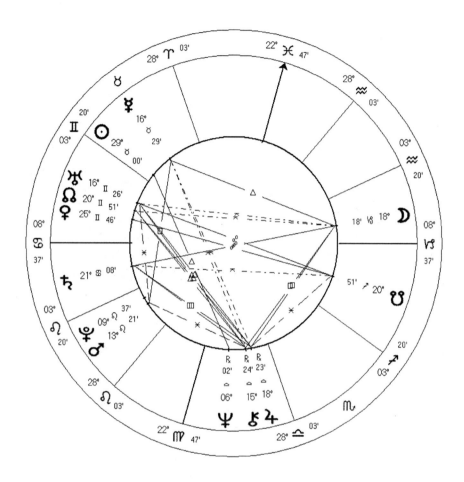

This relationship dynamic is further supported by Jupiter/Chiron in Libra in the 4th House squaring the Moon (as well as Saturn to form a T-square). Jupiter in Libra finds expansion and direction through partnership—in the 4th this is likely to be a spouse or other intimate. Chiron's inclusion portrays a disrupted or hampered relationship (Libra) in need of greater sanctuary (4th House) or emotional care. The Moon square Jupiter accentuates the need for success, to attain the finer things in life (Libra). Ultimately, this T-square promises emotional satisfaction and the attainment of peace once issues of negotiating control are resolved and the heart feels secure.

Cher's Moon is quincunx Uranus in Gemini in the 12th House. This suggests some emotional turbulence has disrupted her centeredness. Gemini includes communication, while the 12th is often an area of inaccessibility or removal, a place of sorrow or loss. It is possible that in a karmic sense, Cher was unable to or blocked from sharing her voice—most likely by the hand of a controlling partner (quincunx to the 7th House Moon). The North Node is also involved, indicating that spiritual lessons entail the development of her ability to communicate (Gemini) and infuse her message with greater inspiration (12th House).

The Moon forms a trine to Mercury in Taurus in the 11th House, which serves as the ruler of the Gemini North Node. There is an innate desire to convey her message (Mercury) to an audience (11th House). As a sensuous sign, Taurus is artistic and simple and singing is one obvious meeting point between this planet and sign. She finds inner peace (Taurus) by spreading beauty and allowing her voice to connect in the world.

Aquarius Moon

An Aquarius Moon faces the challenge of reconciling the planet most interested in forming attachments with the sign most interested in detachment and perspective. Is an Aquarian Moon relegated to a lifetime of emotional disconnection? Let's consider the range of the fixed air sign Aquarius: with the development of consciousness, it is innovative and individuated, trusting in itself and secure with its perspective. An Aquarian Moon may at times be the mark of a true spiritual humanitarian. The struggling version of the story has defiance, eccentricities, emotional unavailability and endless analysis.

Aquarius is about awakening—breaking through limitations to arrive at a new way of being. The path of the Aquarius Moon is to accomplish this feat within the emotional realm. The evolved Aquarian qualities make for engaging and dependable emotional bonding. Before that is achieved, however, there is work to take on—for that is why we are all here.

Why would someone incarnate with a tendency to emotionally detach? We are creatures of love, strengthened by reciprocal nurturance. There is likely some event, or series of events, in the soul history which called for this survival tactic. With the introduction of trauma or removal from sources of nurturance, a natural defense mechanism is to become self-reliant or view life as an observer. The soul *feels* out of touch with itself because it is out of touch with the normal bonding in family or society.

In contrast, there are some cases in which there is a profound love of humanity—the caretaker of the community and liaison to the future. Those with this Moon placement that are further in their growth have incarnated to support progress and collective evolution. The life is less preoccupied with personal concerns and the biography is marked by a determination to help create bridges.

Aquarius Moons become more balanced by learning to "be here now"—to engage fully in the present moment. Much of this involves taking emotional risks in showing others more of themselves, reaching out and connecting through open-hearted joy and trust. By centering awareness in the now, they reorient their own emotional processes.

Another task is to move inward in the pursuit of more advanced levels of consciousness. Aquarians already know how to comprehend reality with a complex and far-reaching scope. It benefits them to now emotionalize that process by extending the heart and sending loving energy compassionately to all. Feeling closer to mystical oneness assists the Aquarius Moon in deepening in relevant ways.

The primary lesson for the Aquarius Moon is to become more active in the personal drama. By so doing, they become the catalysts that emotionally awaken us to move humanity a bit closer to the utopias of our imagination. These people are natural coordinators and overseers of humanitarian progress. With successful growth, they become more emotionally involved in this process.

Marilyn Monroe

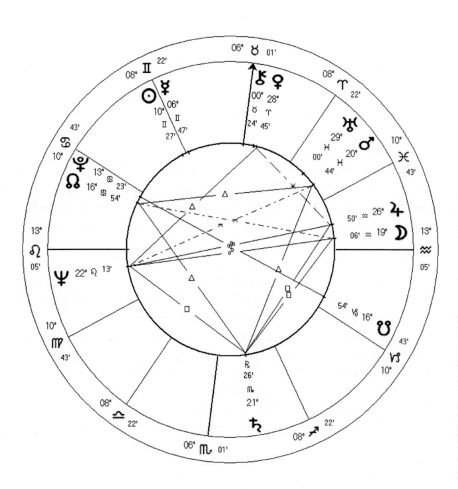

Iconic sex symbol and actress Marilyn Monroe has an Aquarius Moon in the 7th House. There is a vision of an idealized form of relationship. The struggle is feeling out of touch or connected to others in impersonal ways. From another angle, Marilyn may feel married to or in relationship with (7th) the collective (Aquarius).

60

With Jupiter close to the Moon, there are great hopes for emotionally rewarding breakthroughs with significant others. For Marilyn, relationships have a flavor of adventure—she wants to be carried away. Marilyn needs (Moon) to feel loved by many (Jupiter in Aquarius).

The Moon is opposed to Neptune in Leo in the 1st House. As the 1st House indicates the natural persona, Neptune here describes the image she projected in life. There is an ethereal quality to her presentation. In Leo, it takes the form of celebrity and performer, a playful and light-hearted visage. Connected to the Moon through the opposition, there is an emotional need to be seen in such a way—but it also causes conflict and confusion for her. Moon/Neptune implies a yearning, and in this case it is for love and acceptance.

Saturn in Scorpio in the 4th House squares the Moon (and Neptune to form a T-square). At her roots, there is a palpable fear of intensity, a heaviness or severity that exasperates her heart. This Saturn is tightly controlled and even oppressive. It is likely that her home life introduced some unpleasantness that impacted subsequent relations. The work is to uncover the feelings that have been squelched and find a place of emotional strength (Saturn in Scorpio) and emotional perspective (square Aquarius Moon).

The Moon forms a quincunx to the North Node in Cancer in the 12th House. Part of Marilyn's spiritual work entails moving inward (Cancer) and releasing (12th House) emotional material that no longer serves her. Pluto's proximity to the North Node suggests that a confrontation with her pain and wounding is essential for her growth. This corrects the blockage that Saturn indicates.

The Moon is also the ruler of the North Node. Arriving at a new way of relating is very much the idea. With optimal resolution of her lessons, she is liberated (Aquarius) from her struggles and may consciously welcome abundance (Moon conjunct Jupiter). A less favorable outcome is emotional disorganization and being overcome by inner hurts.

Pisces Moon

Pisces is a mystical sign with an otherworldly focus. Its range spans from advanced levels of consciousness, compassion, contemplation, poeticism and unconditional love to escapism, lack of self-definition, impotence, martyr tendencies and the folly of unrealistic dreams. This sign also deals with endings and letting go, which often involves sadness and grief. As a mutable water sign, Pisces has great sensitivity. The Moon here sometimes suggests a melancholic reaction to what is perceived as an uncaring world.

The combination of heightened feeling, but of an impersonal nature, indicates that some souls with this Moon placement feel devotional, even sacrificial. Another possibility is the condition where the feeling nature is flooded with sadness and grief and there is great caution against asserting oneself. Still another example is the emotional tendency to dissolve the self, and this may manifest as alcoholism or substance abuse—the process of self-medicating and thereby becoming ineffectual.

Spiritual growth involves complementing the heightened sensitivity with a call to decisive action. These souls benefit by taking emotional risks and ensuring that their genuine needs are met in the world. When courageous behavior is fueled by love and compassion, an unmistakable mark is left on those who encounter this power. Pisces Moons are learning to be our spiritual leaders.

The tendency for lethargy or complacency must also be transformed. By investing effort and time into the demands of daily living, these souls learn to blend more with the sensual world and therefore reach a greater state of emotional integration. Instead of just good intentions, they can achieve concrete results. This offers emotional well-being through a sense of achievement.

Pisces Moons are in rhythm with the emotional health of the planet. They are more affected than others by the cruelties that often plague this world. It benefits both their individual, and our collective, growth when they learn to take a more active and hands-on approach to rectifying social ills. The gift of compassion can truly transform and mend many hearts.

JRR Tolkein

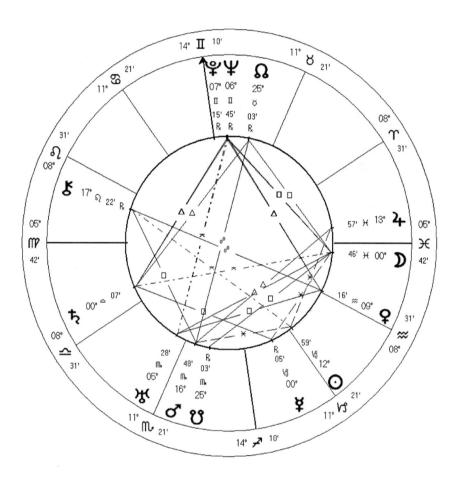

Author of the Lord of the Rings saga, JRR Tolkein has a Pisces Moon in the 6th House. This Moon is used to making sacrifices, while holding onto a vision of better days to come. In the 6th, one has to get down to business—the Moon here in Pisces shows an emotional investment in doing his share to contribute to some collective purpose. This is a modest and well-intentioned Moon, but one holding fast to a yearning.

The Moon is sextile Mercury in Capricorn in the 4th House. Part of the Piscean longing is to exercise his voice (Mercury) in a sturdy and resolute manner (Capricorn)—to work on what is in his depths (4th House). Becoming an accomplished (Capricorn) writer (Mercury) certainly would fit. Tolkein's imagination (Pisces) connects with grounded intention, but the rest of the chart indicates there is much work to do in order to realize this goal.

The emotional need for concrete results is echoed by the Moon's quincunx to Saturn (1st House, Libra), which in turn tightly squares his Mercury. The quincunx suggests that becoming an authority (Saturn) in his chosen artistic field (Libra) lacks a smooth connection to the imagination within his soul. Some form of adjustment and diligence is required to be able to bridge his longing with results.

The Moon squares the Nodal axis—the South Node in Scorpio in the 3rd House and the North Node in Taurus in the 9th House. The Nodes show lessons about the resolution of some form of wounding or intensity (Scorpio) in realms of intellectual activity and perception (3rd), and toward greater comfort and security (Taurus) about following his life path and convictions (9th House). Ruling the South Node is Pluto in Gemini in the 9th and conjunct Neptune. The major wound in Tolkein's soul involves communication (Gemini), and he was likely in a position of giving up (Pluto conjunct Neptune) his dream in order to do what was expected of him or to follow some agenda (9th House).

The Moon is square the Pluto/Neptune conjunction. There is great emotional conflict—quite likely a palpable hurt (Pluto) and sorrow (Neptune) that his needs for realizing and creating his fantasy are unmet. At the same time, the imagination, redemptive and intellectual powers simmer. This Pluto/Neptune conjunction speaks of an incredible reservoir of energy consumed with archetypal and mythic storytelling (Gemini) within the arena of journey and questing for truth and spiritual salvation (9th House).

Uranus in Scorpio trines the Moon from the 2nd House. This suggests that an emotional resource (2nd House) of Tolkein's is a highly charged (Scorpio) need for revolution (Aquarius) or breaking through restriction. He is determined to arrive at new ways of being—a sense of confidence and self-esteem anchors this resolve. Uranus in Scorpio is keenly aware that great psychological transformation is possible—one could argue that some of his characters represent this part of him.

Jupiter in Pisces is loosely conjunct the Moon. This shows a further alignment or identification with epic fantasy quests and limitless ideals. Moon/Jupiter does have an inner confidence that his dreams will, in fact, become realized. It is noteworthy that all of the outer planets make connections to his Moon. Tolkein has a pronounced need to make his mark on the collective. He is attuned to the archetypal and ethereal worlds of imagination and much of his work involves connecting the familiar with the extraordinary.

Forward Momentum

Astute readers may have picked up a theme in these paragraphs. Every sign has a special relationship with its opposite and may learn from it. Part of spiritual growth is to become more emotionally balanced. Opposite signs complement each other and promote equilibrium, bringing in qualities that support greater integration.

Also, astrology is a cyclical system—growth proceeds around the zodiac. Successful work with a particular process naturally brings momentum to the following sign, as each sign builds upon its predecessor.

Although the Moon sign remains the same throughout the lifetime, it connects and learns from the other facets of the system. The Moon learns balance from its opposing sign and looks to the following sign for qualities that support greater development.

Chapter 3
The Moon in the Astrology Chart

Housing the Moon

The natal house where the Moon is placed gives the arena or realm of experience where there is an emotional attachment and familiarity. It is essential to remember that signs are different from houses—it is a mistake to interchange them. Signs are thematically linked with houses such as Aries and the 1st, or Taurus and the 2nd, and so on. However, signs are styles and evolutionary processes geared for growth, and houses are where action is played out. Signs are psychological (how) while houses are contexts of life (where).

The following paragraphs address the Moon within the environment or framework of each of the houses. Whatever house the Moon appears in is where there is fluency and experience. The soul instinctually operates from that realm of life and unconsciously patterns behavior with the house gestalt as a reference.

The 1st House concerns action, behavior, how we naturally approach the world, and one's persona. With the Moon residing here, the soul naturally acts in lunar ways. Many times this results in caretaking or an innate proclivity for hospitality. A person with a 1st House Moon is classically emotional—which may manifest as a heightened sense of caring and sweetness, or defensiveness and reactivity. The assertive function tends to be cautious rather than robust as the Moon is the overseer of survival. When feeling safe, the 1st House Moon displays a hearty ability to form attachments with others.

With the Moon in the 2nd House, the concretizing of lunar qualities is a major concern. This house involves material resources such as possessions, but also inner resources like confidence and self-esteem. A planet in this house may ultimately serve as a bedrock or source of power from which to function. It may also point to qualities that are being developed in order to have that sense of assurance. The Moon here may indicate a soul that is in need of greater poise or solace. Life is organized around the quest for improving inner peace and contentedness. Profiles of 2nd House Moon people range from the self-starter who wants to bolster the checkbook, to the insecure anorexic who struggles to feel whole, to the confident parent calmly adoring his children.

The 3rd House is how the mindset, perceptions and immediate environment are organized. It also relates to siblings and short-distance travel. The Moon in this realm could mean several things, as this is a house of variety and diversity. Among the possibilities is the attachment to learning, reason, or youthful curiosity. There could be a need to be smart, perceptive or to have lightness and spontaneity. The fullness and depth of the Moon has trouble reaching its potential in such an airy house. Sometimes this placement shows an emotional naiveté or even a soul lacking wisdom, so the goal is to further the accumulation of emotional experience. A more developed Moon here is the poet or any person adept at noticing the love that can exist everywhere.

The Moon is in its natural home in the 4th House. This area involves the family system, vulnerability, home and privacy. This placement is indicative of a soul with deep connections to its roots and lineage. There is often a strong need to nest or maintain ties to family members both of the present day and of yesteryear. The sense of privacy makes a person with this placement difficult to know, but once let into the fortress, there is plentiful devotion. Being a personal water house, a developed Moon here suggests someone with a profound sense of self. Alternatively and somewhat paradoxically, it also may be someone who is lonely or unconscious of their needs. Either way there is a predilection to operate within the inner rhythms.

The 5th House includes the self-expression of personality, creative talents, children and love affairs. The Moon here shows a willingness to share the inner world openly, to engage and connect earnestly with life. The focus on sharing with others may result in the attainment of either joy or hurt, as sometimes others are reluctant to reciprocate. In contrast to the 4th House, the Moon here is often a soul that is easier to know. Many times this soul is comfortable with childhood and/or child-rearing. The 5th House frequently alludes to a talent, and with the Moon here it is of a very personal nature. The soul may be attached to displays of affection and unconsciously demand similar displays in return from loved ones. An extraverted nature is common—this may stem from a spiritual legacy of trusting life or conversely a soul that is working in that direction.

The 6th is a house of preparation. It involves health practices, work and service, self-improvement and areas where we pay our dues. As a relationship house it encompasses relations of an unequal nature including mentor/apprentice, guru/disciple or master/servant. The Moon here often suggests a soul striving for something, one who feels weak in comparison to others or a legacy of identifying with underdog or downtrodden positions. The emotional nature is organized in a somewhat fragile or insecure manner. There is an inner need to perform tasks to receive love or nurturing from others. A more developed Moon in this area shows humility and modesty—the helpful and benevolent assistant to others.

We move above the horizon to the 7th House. This is the area of equal relationships: all types of one-to-one interactions including personal friends and marital partners. Opposed to the self-orientation of the 1st, it's how we naturally connect with others. People with the Moon here have an instinctual need to be in relationships and sometimes feel incomplete without them. For some, having the Moon here illustrates a projection of caretaking qualities onto others—for example the machismo male who deflects his softer side. This Moon is prone to entering co-dependent circumstances—this is on the path toward learning interdependence. A developed Moon here suggests a soul who is able to experience a mutual exchange of love.

The 8th House involves shared resources including intimacy, legacies, financial accrual, and making soul contact with others. As a water house, the 8th concerns interpersonal processing, the working through of emotional wounding. Having the Moon located here conveys an emotional nature familiar with, and often in need of, reconciliation with psychic heaviness. There is a pull toward drama and excess as the Moon is becoming more aware of its power and involvement with the darker components of life. Indeed, we have an unconscious planet located in a most poorly lit house—the potential for acting out pain or hurt in the soul is greatly amplified. This Moon has a fervent need to confront its emotional dynamics and to enter circumstances where these lessons may be learned.

Travel, expansion, higher education, philosophy and religion typify the 9th House. In contrast, the Moon seeks to nest and attain stability. A soul with the Moon here often does not feel rooted to a secure base of home life. The attachment to exploration may be stimulating for other planets, but the unpredictability of adventure leads to an emotional nature that is unsettled. Some with this placement may construe organized religion as a parent or source of comfort. On the more developed side is the soul who is aligned with spiritual purpose and a firm sense of morality. A 9th House Moon is able to connect cross-culturally and has a diverse set of lenses through which to view life. Whether or not there is emotional satisfaction is determined by the rest of the chart.

The 10th House involves issues of vocation, reputation, achievement—one's orientation to public life. As the most visible area of the chart, those with the Moon here often have a deep-seated need to be seen. Many times there is some sort of early recognition, or prominent role among other youngsters. Similar to the 1st House, having the Moon here tends to display the temperament openly. Wearing the heart on the sleeve does invite connection, but also turmoil. This is an easy target for adversaries. A 10th House Moon could also allude to a soul with a spiritual legacy involving nurturance or caretaking of some variety in a public fashion. A soul with this Moon position feels important in some way, or has a strong need to be.

A soul with the Moon in the 11th House often feels a sense of inclusion, or on the converse, alienation. This house pertains to allies, groups, community involvement, future aspirations and rewards. A healthy and developed Moon in this area feels popular and cared for by others. In some cases, the Moon here points to a communal living arrangement or some kind of emotional connection with systems larger than the traditional family. A struggling Moon here indicates a lack of emotional roots similar to the 9th House situation. The difference is that in the 11th, there may be even greater estrangement. Some with this Moon placement have a profound need to impact the world. There is a concern for and love of progress.

The 12th House includes institutions, things requiring completion, spiritual practice, as well as unresolved psychic phenomena to reconcile. With the Moon here, there is likely unassimilated emotional material in the psyche. There may be a sense of dealing with loss or the refusal or inability to detach from something dear to the heart. Oftentimes, the emotional nature is lost, excessively private or even suffering with some form of illness. There is a link with institutions and places of confinement. These places serve to facilitate the proper emotional processing necessary to catalyze renewal. Ultimately, a 12th House Moon connects with Spirit and channels that sense of compassion and kindness into personal scenarios. This personal water planet located in a transpersonal water house does connect the heart to the emotional rhythms within the collective consciousness. Successful completion of self-work leads to this lofty promise.

Sign/House Integration

Bringing the processes of a sign to the jurisdiction of a house is essential for grasping the lunar message. The first piece to consider is the nature of the sign—to feel what it could be like to own a particular Moon. Next, how would that evolutionary process function within the context of a specific house? Where is there overlap or dissonance? What gifts or problems could there be? Addressing these questions helps to bring the point of integration.

As mentioned earlier, many beginning students of astrology interchange signs with houses, thereby confusing the essential lunar message. A 2nd House Moon, though, is quite different from a Taurus Moon; a 5th House Moon may vary greatly from a Leo Moon. If we reverse thematically similar pairs, we can see the difference between signs and houses. For instance, let's distinguish the difference between an Aries Moon in the 4th House and a Cancer Moon in the 1st.

A 4th House Aries Moon may be used to experiencing conflict in the home—there is a feisty, protective and flammable quality triggered by close attachments. When acting unconsciously, this Moon may become abrasive, possibly in reaction to some emotional harm it has experienced. This is a Moon that prefers privacy (4th House) but is rooted to a deep-seated need to become powerful.

A 1st House Cancer Moon behaves emotionally. They naturally assume parenting roles, caretaking positions and wear how they are feeling on their sleeves. The Moon is particularly strong in Cancer so this person may come across as needy when triggered. There is the natural tendency to make attachments with others.

In this example it is easy to see very different emotional styles, needs and behaviors. The Aries Moon individual may want autonomy while the Cancer Moon seeks connection. To paint an exaggerated caricature: the Cancer Moon person always has a bowl of chicken soup to share and the Aries Moon may feel the need to throw the soup on a family member for some reason.

Both sign and house placement of the Moon provide instructive, but partial information regarding the unconscious and emotional nature. Combining these two pieces forms a whole that is greater than the individual parts. Houses are how internal consciousness is organized, and how it is projected into the world. By locating a particular style and process (sign) in a house, we can derive more information about how the soul has historically operated to get its needs met. Let's do a few more examples.

A Virgo Moon in the 7th House: This lunar nature tends to be sacrificial and self-critical, although helpful and with sterling intentions. Located in the 7th, themes of serving a partner and giving away one's autonomy are certainly possible. Feeling a sense of insecurity or subservience in contexts of equality leads one to imagine a relationship or marriage clearly defined within precise parameters. The housewife who cooks and cleans for a husband is one such example. The soul is working on (Virgo) achieving a greater sense of equality with others (7th).

A Scorpio Moon in the 9th House: This Moon has experienced emotional intensity (Scorpio) in the area of philosophical or physical exploration (9th). Being wounded or disturbed by religious proclamations or encountering painful realities that have upset a sense of feeling rooted are possibilities. This soul is on a passionate quest for truth, most likely because there are scars regarding this process. Pain involving the concept of Spirit or hostility regarding cultural differences could be part of the story. Someone emotionally indoctrinated into a system advocating enmity is not out of the question. Transformation (Scorpio) occurs when a larger truth (9th) is discovered.

A Sagittarius Moon in the 12th House: This soul may be holding on (12th) to a sense of righteous entitlement (Sagittarius) that no longer serves growth. The lunar nature may have a pronounced need for freedom (Sagittarius) that has met confinement (12th). Someone lonely within his self-created world is yet another possibility. This profile feels heated (Sagittarius), but resigned to the lack of potency indicative of the 12th House. Further evolution proceeds by channeling heart-fueled intention and purpose (Sagittarius) into the discovery of a compassionate and benevolent (12th) spiritual understanding and experiences.

Aspects to the Moon

Another critical piece to consider is the aspects the Moon makes to other planets. Since other planets provide an energetic stimulus, they greatly color the actual lunar energy. Mars in aspect to the Moon gives more urgency and action to the emotional needs while Uranus may electrify or shock the lunar body in unforeseen ways.

Planets in aspect to the Moon are partners. They illustrate how emotional patterns are played out and indicate the habitual behaviors that bring sustenance. They also point to what forces have historically caused problems and how these problems may be worked on. Any planet in aspect with the Moon is intimately involved in the process of emotional nourishment and healing.

Aspects indicate that two energies are linked. The type of aspect gives insight to whether the linkage is smooth (sextile, trine), challenging (square, opposition) or in a state of fusion (conjunction). Smooth aspects to the Moon show emotional strengths—how the person naturally gets needs met and how they instinctually behave. Challenging aspects indicate blockages, frustrations and reactive patterns that stem from past emotional difficulty. Any planet in conjunction with the Moon is intimately a part of the emotional memory of the soul, shaping the unconscious and playing out strongly. There is identification with the energy—for better or for worse.

The following paragraphs posit some examples of how the various planets in (major) aspect to the Moon might influence it. These possibilities are not intended to be all-inclusive, but to give a taste of what the pairing could be like. Planetary energy manifests in a wide variety of ways, and there are no magic statements regarding the interchanges.

The focus here is on "why" such an aspect could be represented in a chart, rather than just a description of "how" it plays out. This approach searches for the meaning behind planetary exchanges. However, the wide range of possibilities as to why such an aspect exists in a chart leaves us with only a thematic understanding—details about the past are elusive.

Sun/Moon aspects will be addressed in great detail later in the book.

The Moon is a focal planet in the chart. Along with the Sun, many astrologers give it more latitude when considering orbs of influence. However, unlike the Sun, the Moon consolidates and likes to hide. Using standard orbs: about 10 degrees for the conjunction and opposition, 7 or 8 for the square and trine and around 4 or 5 for the sextile and quincunx seem right. However, it must be noted that planets occupying the same house or sign are working with similar processes and therefore have some linkage. A good rule of thumb when considering orbs is, "the tighter the better." Where an aspect loses relevance is always speculative.

Moon/Mercury

The Moon in aspect to Mercury connects the unconscious emotional needs to the intellect and communicative function. At the most refined or advanced level, this indicates emotional intelligence. Souls that have integrated these functions successfully have a comprehensive understanding of their feelings and make decisions in prudent and thoughtful ways on their own behalf.

Those that incarnate with a need to develop this interchange further are learning to master the art of emotional intelligence. The busyness and chatter of Mercury has been used as a defensive measure. There is an unconscious pull to use the mind at the expense of sinking into the heart. The need to prove one's intellectual skills, the rationalization of emotions, or feeling youthful or naïve are some reasons why this aspect may appear.

This combination could manifest as a tendency to speak impulsively—the person who blurts out then covers the mouth. The Moon colors the otherwise rational intellectual function in highly subjective ways. Attaining precision and clarity of thought could be a challenge. The gift is the ability to speak from the heart and to balance and consider thought processes in relation to their emotional implications.

Mercury conjunct the Moon brings the otherwise aware and active brain (Mercury) into a fusion with the emotions (Moon). As the Moon is notoriously unconscious, the rational function may be completely submerged. With its associations with survival, the Moon is the stronger energy. The spiritual legacy may include some form of burying logic in favor of automatic responses. This gives a more primitive or instinctual flavor to thought processes. The fusion requires awareness in order to tease these separate functions apart and use them both judiciously and with clarity.

Mercury sextile the Moon allows greater distance and enthusiastic partnering between these functions. The curiosity of an eager child is an example of this exchange. Moon square Mercury could indicate that the unconsciousness in the soul is particularly bothered and upset regarding intellectual functioning. There may be substantial doubt or insecurity regarding one's inherent cognitive abilities.

Having the Moon trine Mercury, one could exhibit harmonious and clever banter and insight. There is likely to be a well-developed emotional connection to the mind, such as someone intellectually confident. Mercury opposed the Moon indicates that the resolution of intellectual issues requires greater confrontation. The heart has distanced itself from the mind, potentially leading to a fragmentation or anxiety in the psyche. The work is to learn (Mercury) about the feelings (Moon) through connecting with others.

Moon/Venus

This combination portrays a strong connection between the emotional "needs" (Moon) with the more casual "wants" (Venus). What we want, including socialization or achieving peace and comfort, is brought to greater urgency. The soul *requires* cooperation from other people, the accumulation of possessions or indulging in leisure to feel emotionally secure and happy.

We all need others—this is healthy and necessary. Those with this interchange have the need more pronounced than most, and there is likely some work involved in its integration. The goal is to develop the intimate function in ways that may provide greater union and fulfillment. If not, whatever neuroses that exist in the emotional unconscious are played out with others.

Those that have already gone through impressive soul development have quite an asset. There have innate diplomacy skills and a solid base of operations that govern emotional behavior. However, most of us are unfinished works and the task is to learn how to connect, share and find emotional gratification through relationships which will ultimately produce inner calm. The spiritual history likely shows some form of heightened expectations of others. The Moon and Venus are both gentle energies that seek pleasantness and accord. This pairing ultimately promises gracefulness and harmony after the resolution of unconscious tendencies that may be hindrances.

A conjunction between Moon and Venus blends to create an inner need to form pair-bonds and have deep friendships, or a heightened need for pleasure. It becomes very important to share the self with others—to *really* get to know another or at least open up oneself for others to see. A challenge is the increased chance of getting hurt by others and becoming too clingy in relationships. Another strong possibility is a situation where relational needs are so hidden and private that the self is one's best friend. Learning to get in touch with and honor the need for connection is the work.

The sextile between these planets shows an eagerness to connect with others, a temperament of engagement and trust. It is like the openness of a child approaching another at a playground, "Can I play with you?" The square shows a more troubling relational dynamic. The inner needs are somehow at odds with forming connections—and the possibilities are plentiful. There may be an unconscious need to sabotage friendships stemming from a karmic pattern of hurt or mistrust. A soul could inappropriately confuse friendship with love and put heavy emotional demands on others. There could be challenge in giving and receiving intimacy in a fluid and fair manner.

The Moon in trine to Venus contributes to likeability. This aspect has the mark of friendliness which many times leads to popularity. Since relating comes easy, the challenge is to complement this disposition with other skills such as honesty and clear boundaries. The opposition between Moon and Venus often indicates a history of interpersonal conflict and misunderstandings with others because of perceived slights and offenses. There is a strong need to build bridges, but the building is fraught with emotional negotiations and compromise. There is a hyper-attunement to relating and this aspect shows the greatest potential for projecting one's needs onto others.

Moon/Mars

Both of these energies are highly charged. Come hell or high water, an activated Mars satisfies its cravings. In the same vein, the Moon requires its needs to be met or else there is great upset or hurt. The combination makes for a feeling nature of urgency and passion. A soul with this pairing has integrated its experiences in a volatile manner. There is undoubtedly some form of wounding that has occurred that raised the temperature of the usually placid lunar lake.

There is likely a frustrated need within the soul calling for resolution. The ability to assertively get what one requires, and live life according to one's impulses, is in hot pursuit of better outcomes. The soul has felt some degree of anger or explosiveness and channeling the energy constructively is necessary. Those who come from the higher end of the evolutionary spectrum have been adept at being warriors in some way. Most with this combination have that aspiration.

The potential for lashing out unconsciously is quite likely here. The healing method involves action and direction, to courageously follow one's heart. Those who act without being in touch with underlying motivations are bound to create or find conflict. This gives the chance to learn how to reconcile these inner needs.

Moon conjunct Mars suggests an underground need for aggression or emotional conflict. There is a substantial emotional protective urge, likely stemming from a karmic familiarity with war-like themes—be it literal or psychological. This Moon feels angry. This pairing functions covertly, more like a counter-puncher. A Moon/Mars conjunction may manifest as a selfish tendency to run roughshod over others. At the other extreme is the condition where pro-active self-extension is quashed and the self turns inward to protect the simmering inside. A lid is put on the boiling water—and eventually an explosion occurs.

The sextile tempers the combination somewhat and yields a high-spirited disposition. The ability to act from a position of emotional strength is more rooted in the soul. The square presents quite a formidable challenge. The feeling nature seems to unconsciously find upset and hurt, creating a cycle of expectation of this outcome. The assertive drive runs contrary to the protective function, producing many obstacles to getting authentic needs met. There could be a tendency to become attracted to scenarios and people who exude uncomfortable energy—the purpose of which is to learn how to manage conflict more adeptly.

The Moon in trine to Mars suggests adeptness with emotional management and the assertion of intent. These people have a consistency between knowing what they need and effective action to fulfill the longing. The opposition is often played out in relationships. There is willingness, sometimes an eagerness, to engage in conflict. This person is the button-presser or antagonist who likes to chide people. The lunar memory has been opposed by aggression in some way. To balance the books, there is a need to push it back outwards. Knowing the correct battles to wage is the lesson.

Moon/Jupiter

This combination shows an emotional need to make an imprint upon humanity. Jupiter fuels the Moon to find meaning and feel comforted by a higher order in the world. The soul has integrated a code of living, or has faced great struggle in attaining this sense of moral imperative. The desire to make sense of life has been an inner longing. The spiritual quest we are all on is particularly emphasized in this combination.

The proverbial quest is often misguided by prescriptions from others. Many have been emotionally indoctrinated into belief systems that fail to deliver what they promise. This is a passionate pairing that may fuel rigid or dogmatic behaviors. Some may even be angry at Spirit or a personal conception of the divine. The more advanced souls have been able to find and deepen their sense of purpose. Most anyone with this combination is working toward that ideal. There is likely soul familiarity with the process of wrestling with philosophical or religious feelings.

Jupiter contacts with the Moon tend to enliven and inflate emotional tendencies. With such a large and spirited planet, there could be an exaggeration of one's behavior, an impulse to live large. Also possible is the folly of unrealistic expectations or grandiosity regarding one's importance. Growth is furthered by teaming needs with the action necessary to actualize intention.

Moon conjunct Jupiter shows an alliance between these functions. The soul feels jovial, adventurous or in need of risk-taking. There is an optimistic flavor, an innate trust in the benevolence of life, but one pitfall is having great expectations that life and others will always provide satisfaction. The shielding from unpleasantness may bring alarming reality checks.

The Moon in sextile to Jupiter suggests the mark of the pioneering spirit who leaps before looking. This outgoing aspect tends to equip a person with goal-directed behavior—the zest for engaging in life is infectious and inspiring. The square configuration shows more a frustrated need in pairing the self with a sense of mission. The emotional resolve to live fully or

80

make an impact has met obstacles and thereby created the condition of restlessness. Like shaking an unopened can of soda, there is a frustrated need for release. Further growth is achieved by attuning within and taking clear action on behalf of a calling.

The trine is easier. When it connects these two planets, a smooth partnership between inner life and outer circumstance is possible. This blending makes for a naturally content disposition that seems to act in alignment with the inner compass. The challenge may be one's own exaggerated expectations and unwittingly upsetting other people by not understanding one's emotional impact on them. When the Moon is opposed by Jupiter, there's a feeling of "almost making it." Goals and aspirations seem to be just out of reach—unable to be brought to fruition. This frequently results in ascribing rewards onto others and thus setting up a dynamic of jealousy or envy. Many times, there are expectations that others can and will meet one's inner needs. The lesson is to rely on the self and to find greater purpose within.

Moon/Saturn

One of the more serious and austere of all planetary combinations is between the Moon and Saturn. The emotional history of the soul is connected with fear, blockage, hardship or having experienced sobering realities of some sort. The "heavy heart" encapsulates this energetic exchange. In some cases, past life experiences have made the soul cold, wizened and paralyzed by dread or trepidation. At best, there is a sense of seasoned pragmatism, the bittersweet embrace of life knowing that it can deliver heartache at any turn. Moon/Saturn recognizes the frailty of existence and is learning to use wisdom to open channels of compassion.

The cautious and serious quality of Saturn doesn't easily mix with the vulnerability of the Moon. The soul has had to wise up and take care of things. There is a sense of emotional responsibility which often undercuts the carefree spontaneity of youthful fancy. Not all souls with these aspects could be considered "old" or "wise;" rather they have felt some burden in which youth or innocence was compromised.

Moon/Saturn contacts are quite common—illustrating the universality of difficulty people have with emotional management. Saturn may shut down the Moon, squashing, limiting and controlling it. Nevertheless, there is great potential for spiritual maturation. These contacts do tend to bring a soul into a more complete fruition.

Saturn conjunct the Moon portrays an emotional alignment with the fearful and heavy description above. This can manifest as a person who prefers not to invest emotionally in others—likely the result of having a spiritual history that includes poor nurturing or a series of difficult emotional connections. The soul has experienced a paucity of sustenance and incarnates in a similar predicament to learn to work through it. Effort is required to learn how to get in touch.

Saturn sextile the Moon has a flavor of emotional security or confidence with a readiness to hold positions of power. The usually changeable emotional nature is steadied while the externalization implied by the sextile yields high self-efficacy. The square shows conflict with maturation, a thwarted sense of emotional satisfaction and possibly depression. There may be little awareness of unconscious tendencies as Saturn tends to deny and repress. It some cases, the soul is frozen. Ultimately, the transformation into a solid, secure and grown-up disposition is developed.

The trine shows more of a seasoned nature. Confidence, integrity or the need to be in charge, are some manifestations. One challenge is lethargy. Without a stimulus or urgency to exercise the gift here, the soul may deflect responsibility. With Saturn opposed to the Moon, power struggles with authority are common. There is some disconnection between the inner needs and how these needs are met by others. Feeling oppressed or expecting parenting is unconsciously ascribed to others. Learning to welcome one's own sense of stature and accountability gradually lessens the interpersonal dynamic and builds inner confidence.

Moon/Uranus

In approaching the feeling nature of this mixture, it is important to keep in mind how inward and protective the Moon is in contrast to Uranus, which operates outside of the parameters of the status quo—the known and familiar. Picture a bizarre clown, gesturing wildly and speaking a made up language, holding a frightened puppy. This combination of energies is perplexing and unsettling. Likewise, a soul with this contact has been through experiences that have made a similar impact. A sense of emotional alienation, incredulity or jolting wildness has been absorbed.

Unpredictability is a major component to Uranus. Souls carrying this combination have likely assimilated into the psyche remnants of experiences that were disruptive in some way. Whereas the Moon likes to maintain continuity of nurturance, Uranus is uprooting. The more advanced souls with this aspect have been able to roll with the changes and have used the jolts in interesting ways. However, Uranus by its very nature is unstable—and when in contact with the Moon, it becomes unnerving.

Indeed, this combination describes emotional conditions that tend to be extreme. The restless and uncompromising energy of Uranus simply jars the more vulnerable and receptive inner life. These contacts potentially serve to awaken and even shock the unconscious into greater freedom and individuation.

The conjunction points to major disruptions in the unconscious emotional body. There is likely to be some form of trauma that needs to be reconciled and integrated. There may be little expectation of attaining comforting nurturance. In many cases the soul incarnates into a situation where love is given erratically if at all. Healing requires a descent into the unconscious to make contact and come to terms with difficult feelings. This frees the emotions and eventually lessens their impact. The result is liberation, the goal of healing this conjunction.

The sextile is obviously less severe. This combination portrays a soul with an excitable emotional nature—wired and rearing for stimuli. The soul is accustomed to activity and likes to shake things up. The challenge is an attachment to unstable or eccentric behavior patterns. The square shows an inner disquiet that is more troublesome. The emotional needs are either out of touch, highly unusual in some way or inappropriate in expression. The soul may feel a sense of weirdness and alienation and conclude there is pathology.

The trine between the Moon and Uranus shows some comfort with off-kilter or highly individualized feeling states. The soul is familiar with some degree of wildness and is naturally at home with diverse internal states. This aspect may indicate a soul with command and knowledge of itself. The opposition suggests a pattern of working though troubling emotional material with others. There is an unconscious presumption that relationships bring instability, which stems from a karmic pattern of this nature. Further growth requires the recognition of the pattern and the willingness to take measures to negotiate with one's emotional turmoil in a more conscious way.

Moon/Neptune

Out of the three outermost (transpersonal) planets, the Moon has the smoothest time integrating with Neptune. Both energies are loving, soft, serene, seeking connection and compassionate. The major difference is that Neptune is selfless while the Moon has urgent, self-preoccupied needs. This often results in an emotional nature that is filled with longing, a sense that life can be more fulfilling. This preference to cling to idealism or transcendence may distance the self from its more basic and primal needs.

Emotional confusion, deprivation or some form of dis-ease may be indicated by such a combination. Themes of tuning out through substances, television or fantasy are common. The underlying reason why a person behaves in such a way is from repeating past-life emotional coping strategies designed to ease pain. We dissociate from unpleasant stimuli, and lose ourselves in the process.

The dreamy quality of Neptune is like a great reservoir of love and potential. Filled with possibility, there is an almost irrational need to make contact with something redemptive and uplifting. This need is often the result of being in conditions that do not deliver sufficient sustenance. We often turn to Spirit in the more dire moments, in the most perplexing conditions. A seasoned or evolved soul with this combination carries the mark of the mystic—those that have been able to absorb and integrate an experience of Spirit.

Neptune conjoined the Moon may illustrate a high degree of emotional unconsciousness—authentic needs may be out of reach. It may also suggest that the urge to connect with Spirit has similarly become unconscious and is rendered inaccessible. Deep inside is a palpable longing, but without shining awareness internally there is little chance to access the gift. In some cases, the soul may be authentically engaged with transpersonal compassion and benevolence. This is the soul of a visionary, and the emotional need for this aspiration comes in many gradations of health and well-being.

The Moon in sextile to Neptune shows a serene disposition that actively wishes to channel peacefulness into the world. The soul has likely experienced expanded states of union in its history and may behave in accordance with it. The square suggests that there has been a great need to achieve more connection with love and healing attachments which have been denied or elusive. Underneath everyday awareness could be sadness, loss or dejection. Further growth requires the suspension of feeling estranged and the cultivation of relations that promote greater harmony and unimpeded sharing.

The trine aspect points to a state of emotional affinity with Neptune's spacious territory. There is likely trust in the goodness of humanity. This could be a soul with contemplative experience or, conversely, one with innocence or even gullibility. There is a pronounced instinctual need for flowing relations based on some positive set of karmic experiences. Neptune opposed the Moon often suggests deception or poor relational boundaries. This could be the result of a pattern developed over lifetimes of having relationships that are not trustworthy or clear. The soul eagerly wants to connect love with spirituality as a remedy for prior let-down or confusion.

Moon/Pluto

Perhaps the most intense combination in all of astrology is between the Moon and Pluto. The extremity and urgency of Plutonian processes brought to the vulnerability and tenderness of the Moon equates to an inner life of utmost passion, forcefulness and at many times deep emotional wounding. The severity of the condition is in equal measure to the powerful potentials available upon successful healing and resolution.

The frequent mention of transformation with Pluto has great relevance when paired with the Moon. Here, we see emotional breakdown as fuel for breakthrough. Those that incarnate with this combination have unfinished work to do in channeling the power of psychic wounding into constructive uses. Volcanoes need to erupt in order to release the building tension. In a similar way, there is great intensity simmering within that requires management and healing.

Those who have this combination likely have been involved in extreme circumstances to have absorbed such power. Prior lives have left an enduring mark, and the current lifetime involves engagement with the psychic material. The potential for deep, authentic and life-altering intimacy is attainable for those willing to pursue a path of growth.

Fusion of the Moon and Pluto often signifies unconscious rage, severe psychic hurts, abuse or manipulation regarding the use of power or any other emotionally damaging experiences whose imprint has gone underground. The soul is in a state of alarm, desperately seeking the reclamation of solace. This demarks a soul that has been involved in some of the most tumultuous dramas imaginable. The healing journey is a long process of soul retrieval and transformation—the pitfalls of using this strength unwisely and unconsciously are great.

Having the Moon configured in a sextile relationship with Pluto positions a person to use the wisdom and potency gained in prior lives for active purposes. The soul is familiar with the darker realities of the human condition, and has been able to use the lessons of these experiences with skill. The square insists that integration between these energies has been problematic, and it's now necessary to work with them unflinchingly. The necessary friction of the square tends to give the Moon/Pluto exchange many guises, seemingly at every turn. The soul is unconsciously drawn to people and situations that trigger emotional upset and wounding. By navigating the Plutonian waters, a soul learns how to be with itself, manage its emotions, and find power in vulnerability.

The trine shows a far smoother history of working with this intensity. The soul has become adept at understanding and connecting with others from an emotionally sound and mature disposition. Using emotional material as fuel for catalyzing growth has become a resource in the soul. One would need to realize that not everybody is so skilled at this type of exchange— the hazard is to unwittingly alienate people who aren't.

The opposition brings the interpersonal component to its strongest expression—with the Moon and Pluto this means intimacy is the battlefield. This aspect indicates that one's needs (Moon) have met opposition in psychologically challenging scenarios (Pluto). This has resulted in a suspicion or expectation that intimacy needs cannot be met by others. Many times, disturbing material is projected upon others, creating a lengthy portfolio of emotional crises. A soul with this aspect has undoubtedly been quite upset and injured by the actions of others and now has the inclination to seek out further evidence that the world is damaging—or to finally realize the soul can be healed through connecting authentically with others.

Into the Deep

In the astrological system, the element of water pertains to emotions, processing and healing. In order to move forward, one must reconcile the emotional struggles within the soul. As discussed throughout this chapter, the Moon plays the prominent role in this undertaking.

The other water planets are Neptune and Pluto, which are associated with the signs of Pisces and Scorpio and houses 12 and 8, respectively. These planets, signs and houses are relevant and very much a part of emotional/spiritual growth. However, it must be noted that the Moon (along with Cancer and the 4th House) is more personal. Scorpio and Pluto have connections with social and interpersonal issues while Pisces and Neptune extend to the transpersonal. These energies involve forces outside the personal realm that impact the shape of the unconscious. They are broader in scope and deeper within the psyche.

Much has been made of Pluto in evolutionary or soul-focused astrology, and rightfully so. It represents the greatest injuries we have sustained, the wounds most in need of healing. Neptune tends to be less of a focus but also conveys places where there may be emotional issues such as sadness, grief, disillusionment and longing. Spiritual growth must ultimately address the terrain of both Neptune and Pluto.

Since these areas of the unconscious are remote, they are difficult to access. We are connected to the interpersonal and transpersonal through the personal—we touch these areas *through* the Moon. One analogy to use is digging in the ground. If we descend into deeper and deeper layers, we eventually run into the wounds that are buried. Pluto and Neptune are connected to these sensitive areas of the unconscious, but the Moon is the entire ground. One cannot work with deeper processes without the necessary mechanism that allows contact in the first place.

Digging in the dirt of the psyche will ultimately lead you to all corners of the unconscious. By working through whatever issues are pertinent to the energies of Neptune and Pluto, the entire ground of the unconscious will shift. This will certainly provide irrigation and allow Moon seeds to grow more strongly into radiant flowers. All water processes involve emotional/spiritual growth—the Moon is how they become accessed.

Conclusion: General Interpretive Guidelines

The major factors in interpreting the Moon are sign, house and aspects. These factors provide an extraordinary level of detailed information as to how a soul feels. Intellectual analysis only gets an astrologer so far, and with the Moon, it may actually sabotage understanding. The best way to comprehend the Moon is by entering its emotional language. Connecting the heart to the symbols deepens one's grasp.

Every sign has a different feeling component. The Moon accesses a particular sign in highly subjective ways, and these styles and processes are taken personally. Touching in with what Virgo or Sagittarius feels like opens the intuitive channels and allows the astrologer to empathize. Whereas Jupiter or Mars latch on to more active qualities in a sign, the Moon deepens and absorbs its nature. It is useful to spend a few moments contemplating the feeling states that emerge.

The essential nature of the Moon is located in a specific house. The house defines the area of life where there are attachments and needs. However, the house location is not as much an anchor as the sign. This is because houses are fluid areas and malleable. They *host* energy rather than indicate its elemental character.

Planets making aspects to the Moon not only distribute its influence elsewhere, they energetically color and inform the lunar profile. Again, it's essential to attempt to feel the other planets involved. What does an opposition to Saturn or a trine to Venus feel like? Each planet has a broad scope. Integrating with the Moon narrows them down to personal issues of protection, survival, needs, temperament and instinctual behaviors. The Moon and its aspected planets synergize into newer psychic constructions—the sum is greater than the parts. This is most evident with the conjunction, but all aspects show some form of joining between planets. The orb (degrees of separation) of influence provides information about how strong or weak the relationship is.

Any planets in the sign of Cancer are also connected to the Moon since it rules these energies. The house with Cancer on the cusp is also an area where lunar energy is naturally distributed. In the case of a Cancer rising, the Moon becomes the chart ruler. Ruling the pivotal 1st House, which concerns choices, action and persona, the Moon has great influence on behavior. The possible gift is to act wisely in accordance with what's inside oneself. The struggle is behaving unconsciously. It's important to note that the entire lunar profile shapes the personal expression. Every Cancer rising individual is being powered by a unique Moon.

Special consideration is usually given to planets that are "angular" (residing in houses 1,4,7 or 10). These houses initiate activity and open new sectors of the chart: action (1st), roots and home life (4th), relationships (7th), and career (10th). The Moon's natural home is the 4th House, so this location indicates a strong lunar disposition attuned to family, privacy and introspection.

Grasping the Moon is a powerful way to begin a chart analysis. More than any other planet, it shows why, how and where someone is coming from. It relates directly to past life and early child influences and carries the greatest personal depth of all planetary energies. The human drama is marked by vulnerability and our innermost needs, which require acknowledgement and the intention to work through emotional issues. The payoff is the ability to successfully bond with the self, others and the collective.

Chapter 4
The Lunar Nodes: Chronicles of Lessons

The Nodal axis in the chart is full of mystery and intrigue. Many astrologers do not use it at all—and those who do interpret its meaning in various ways. Some view it as being related to maternal or nurturing issues, while others believe it's involved with the psychological integration of solar and lunar functions. Many understand the axis as somehow pertinent to development, but the spiritual view that accepts reincarnation is not yet broadly popular.

Here, it is assumed that the Nodes relate directly to the central soul lessons being worked on. The Nodes are at the intersection between past (Moon) and present (Sun) and portray the themes, situational determinants, areas of familiarity and reflexive behavior patterns that helped shaped the lunar unconscious. As is the case with the Moon, the level of consciousness present with any pair of Nodes cannot be gleaned from the chart. We are all works in progress, and it is prudent to view the Nodes as having both assets and challenges. A soul incarnates to attain advanced levels of growth, so struggles are assumed to be part of anyone's spiritual history.

Perhaps the most important (and curiously overlooked) facet of the Nodes is that they are the Nodes *of the Moon.* Therefore, they relate directly to the Moon itself—specifically, how the unconsciousness of the soul is developing. Interpreting the Moon with its Nodes provides integration between how a soul feels (Moon) and the main lessons it's addressing (Nodes).

The Moon is the unconscious, emotional memory of the soul that is carried from lifetime to lifetime. It is pure feeling.

Using words or ideas to capture the essence of the Moon can actually bring us away from it. In contrast, the lessons of the Lunar Nodes are appropriately understood through analysis.

Whereas the Moon depicts attachments, instincts, defensive strategies and needs, the Nodes convey a whole other set of qualities. The South Node represents what the soul is familiar with, including the soul's natural tendencies and inclinations, the usual ways of approaching and processing one's life. It also conveys the inherent strengths and resources accrued from the past.

Familiarity leads to habituation and repetition, which produces a solid and consistent character. It also leads to a crystallization of patterns which inhibits newer creative expressions. The "familiarity factor" of the South Node is part of what some call our karma. The definition used here is that karma is the interrelationship we have with the world based on our actions and the results of those actions. Unlike the hidden and instinctual Moon, the South Node has more to do with how past lives were actually lived.

Theoretically, we have lived many lives. The totality of a soul's experience may never be fully understood. The Nodal profile helps narrow the focus to present life issues. In a meaningful and intelligent universe, it is reasonable that the most pressing imprints from the past are detectable.

The South Node describes lessons to be learned—work that the soul wishes to address. At some point in the past, set behaviors and inclinations have brought us to crisis points. At these times we are challenged to regroup and move beyond the predicament. These "rocks on the road" can overwhelm and even defeat us. The planets connected to the Nodal axis by aspect and rulership show us not only the energetic forces that shaped us, but also the ways to successfully overcome past struggles.

The karmic profile can be interpreted abstractly as a set of psychological traits or concretely as a biographical storyline. Either way, certain themes emerge that point directly to the lessons being worked upon. The abstract/psychological interpretation is more general and gives greater latitude to what

92

actually occurred in past life scenarios. However, being less tangible, it is harder to grasp the spiritual struggle. A concrete/biographical storyline provides greater animation and form and is easier to understand.

Critics of evolutionary astrology argue that it is impossible to know the actual stories of past lives, and thus, this analysis is too speculative if not disingenuous. It's important to keep in mind that the *themes* from the past are what is most relevant, not the details. Whatever story is gleaned may well be factually inaccurate, but if it is thematically consistent with the symbols, it will resonate with the chart owner. It provides a sense of the dynamics in play. The emotional connection with the story is the verifying factor.

The North Node is the direction in which a soul seeks to travel. Always in the opposite sign and house from the South Node, it is where the soul may expand to incorporate new skills and experiences. Since the South Node is familiar and habitual, it takes concerted effort to keep momentum toward the North Node. Ultimately, a balance may be attained. Astrology largely concerns the reconciliation of polarities, and nowhere is this more evident than with the Nodes.

The movement toward the North is in no way a dismissal or condemnation of the South. In fact, South Node attributes are so well-developed and such a part of the soul legacy they cannot be erased (nor should we want to). It would be like forgetting the skills learned in elementary school such as arithmetic or tying one's shoes. Striving to reach the promise of the North Node *complements* spiritual growth and makes the soul more well-rounded and whole. Achieving a sense of mastery through the Nodal lessons would include proficiency with both; at birth only the South is familiar.

The North Node is a clear statement of what the soul wishes to accomplish in the lifetime for greater emotional completion. It's a wonderful gift to have astrology reveal this major intention, but it's important to keep in mind that fulfilling its possibilities is never easy. Consider a sailor who spots land after many days at sea—there is still a journey ahead to reach the mooring. Many of us are adrift and never reach the destination, but at least the North Node informs us of what our promised lands are like. As soon as we relax our conscious efforts to grow in this direction, we tend to fall back upon the gifts (and repetitive patterns that further our struggles) already established (South Node). It takes solid intention and persistent effort to maximize the potentials of the North Node.

The Nodes in the Signs

The Nodes always occupy a pair of opposing astrology signs and concern the interplay within the polarity. Opposing signs have such a dynamic interaction because they complement each other. Incorporating both sides of a pairing brings greater wholeness.

For example, a chart may have a South Node in Virgo in the 3rd House. This soul has a piercing, analytical mind, capable of great reason and intellectual prowess. The North Node would be in Pisces in the 9th. The soul, already familiar with knowledge and education, may choose to expand its scope into philosophy, spirituality and more systematic thinking. Of course, the Virgo skepticism and "small pond" mentality of the 3rd House would have to be reconciled in order to realize the limitless, mystical Piscean qualities within the "big pond" realm of the 9th. Nevertheless, there is a continuation with learning.

The house placement of the Nodes gives crucial information about the contexts of the soul lessons being addressed. Any of the 12 Houses will move the Nodal profile dramatically in particular directions. In a sense, there are 12 different versions of any of the Nodal characteristics. To take it even further, the rulers of the Nodes also play key roles in describing how the lessons conveyed by the Nodes are carried out. The following paragraphs on the sign polarities are general and brief with some examples of house placements.

Aries/Libra

Those with the Nodes along this axis are learning about the dynamic of I-Thou relationships. Aries defines itself and holds fast to its autonomy in relation to others. Libra is other-focused—sometimes in ways that do not honor self-will or determination. Having the Nodes here suggests that a balance between self/other is lacking in some way. An Aries South Node is learning to complement an already established self-orientation with more sensitivity about how personal behavior impacts others. In contrast, a Libra South Node is learning new ways of behaving based on established social mores and awareness of others' needs.

Aries South Node: Whereas an Aries Moon may indicate a soul that feels angry, thwarted or somehow emotionally motivated for conflict, the Aries South Node portrays the theme in a more externalized or biographical way. There is actual experience with Aries scenarios in which the soul has been embroiled. An Aries South Node is self-preoccupied and used to defending itself in some way. The approach to the world is with the guard up, and others are seen as antagonists. "One needs to be prepared for battle" is a wise attribute to have when a situation calls for it, but much of life is not about conflict. Effort in peaceful endeavors (Libra North Node) balances this inclination.

An Aries South Node in the 10th House may be familiar with public displays of courage and could have held leadership positions. With a 4th House Libra North Node, there is the intention to create a balanced and pleasing environment in the home, perhaps to raise a family. The soul may use its gifts of assertion and self-awareness to provide a home that offers a sense of dignity and grace to its residents.

An Aries South Node placed in the 6th House may suggest involvement with military (Aries) service (6th House). With the Libra North Node in the 12th, one's asked to seek greater peace and equilibrium (Libra) and to let go (12th) of psychological scars from past battles, and to learn how to connect more with Spirit.

Libra South Node: A Libra Moon is gentle, pleasing, and has an instinctive need for harmony. A Libra South Node has been a peacemaker. It has a natural proclivity for diplomacy but also has refused to actively stand up for itself in some way or habitually chooses the path of least resistance. Many with this placement are familiar with marriage or other long-term relationships and naturally gravitate to pairing with others as a way of self-definition. The North Node in Aries points to a need for greater self-orientation and to enter roles that can effectively utilize the social skills. The soul seeks risk and involvement in situations that call for bravery and/or determination. This may mean tackling a great work of some kind and following it through to its conclusion.

A Libra South Node in the 9th House shows a reliance on others (Libra) in the formation of belief systems (9th House). A soul that has been part of a social congregation that promotes inclusiveness and equal sharing is a possibility. There is likely an attachment to living by a code of behavior (9th House) to maintain psychic equilibrium (Libra). An Aries North Node in the 3rd illustrates that spiritual growth involves courageously (Aries) using one's own cognitive abilities (3rd) to discover new ways of understanding. The intention is to think (3rd House) for the self (Aries).

With a Libra South Node in the 8th House, peacemaking roles in interpersonal conflict, strife or psychologically disturbing venues are indicated. Being married to someone else's power, resources or even being under a partner's control are possibilities. The Aries North Node in the 2nd House seeks to develop self-reliance, confidence and inner fortitude. The lesson is not only to become stronger (Aries) but also to create inner contentment and personal security (2nd House).

Taurus/Scorpio

Taurus and Scorpio function along the axis of fortification versus risk. Souls that are comfortable or serene within (Taurus) often choose not to venture into intense scenarios. Souls that have habitually acted in risky ways (Scorpio), or have been caught up in dramatic situations, benefit by being settled and embodying greater calmness.

This axis also has a relational correlate—how we are secure in the self (Taurus) vs. sharing and exchanging with others (Scorpio). However, the dynamic largely concerns the interplay between stability and inertia (Taurus) and complexity and change (Scorpio). A Taurus South Node is learning to use its earthy self-reliance in circumstances that foster emotional and psychological growth. In contrast, a Scorpio South Node is striving to reach greater stillness in order to balance a spiritual history too familiar with drama.

Taurus South Node: A Moon in Taurus may indicate a sensual quality to the feeling nature, perhaps an emotional need for safety or someone genuinely at peace with the self. A Taurus South Node may belong to a soul familiar with Taurus pursuits such as gardening, money-making, the arts or massage, who approaches the world with an expectation of naturalness and ease. Adam and Eve were expelled from the Garden of Eden to experience more complex truths, and having a Scorpio North Node is a similar program. It is time to confront and integrate what has been previously unspoken, ignored or driven into the unconscious.

Entering the labyrinth of the taboo, the dark, the unseemly and even the twisted is understandably something most of us avoid in everyday life. However, Scorpio truths are part of the human drama and involvement with such subjects not only rounds out the Taurus South Node's life education, it also makes them more emotionally powerful.

A Taurus South Node in the 7th House is a steady and dedicated (Taurus) partner familiar with bonding and connection (7th). This seems like a preferred disposition but the Nodes convey lessons. It's quite possible the soul has been in stultifying arrangements that limit spiritual advancement. A Scorpio North Node in the 1st is a bold statement about finding one's own unique power and assuming greater responsibility, if not leadership positions (1st House).

With a Taurus South Node in the 12th House, a soul is likely to be comfortable or stuck in reclusive positions such as in a monastery or prison. This configuration speaks of a soul that benefits by working on (6th) and improving psychological processing skills (Scorpio). Being in intense and even turbulent environments (such as an emergency room) assists spiritual growth by introducing the element of unpredictability. Working hands-on (6th House) with the gripping moments of this human drama (Scorpio) is beneficial.

Scorpio South Node: A Scorpio Moon has a volatile and intense emotional disposition whereas a soul with a Scorpio South Node has been involved in dramatic circumstances, but may feel (Moon) differently about the involvement. Nevertheless, this placement shows a proclivity towards entering highly charged situations and assuming roles that tend to make others uncomfortable. Examples of this Nodal placement include the detective, therapist, hypnotist or any other role that probes deeply for inner truths. This probing, and often dark preoccupation, is balanced by learning about simpler and less tumultuous endeavors. It benefits those with a Taurus North Node to involve the self with people and activities that promote calmness—to harmonize with nature (both external and internal) with a lower heart rate is called for.

A Scorpio South Node in the 1st demarks a soul that is responsible for behaving in powerful and even imposing ways. This is the disposition of a highly motivated seeker of life-altering experiences. Having control and autonomy is of utmost importance. Freedom with sexual and/or psychological assertiveness is prized. A Taurus North Node in the 7th is learning to become more trusting and comfortable (Taurus) partnering in egalitarian ways (7th House) and finding contentment in the company of others.

Having this South Node in the 3rd House speaks of an intellectual inquiry into places of darkness, sexuality or power. This Node is highly focused and probing. This South Node may be hurt or manipulated (Scorpio) by what it was taught (3rd House) in prior lives. To complement this disposition, expanding

98

one's mind (9th) and coming to greater appreciation of the vastness of Spirit heals. Making peace (Taurus) with the belief system (9th House) is warranted.

Gemini/Sagittarius

This polarity deals with perceptions and viewpoints. The difference is between an open-ended inquiry (Gemini) and finding solid convictions (Sagittarius). Both share a willingness to learn and venture forth. These signs seek to understand the world (Gemini) and develop an approach life (Sagittarius). Gemini tends to be innocent, curious, open-minded, generally youthful and logical. Sagittarius is seasoned, has opinions, and advocates morality. It tends to discount logic as the final arbiter of larger truths.

A Gemini South Node is skilled at questioning but would now benefit by finding clear direction—to choose one horse to ride, and ride it with vigor. The curiosity about life (Gemini) can be brought into a spiritual path (Sagittarius). In contrast, a Sagittarius South Node can be rigidly aligned with pat answers and needs more information, variety and openness. The foundation of wisdom (Sagittarius) is ready for open-minded communication and teaching (Gemini).

Gemini South Node: Many times, this South Node shows a youthful spiritual condition, the *puer* or Peter Pan who resists growing up. Those who choose to remain immature are prone to irresponsibility, ineffectuality or lack a firm moral compass. They are learning that life is far more than a pursuit of the trivial. Whereas a Gemini Moon shows an emotional disposition that uses rationalization as a survival tactic, a Gemini South Node suggests a general approach to life. Some examples of the open-minded disposition are found in the student, journalist, writer and all types of the "scientist," using a broad definition.

A Gemini South Node placed in the 4th House implies that the home is where schooling takes place. The family lineage is one of learning and there is an expectation to become intellectually adept. The home life may also have conflicting messages and elements of chaos. The soul may be rooted to indecision resulting from unclear messages received. A 10th House Sagittarius North Node is a declaration to become proficient and authoritative in the world, fueled by an unwavering passion to make a difference.

Having a Gemini South Node in the 2nd House reveals an alignment with reason. Being an earth house, the 2nd is where we are prone to calcify and become stuck. It is what's "mine"—be it material or psychological. With a Sagittarius North Node in the 8th, evolutionary advancement occurs when the soul enters realms of greater psychological complexity and finds a sense of meaning there. The soul intention is to seek and risk new levels of profundity and engagement with life.

Sagittarius South Node: A Sagittarius Moon has an emotional need to be right and assert its sense of adventure. A Sagittarius South Node may suggest an explorer, religious figure, philosopher or politician. The soul approaches life from the certainty of purpose and direction. These souls know that life is meaningful and there is a responsibility to do something with our precious moments. However, the extreme Sagittarius struggles with dogmatic, rigid and even controlling behaviors as seen with fanatics, terrorists and religious zealots. This placement is in need of more input and experience to truly see the big picture. The freshness and fascination of Gemini is the complement.

A Sagittarius South Node in the 12th House is a religiously oriented placement. The contemplative arena of the 12th is infused with a doctrine or philosophical protocol. This very well could be the mark of an ascetic, nun or anyone who has made great sacrifices (12th) for a religious understanding (Sagittarius). This is certainly laudable, but it may also be unbalanced. Further growth is attained by reentering the everyday world. Engaging in service, mentoring and other realms where one could be useful (6th) with a desire for further learning (Gemini) brings a newfound discovery of possibilities.

In the 5th House, the Sagittarian South Node operates in areas of children, fun, creativity and involvement in social/romantic settings. A soul with this configuration feels entitled to live life fully and bask in the present moment. There is an allegiance to freedom. Further growth becomes possible by attending more to the future, global issues and group membership (11th) with an attitude of openness to whatever needs to be done to be of help. These souls are learning (Gemini) to connect with the wider world family (11th).

Cancer/Capricorn

Cancer and Capricorn both concern influence. The difference is between private influence as seen in the home and the public influence of a vocation. These cardinal signs address issues of initiative and tend to be conservative, thorough and tenacious. The difference can be thought of as soft vs. hard. Cancer is sensitive, empathic and emotional, while Capricorn is results-oriented, disciplined and not easily swayed by sentiment.

Having the Nodes along this axis is not as much about the emotional temperament (Moon) but about roles, behaviors and lessons. Those with a Cancer South Node are learning to invest the heart more in visible, public, and effortful ways to sculpt a body of work. A Capricorn South Node benefits by investing more in family, inner well-being, emotional understanding and finding strong roots.

Cancer South Node: A Cancer Moon is in touch with feelings. Souls with this South Node are heavily invested in a family or personal mythology that has defined them. They're likely to be holding on to age-old imprints that have been passed down. These imprints have had tremendous impact on decision-making and life choices. An example would be someone born into a prominent family and expected to follow a script. The Cancer quality brings a sense of nurturance, support and familiarity.

Capricorn follows rules too, but they serve personal ambition. Having the North Node in this managerial and largely autonomous sign is to separate from the pull of expectation and reorient to a sense of being one's own authority. In some cases, the Cancer South Node accrual of experience will be a welcome support to one's calling—in other cases it may be too restrictive and filled with a vacuum-sealed agenda. Cancer South Nodes are learning to accept greater self-responsibility and to wield a power of their own design.

This South Node placement in the 7th House brings nurturing, consolidation and loyalty to partnerships. There is a tendency to feed the needs of the relationship to ensure its preservation. Taking care of, or expecting care from, others can also be part of this configuration. Capricorn North Node in the 1st has a strong level of self-definition and behaves in accordance with personal, rather than relational considerations. The soul wishes to work diligently toward a goal and find self-respect and integrity through that process.

A Cancer South Node may be in the 10th House. Here there is familiarity with a public role as a nurturer of some sort. Mother Theresa or other emotional diplomats come to mind. The drive is to care for the world, or in some cases, to care for one's reputation. A Capricorn North Node in the 4th seeks to become more rooted to one's personal strength. Instead of parenting through vocation, the soul may be interested in more private, contained and in-depth nurturing of one's own kin.

Capricorn South Node: Whereas a Capricorn Moon may struggle to connect with feelings, the locus of life orientation with the South Node in this sign has been on vocational or public issues. The soul is used to hard work, surviving the slog toward accomplishment and generally avoiding things that get in the way. There is trust in what works—a more traditional and even vigilant exercising of security. There is a protective and sometimes even isolated quality.

Structure is priceless but it also leads to hardening. A Cancer North Node seeks to bring in fluidity to what is rigid. The next lessons about heart are being learned, and this may involve family, introspection or whatever facilitates a deepening of feeling. A Capricorn South Node is becoming more able to let go and trust in the fragility of this human condition.

A Capricorn South Node in the 9th House may well bespeak conservative religiosity. Being part of a structure (Capricorn) that provides meaning and life direction (9th) is familiar. Solidity here leaves little room for variation, so having a Cancer North Node in the 3rd corrects the imbalance. Exercising the faculties of the mind, becoming aware of new perceptions and asking questions are 3rd House material. Doing this from a soft, compassionate and sincere (Cancer) disposition allows the evolving soul to embrace new understandings of the human drama.

With a Capricorn South Node in the 6th House, a much different story emerges. This could be the hardest working combination of all. Assuming responsibilities to ensure survival through enduring constant drudgery has worn out the soul. In a karmic sense, the soul has been through many trying tests. With the Cancer North Node in the 12th, nourishment through connecting with Spirit is part of the intention. Opening the heart to the transpersonal uplifts and refreshes the soul. Falling in love (Cancer) with Spirit (12th House) brings priceless reward and development.

Leo/Aquarius

Leo and Aquarius address the interplay between individuality/personality and collectivity/sociology. Every performer (Leo) needs an audience (Aquarius) and within every group (Aquarius) emerge particular personalities (Leo). Those with work along this axis are keenly aware of how connected an individual is with the group and may choose to work on identifying with the opposite polarity.

There are many possible reasons why some people don't participate in life: trauma, exile, overly rational disposition, feeling different, estrangement and disability are some examples. These themes and others are possible with an Aquarian South Node. Conversely, some souls become too identified with personality, self-expression, living large, self-consciousness or indulgence (Leo South Node) and would benefit from a more global and detached perspective.

Leo South Node: Having this indicator does not necessarily mean the soul has been in positions of royalty or celebrity although that is a possibility. It means that past lives were organized in a self-centered way and created an imbalance. A Leo Moon feels special and has an emotional need for attention and to be well thought of. The South Node in Leo is more a statement about the karma accrued from past lives.

There could be a spiritual legacy of privilege or living life in a robust way which contributed to narcissistic tendencies. Leo is incredibly generous and giving but is uninterested in collective issues. Learning to contribute to and participate in humanitarian causes and concerns in some way brings greater balance. Whereas Leo basks in the present moment, Aquarius has an eye on the future.

A Leo South Node in the 10th House is the placement where it's most likely that fame or celebrity is part of the soul's history. The 10th concerns public roles and reputation, and with Leo, there is a memory of visibility. The Aquarius North Node in the 4th House indicates that greater individuation unfolds in more private, introspective and family realms. The cutting edge of future potential (Aquarius) is located within, and with solid attachments to loved ones.

A Leo South Node in the 8th House has sought and enjoyed vital expression in deep soul merging with others. There is possibly an over-identification with partners' well-being or the rewards they may have access to: pleasure, monetary resources, as well as sexuality. The soul feels good (Leo) by entering transformative connections (8th). The intention is to become more grounded, contained and secure (2nd) in one's individuality (Aquarius) and derive strength from one's self-esteem.

Aquarius South Node: An Aquarius Moon often is distanced from emotions while an Aquarius South Node may belong to a soul that is in some way out of sync with the norms of society. Some among us are the revolutionaries, paradigm shifters, rebels, outlaws and eccentrics. Many of these souls march to the sound of their own drums and refuse to care what others think.

These souls have experienced some form of marginalization, or possibly shock or trauma. Disability in some form, whether physical or psychological, renders a soul unable to actively partake in everyday life. A Leo North Node indicates the necessity to be more present and involved. It entails the development of a unique personality and creative gift to share.

One possibility for an Aquarius South Node in the 5th House is a soul that may have suffered some form of trauma (Aquarius) in childhood (5th House) or was unable to share itself openly. Another possibility is a soul legacy of being different (Aquarius) in social spheres (5th House) and likely misunderstood. The soul is moving towards investing magnanimously (Leo) in global issues (11th), to be vital and engaged in groups and causes. This personal investment (Leo) in the world (11th House) corrects the imbalance of removal or peculiarity.

With an Aquarius South Node in the 3rd House, a scientific mindset capable of observation and detachment is noted. This is someone who prefers using a microscope or fantastic gadget compared to directly experiencing the rhythms of life. Investing heartily (Leo) in far-reaching and even exotic (9th) adventures brings wholeness and spiritual growth.

Virgo/Pisces

Virgo and Pisces both seek advancement, healing and resolution. Virgo has a hands-on approach while Pisces surrenders into consciousness and learns to reach perspective. Ultimately, Pisces yearns to let go of or resolve pressing issues. Both of these signs deal with making sacrifices and reaching a place of humility. This orientation to advancement can be channeled into its polarity through a willingness to become either more focused or spacious with the intent.

Those with a Virgo South Node have been in obedient or subservient roles and are familiar with performing hands-on tasks in the world. They find meaning through contemplative, expansive and more fluid activities. With a Pisces South Node, the soul has given its potency or visibility away and benefits by an earthy or structured routine.

Virgo South Node: A Virgo Moon may have a restricted emotional nature or the need to be of assistance. The South Node here is the mark of the servant—and when defined broadly, this means many things. Those that have made sacrifices to put others' needs ahead of their own are used to servitude. This certainly includes work, but also service to a partner, a cause or a religion may be included depending upon the house position. Virgo themes include self-denial or even punishment.

A Virgo South Node may be a workaholic or become wrapped up in minutia. Pisces endeavors such as meditation, merging with nature, transcending ego limitations and being more "loose" assist in soul development. Becoming adept at the spiritual arts, enhancing the creative functions and learning to see the illusory (even dreamlike) quality of life are helpful remedies.

Having this South Node in the 11th House portrays a soul that has put the needs of the world before the self and has made many sacrifices. This is a vigilant and tireless humanitarian who just can't say "no" when help is needed. "Sure, I'll volunteer for the Sierra Club, I'll fit it in somehow." A Pisces North Node in the 5th suggests it's time to lose oneself (Pisces) in the present moment and become absorbed in fun, personal experimentation and simpler activities.

With a Virgo South Node in the 4th House, family responsibilities are called to mind. This soul has been sheltered, hidden and its fingers are worn thin from work. One possibility is the mother busy raising a house full of children or even a slave (Virgo) on a plantation (4th). A Pisces North Node in the 10th shows the intention to have an imaginative (Pisces) career on one's own terms. Making movies, being an ambassador of compassion or a meditation instructor are some examples.

Pisces South Node: A Pisces Moon may have great emotional sensitivity, a reservoir of compassion for others or be dealing with unresolved sadness and longing. A Pisces South

Node suggests a karmic history where self needs were sacrificed in some way. Like a feather blowing in the wind, there isn't an anchor in this placement. Being consumed by relationships, a career, family, a spiritual program or whatever the entire Nodal profile suggests became problematic. Virgo qualities of steadfastness, attending to detail, discernment and a commitment to growth are sought.

Another possibility would be past lives of invisibility brought on by imprisonment, substance abuse or contemplative retreat. Showing up fully is required to achieve the lessons of a Virgo North Node. Another theme along the axis of Virgo/Pisces is tightness/looseness. Some with a Pisces South Node have had loose morals, poor impulse control or undefined understandings of how to proceed through life. Virgo has many guidelines and develops a firmer program.

A Pisces South Node in the 7th House speaks of the tendency to make sacrifices for a partner—almost to give away one's sense of control. Pisces is poorly defined as it is, and in the 7th there is the propensity to follow another's lead. A Virgo North Node located in the 1st House advocates greater autonomy and sharper self-definition (Virgo) through one's actions (1st House). Working diligently at a craft or personal self-improvement regimen increases viability and personal power.

With a Pisces South Node in the 1st House, the looseness of the sign has behavior correlates. This profile suggests someone who prefers not to be bound by routine, but free to act on whatever whims arise. Virgo in the 7th is becoming more aware of others and is cultivating interdependence. The lesson is to develop (Virgo) equal relationships (7th).

Housing the Nodes

As is the case with the Moon and every other planet in the chart, the Nodes are always located in houses. With the Nodes, it is more accurate to think of them as occupying a pair of houses. They will always span 1 of the 6 polarities of opposing houses.

Before proceeding to sign/house integration, here's a quick summary of these 6 polarities.

When the Nodes fall along the 1-7 axis, issues of self-orientation vs. others require greater balance. With the South Node in the 1st, the alignment is with the self: one's desires, behaviors and choices are at the root of the karma. Learning to take others' needs into consideration is being cultivated. With the South Node in the 7th, the lessons to resolve are within the realm of relationships. The energetic transmissions received from others caused some form of problem that is calling for resolution. The healing method is to take control and act decisively on behalf of self needs.

The 2-8 axis concerns personal resources vs. merging with others. A 2nd House South Node illustrates that lessons involve a preoccupation with security, money, bolstering one's sense of esteem or refusing to take risks. There could be a component of fear. The 8th is perhaps the scariest of the houses. With the North Node here, it benefits the soul to enter the terrain of intimacy, darkness and learning how to exchange with others on all levels. A South Node in the 8th indicates the reverse. Here, a soul has lost equilibrium in turbulent waters of psychological crisis, dependence on another's resources, or powerlessness in intense energetic scenarios including catastrophe. With a North Node in the 2nd House, qualities of feeling anchored and secure in the self are necessary to develop.

Having the Nodes along the 3-9 axis suggests that work involving the mindset vs. spiritual direction requires attention. A soul with a 3rd House South Node is familiar with the lower mind: logic, rationality, questioning and the accumulation of data. The 9th House North Node asks the person to do something meaningful and to venture into realms of the higher mind such as intuition, philosophical speculation and the like. The adherence to 3rd House faculties has reached a point where it no longer serves soul growth to remain so dispassionate about life. A 9th House South Node suggests a soul that is aligned with convictions but they are likely to be ill-informed or reached prematurely. A 3rd House North Node requires an opening of the mind to more possibilities and a trusting of one's perceptual abilities to make sense of the world.

The 4-10 axis concerns family vs. vocation. Simply stated, the soul is quite comfortable operating in one of these realms and it's appropriate to stretch the self to understand the other. The 4th House South Node shows familiarity with private matters, familial expectations and legacies, remaining hidden or sheltered from the world. It behooves the soul to break free from whatever internal pull there is to remain so concealed and to fashion a life on one's own terms in the public world. The 10th House South Node is used to positions of authority, power or visibility. The soul defines itself through its achievements or roles and is reluctant to settle down. There may be a spiritual legacy of worldly expectation that is rectified by welcoming in feelings of self-love or the softness of nurturance from a family system, both of which are indicative of the 4th House North Node.

With the Nodes occupying the 5-11 axis, lessons pertaining to personality, social involvement, childhood and creative pursuits vs. a more global or communal focus are indicated. A 5th House South Node is used to living within the present without regard for the greater world family and the future evolution of the collective. The soul intention of an 11th House North Node is to connect more with progressive groups. The converse is the South Node in the 11th, where an alignment with collective forces or group identification has superseded personal expression. A 5th House North Node asks souls to connect more with spontaneity, to develop a talent or involvement with recreation.

The 6-12 axis involves attention to tasks of daily living vs. the release into a more expansive consciousness. A 6th House South Node indicates a predilection to perform the necessary functions to make the world operable. There is often marked responsibility and a dutiful nature. The 12th House North Node finds balance in learning how to let go and reorient the self towards a spiritual vision, to reap the fruits of contemplation and compassion for the health of the collective. A 12th House South Node is familiar with some type of removal or retreat and it serves development to now attend to more mundane realities. Some with this placement have been imprisoned, made impotent through illness or have preferred to be in some way invisible. Those that have attained meditative acumen are now asked to be mentors or tutors preparing others for more advanced growth.

Sign/House Integration

As in the case with planets, the Nodes are within signs and occupy houses. Integrating the archetypal processes of the signs within the confines of the houses brings precision to the interpretation. Signs are best thought of as psychological while houses are contexts of life. (Whereas Cancer involves feelings, the 4th House is an orientation to the home. Sagittarius is the process of developing a life mission while the 9th House is where that becomes played out). The combination of sign and house yields a whole greater than either of the parts. Here are a few more examples of this integration.

A South Node in Taurus in the 9th indicates a soul familiar with finding comfort and simplicity in a belief system including those in religious or educational settings. Taurus is a fixed earth sign, and the nature of the connection is firm and reliable. Membership in a congregation or institution of higher learning has brought a reliable sense of meaning and understanding of the world. The North Node in Scorpio in the 3rd House suggests a need to intellectually investigate the world trusting one's own perceptions. Ultimately, there is new information accumulated that provides a far more complex and multi-leveled grasp of the meaning of existence.

With a South Node in Libra in the 4th House, the soul is familiar with a pleasant home environment. Manners, expectations and following social scripts are likely to be ingrained. Feeling rooted to privilege or accepting the limitations of the familial code in order to remain in good graces has been readily accepted. This is a soul that doesn't want to rock the boat, for it is like a comfortable yacht. A North Node in Aries located in the 10th House is a statement about taking command of one's reputation and forging a vocation that demonstrates passion and conviction. The lesson is to boldly take risks and free the self from being defined as part of a family unit.

A Pisces South Node in the 2nd House shows a nebulous and uncertain relationship with one's sense of potency and self-esteem. Past lives may be marked by escapist tendencies or ineffectuality. There could have been illness of other impediments to assuming control and using one's power. A North Node in Virgo in the 8th is an intention to ardently work with others in the pursuit of greater intimacy. The intention is to fully engage in edgy experiences in order to overcome tentativeness or the habitual pattern of tuning out.

Chapter 5
The Nodes in the Astrology Chart

The Moon holds deep soul memories as feeling states in the unconscious. When we tune in to our Moon, we may discover joy, pain, love or sadness and have little idea how it got in there. These emotions act as a foundation and heavily influence the temperament. The Lunar Nodes play the necessary role of giving information as to why the unconscious is in a particular state. Therefore, the Moon and the Nodes are intimately related.

The Nodes illustrate the focus in the present life. Out of the entire soul history, certain dramas and lessons are chosen for attention. This is based on what the soul is ready to address, what is necessary to explore, and also how the soul may use its experience for the collective good.

Using the analogy that threads throughout this book, the Moon is the underground seed and the Sun shows the flowering of potential. The Nodes are like the gardening—the work of tending the soil to maximize the outcome of the seed. Following the prescriptions of the Nodes assists the seed (Moon) in surviving and ensures the eventual blooming of the flower (Sun).

The best way to illustrate this process is to give a detailed example. Let's use a Pisces Moon in the 9th House; and the South Node in Taurus in the 11th/North Node in Scorpio in the 5th. This discussion will segue into other facets of the Nodes including planets that rule the Nodes and those that make aspects to the Nodes.

A Pisces Moon is the least attached to incarnated life. It reflects the soul of the mystic, the escapist or the grief-stricken. It has a palpable sense of longing—an idealism that someday the world can indeed become closer to what is imagined. Through integrating awareness and vitality, the Pisces Moon learns to channel compassion and love out into the world. A failure to evolve renders it impotent, lonely, and ultimately hope is abandoned.

This Pisces Moon is situated in the 9th House. The emotional need has been to understand Spirit—or to quest in search of something meaningful. Themes of travel and expansion are indicated. This is the mark of the gypsy or spiritual seeker—a soul in touch with the awe of possibility.

The South Node appears in the 11th House and in Taurus—a statement about safety (Taurus) in numbers (11th House). Community, clan or tribe consciousness, being part of a collective body are familiar to the soul. Such a group may have provided comfort and tangible security (Taurus). This soul has a well-developed sense of belonging, of being part of a routine and performing hands-on works. A member of a kibbutz or some other culture that lives off the land is a possibility.

It appears that this gypsy soul, with its wanderlust and desire to contact Spirit, was limited by the everyday responsibilities of making a community work. A bright version of the story would be someone who shared spiritual endeavors with group members and developed a strong soul connection through such practices. Here, the Piscean qualities of compassion and mysticism would be enhanced. A harsher version would be the condition where the demands of everyday life became overly burdensome and there was only sadness and longing for Spirit (Pisces), a desire to travel and get away from it all (9th).

Wherever this soul may be in its growth, there is more work to address. The North Node is in Scorpio in the 5th House indicating that it would benefit the soul to become more daring, psychologically complex and passionate (Scorpio) about individual self-expression and creativity (5th). We notice a movement away from "safety in numbers" and into the depths of individuality. This soul wants to get to know itself more intensely, and through that process, share something original.

By moving in the direction of the Scorpio North Node, this soul can help bring greater nourishment to the Pisces Moon. The Lunar need is to contact Spirit. This Nodal scenario suggests that Spirit is found with an inward journey. By discovering the complexity of the individual psyche, learning the art of intimate engagement with other souls and being authentic in the moment, the Lunar need for spiritual expansion is met. The 5th House emphasis is also performance related: the outward expression of what is discovered inwardly. The Piscean inspiration within the Moon may be channeled into poetry, music or some other form of artistry.

The challenge is to release the desire for safety (Taurus) and affiliation (11th House) and to emerge as a unique individual with original talent. It is a risk (Scorpio) to show the self (5th) to an audience. It is a challenge to probe one's psyche and share (Scorpio) in an open, honest and heartfelt way (5th). Being an investigator (Scorpio) of the present moment (5th) or a psychologist (Scorpio) working with children (5th) are new and exciting areas for spiritual growth. Moving toward the North Node brings healing, sustenance and liberation to the Moon itself.

Energizing the Nodes

The Nodes are in signs (styles, processes) and located in houses (realms of experience). They point to the lessons being addressed. An influx of power is needed to boost the evolutionary processes into action. The planets do this by energizing the Nodes in two ways: planets ruling the Nodes, and planets making aspects to the Nodes.

The ruler of the South Node provides important information about the nature of the drama unfolding, the forces that animate the story. Depending on the planet and its house, the ruler may display a variety of properties. For instance, if the South Node ruler is the Sun in the 1st House, the drive of the life force is largely responsible for the South Node conditions. In the 11th House, global forces beyond one's control are likely.

115

Just like the South Node, its ruling planet is familiar to the soul. It suggests repetitive behavior patterns and has a dominant streak in the psyche. It may indicate a well-developed function that can operate with little effort. This planet can activate mindless repetition if used unconsciously. It may also serve as an important catalyst for spiritual growth if it can expand its range of expression. Since this planet is part of the problem, it is also part of the solution.

The planet ruling the North Node illustrates how the intention of the North Node can be achieved. The Node points to an evolutionary process (sign) located in a house—a statement of potential, the beacon in the distance. The ruler is the energetic power to move closer. The sign, house and aspects it makes give further information about how it connects in the chart and what assets and challenges it faces in the journey.

Like the North Node, its ruler may seem unfamiliar. It suggests the cutting edge of advanced growth if done well. Effective application of the ruler's positive qualities assures much growth. If one is blocked, chooses not to invest, or is simply unaware of the spiritual gold represented by this planet, the ruler's energy still remains in the psyche. A person may confront representations of it in the world designed to bring greater awareness to it. Like all planets, if not addressed consciously, the ruler will present problems.

Let's return to our example and use Venus in Cancer in the 1st House as the ruler of the South Node. This Venus placement indicates a friendly and nurturing (Cancer) disposition or persona (1st House). This person naturally behaves (1st House) in a pleasing manner (Venus) as a caretaker (Cancer). This is certainly someone non-threatening, likely to be classically feminine in temperament regardless of sex, loyal, thoughtful and calm. We can surmise that the role in the community may have been as a cook, nanny or someone involved in real estate. The person takes an active role (1st House) in ensuring that conditions in the community are hospitable (Cancer) and in good shape (Venus). Integrating the knowledge we have about Taurus (South Node), we can also see a potential for pottery, ceramics, basket-weaving or any other art that could serve a useful function—particularly the culinary arts (Cancer). We notice many capabilities in this 1st House Venus in Cancer, but it may also limit the expansion into spiritual enrichment that the Pisces Moon craves.

Now for the North Node, we can imagine its ruler, Pluto, in the 3rd House in Virgo. A 3rd House Pluto has a wound involving education, learning, perception, or possibly siblings. A possibility is someone who wanted to learn more and advance intellectually, but didn't have the opportunity. It can also indicate learning difficulties, making schooling a source of embarrassment, challenge or pain. In any case, there is a need to meet the challenges and increase the scope of the intellect.

This Pluto is in the sign of Virgo, giving another piece to consider. Many disregard the outer planet signs and consider them "generational" but my experience indicates that all parts of the chart are useful and personally relevant. Here we may have a soul that doesn't feel it is good enough or excessively self-critical in intellectual matters (3rd House). There may be a wound in the application of effort (Virgo)—either someone who gave up or worked the fingers raw and was still unsatisfied.

Working diligently (Virgo) on educational matters (3rd House) assists in actualizing the Scorpio North Node. The 8th sign is extraordinarily complex, ranging from painful struggles to feeling ecstatic. In order to have social involvement (5th House) with this degree of intensity (Scorpio), one needs to be prepared and knowledgeable about the terrain. Virgo is most interested in improvement and results and the 3rd House is full of fascinating data. Bringing this concentrated (Pluto) but curious (3rd House) focus to areas of connection (North Node in the 5th House) makes lively and rewarding intimate exchanges.

If we regard the 5th House North Node for its associations with talent or creative self-expression, the ruler may play an important role. The 3rd House is where we are open to learning, and Virgo involves crafting a skill. This Pluto indicates a complete immersion into the processes of learning (3rd House) as preparation for self-expression (ruling 5th House North Node).

Developing this Pluto will ultimately help heal the Moon. Pisces in the 9th wants to feel connected to the universe in a cosmic or transcendent way. Developing a precise (Virgo) understanding (3rd House) about the nature of life can assist in preparing one to merge with it from a broader understanding. Then, life is not bound to the limits depicted in the South Node drama. The soul feels more secure in itself, and better able to achieve its intentions.

Planets Aspecting the Nodes

The other way that planets energize the Nodes is through aspects. Planets that make significant aspects to the Nodal axis are integrally involved in the spiritual lessons pressing for resolution in the present life. They are an intimate part of the soul journey and may have either been difficult lessons (challenging aspects) or qualities and strengths used effectively (supportive aspects), but also may have contributed to dramas that now need to be addressed.

Planets conjunct the South Node are generally identified with the soul. At the bus station may sit the grizzly bear or the golden retriever. If a planet is with the South Node, its energy is highlighted in the present incarnation. The soul experience is marked by the planet's qualities and it is natural to behave in accordance with its nature. However, house position plays an important role that modifies the relationship. If the South Node conjunction with a planet occurs in one of the relational houses, the planet suggests what is experienced in those realms as part of the karmic drama (South Node). It conveys general characteristics of the chart owner, but the particular lessons are most applicable in relational settings. As is the case with all planets, they can be projected onto others.

For example, someone with a 7th House South Node conjunct Pluto arrives with heavy relationship karma to work through. Intense relationships with powerful "others" have resulted in substantial wounding for the soul. So the spiritual condition to resolve (South Node) is marked by interpersonal

118

hurts (7th House Pluto). Pluto is the chart's owner, but it will be experienced as if it is coming from another (7th), and this catalyzes the planet for processing and eventual healing.

Planets in opposition to the South Node are outside forces that countered or antagonized the soul. They too are familiar, but not integrated and are often feared or estranged from the soul. Successful growth requires a confrontation with the planet, to welcome it, get to know it and ultimately to become and integrate its power.

Mars in Capricorn may oppose a Cancer South Node. The softer, more private qualities in the soul were opposed by some type of aggressive and authoritative energy that created karma. The possibilities are numerous and include malevolent forces at a job, domineering others, violence or malicious energies. The house placement would give further clues. The soul arrives disempowered, and the work is to cultivate the Capricorn North Node qualities of toughness, authority and perseverance and to embody the assertive, leadership energy of Mars. Moving toward the North Node, the soul is becoming an empowered and more conscious version of what previously defeated or antagonized it.

Planets that square the Nodes reveal forces that were problematic and difficult to integrate. Whereas the opposition is more classically relational, the square shows a general sense of inner discord or strife. For example, Saturn in Virgo may square a Gemini South Node. The curious, youthful South Node had trouble with discipline and sculpting a body of work. An institution (Saturn) may have been overly critical (Virgo) of the soul and rendered it fearful.

In order to proceed to the North Node, the planet in square aspect to the Nodes must be integrated and used as a resource. The usual scenario is that a person will initially feel blocked by the planet and gradually learn to master it. In this example, the Sagittarius North Node has conviction, purposeful behaviors and direction. Part of the growth is to perform hands-on work (Virgo) and attain a level of mastery (Saturn) in one's vocation, thus providing spiritual direction (Sagittarius North Node).

Sextiles and trines suggest supportive qualities in the soul and are different in how they connect into the world. The sextile is closer to the conjunction and is more aligned with personal choices while the trine is closer to the opposition and has more of a relational feel. The sextile tends to be more impulsive and the trine more seasoned.

Planets forming sextiles and trines to the South Node indicate resources or strengths the soul has at its disposal. Depending on the developmental level of the soul, and severity of the karma present, sextiles and trines may also be contributing factors to the struggle. They may show how a person's strengths also can be vulnerabilities, such as a brilliant intellectual who has no idea of how to relate to others.

An example is Jupiter in Pisces trine a Scorpio South Node. The soul has a metaphysical or transcendent (Pisces) understanding of the universe (Jupiter) that was an inspiration to others. This could have resulted in wounding (Scorpio) dramas. Witness the case of Galileo or other philosophers who rocked the boat. Many were persecuted (Scorpio) for their belief systems (Jupiter). The soul wants to develop a sense of security (Taurus North Node) and to use the philosophical acumen to do so.

Let's continue with the example begun earlier with the South Node in Taurus in the 11th and add Uranus squaring the Nodes from the 2nd House in Leo.

This natal placement of Uranus presents a major crisis to the development of the soul. The 2nd House concerns resources, both internal and external, that bolster a person's security, esteem and confidence. When the 2nd House poses no difficulty, we proceed with self-assurance—forging ahead to achieve our goals. When there are pressing issues here, we tend to lack the conviction, know-how or means to attain the desired outcome. By being outside the Saturnian boundary, Uranus points to conditions that were not part of the status quo, the consensus reality of the soul. There is a need to incorporate the Uranian attributes in order to heal a sense of estrangement.

The sign (style and evolutionary process) provides the information about what needs greater development. Leo qualities such as spontaneous expressions of joy, a sense of engagement with life, and openness to creative outlets were problematical. The 2nd House placement suggests that the chart owner either lacked the necessary tangible resources to fulfill the creative pursuits or the confidence and determination to actually draw down inspiration into manifestation. Perhaps responsibilities to the group precluded and thwarted attempts at personal development.

The path of individuation (Uranus) is to gain confidence (2nd House) about one's creative expressions (Leo). With this solid foundation of talent, movement toward the North Node (5th House, Scorpio) becomes possible. Bolstering the sense of radical self-allegiance (Uranus) to one's creativity (Leo) equips the self to proceed in a daring, passionate and risky way (Scorpio) in the expressive realm of the 5th House. The person is learning to say, "This is me, like it or not. I have something to share, something I've put a lot of effort into—I believe it's my gift to the community." The polarity of the 5th House is the 11th, and the completion of the work is to integrate the new skills into the entire Nodal axis.

Chart Examples of Nodal Lessons

Following are some examples of celebrity charts to illustrate how the Nodes indicate the central lessons being addressed in the lifetime. At the end of the book are several more examples of the Nodes—included with analyses of the Sun and Moon.

Mahatma Gandhi

Spiritual leader and political activist Gandhi has an Aquarius South Node in the 4th House. He is familiar with processes of change, revolution, questioning authority and is also comfortable with outsider status. In the 4th House, these processes are deeply within him, connected to his roots and homeland. He was likely nurtured in the home (4th House) to be true to himself

(Aquarius). This is a revolutionary (Aquarius) lurking privately (4th House).

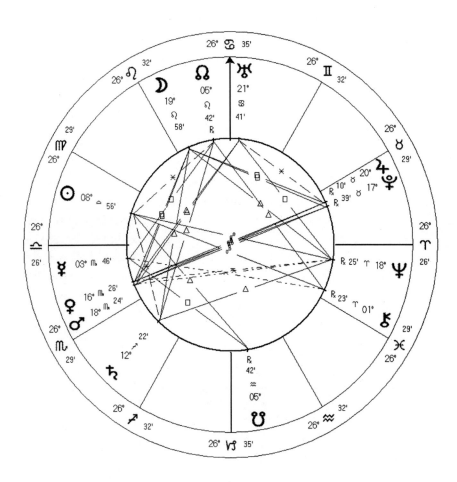

Uranus in Cancer in the 9th House rules the South Node and brings the revolutionary spirit to religious and political arenas. He believes (9th House) in the liberating power (Uranus) of the heart (Cancer). Connecting back to the private nature of the South Node (4th House), the ruler suggests Gandhi was unable to fully manifest (Uranus) what he knows (9th House) inside of him (Cancer). His soul intends to work on unmanifested (Aquarius

South Node) political/religious ambition (ruled by Uranus in the 9th).

The North Node is in Leo in the 10th House. This statement about public visibility (10th House) and having a big presence (Leo) perfectly complements his growth. He can use the established Aquarian resources in ways that impact the world. The philosophical intentions (9th House Uranus) can be further combined with leadership qualities by moving towards the commanding North Node.

The Sun is the ruler of the North Node and sits in Libra in the 12th House. The solar intention is to radiate diplomatic and peaceful energy channeled from a spiritual source. The 12th House engages deeply in meditative practices and often renounces the trappings of the material world. Gandhi's soul is learning even greater spiritual (12th House) equanimity (Libra), perhaps even to be a martyr (12th House) for peace (Libra). However, the North Node does want to secure a position (10th House) of charismatic (Leo) leadership.

This Sun is trine the South Node indicating that Gandhi's soul has already developed much of the solar intention—he can pick up where he left off (Sun sextile the North Node). The Sun is also sextile Saturn in Sagittarius connecting the life force with philosophical/religious (Sagittarius) authority (Saturn).

Mercury in Scorpio in the 1st House squares the Nodal axis. His soul intends to speak truths ardently. Considering the 4th House placement of the South Node, his message was previously hidden. Connecting Mercury up to the 10th House brings his powerful (Scorpio) voice to public venues. Gandhi's 10th House Leo Moon has a need to be a charismatic public figure. The present lifetime maps out a strategy for him to achieve this.

Helen Keller

An inspiration to all, and champion for people with disabilities, Helen Keller has a Cancer South Node in the 8th House. Her soul is accustomed to needing (Cancer) others' support and resources (8th House). This watery combination does account for her overcoming impetuous behavior, and working through incredible frustration as a youngster. This South Node suggests dependency and volatile emotional relationships.

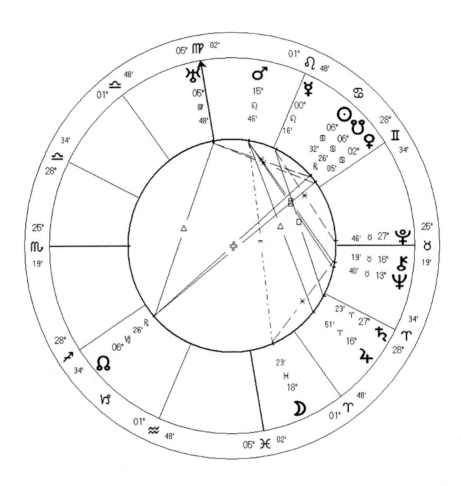

The Sun is tightly conjoined the South Node. The Sun, as the prime indicator of the present life force, is aligned with lessons from the past. For Helen's growth, it is necessary for her to re-experience and to embody this emotional disposition again, perhaps to use it in more creative (Sun) ways. By increasing her awareness (Sun) of her trying lessons, she can then proceed to develop powerfully loving relations (Cancer in the 8th House).

124

Venus in Cancer is also conjunct the South Node. This further emphasizes the need (Cancer) to connect (Venus), even to rely on others (8th House). In the 8th, her darkness and psychic pain need nurturing through intense interpersonal relationships. With successful spiritual advancement, Helen herself is able to nurture others who struggle.

A Pisces Moon in the 4th House rules the South Node. This suggests that the karmic story is played out in the arena of the home (4th House), with those she dearly loves, and to whom she may give power (Pisces). This Moon is quincunx Mars in Leo, which explains the expressive bursts of anger and frustration, and sextile Chiron in Taurus in the 6th House, which actualizes in bodily (Taurus) disability (Chiron/6th House).

The North Node is in Capricorn in the 2nd House. Helen is working toward self-reliance, fortitude and a strong sense of self-worth. Capricorn also wants greater visibility, which corrects her tendency to hide in her struggles. This North Node is grounded and tough, striving for the attainment of autonomy, survival and wisdom.

Ruling the North Node is Saturn in Aries on the cusp of the 6th House. Aries emphasizes independence, while the 6th House suggests self-improvement, health issues and mentoring. Saturn in Aries potentially heralds leadership—in the 6th House, it is applied to the assistance of others to overcome obstacles. As a child, this Saturn must have felt like an incredible burden to others. She lacked (Saturn) autonomy (Aries) and was in a position of weakness (6th House). The gift is that over time (Saturn), she becomes a leader (Aries) for the underprivileged or disabled (6th House)—and this carries out the North Node intention.

Also of note is Uranus in Virgo in the 10th House, which sextiles the South Node and trines the North Node. From the perspective of the South Node story, Uranus in Virgo shows an unconventional (Uranus) service (Virgo) career (10th House). In past lives, it is reasonable to conclude that Helen was involved in assisting (Virgo) others, particularly those who are not a part of the mainstream (Uranus). This asset is applied to the present lifetime, where Helen is to assume greater authority (Capricorn North Node) in such matters.

As the Nodes of the Moon relate to healing the Moon itself, her sensitive Piscean nature becomes stronger and able to pursue its inherent gifts. As an adult Helen said, "I am happy all the day long because education has brought light and music to my soul."

John McEnroe

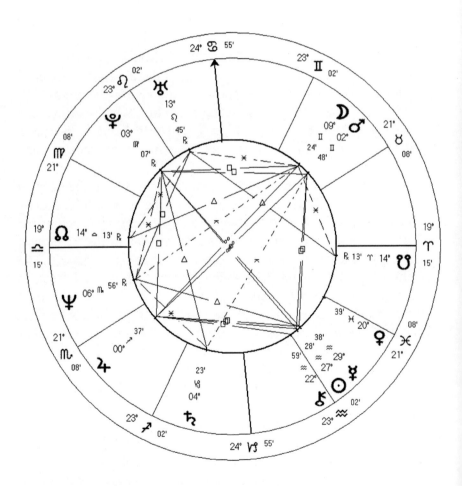

Tennis legend and sardonic celebrity John McEnroe has the South Node in the 6th house and Aries. His soul has likely been in subservient positions (6th house) where he needed to fight and claw (Aries) his way forward. This is the mark of the underdog who wants to defy all odds: the inner city youth wanting to rise from poor conditions and make it to college, or the slave who refuses to accept his position and challenges the master. McEnroe is familiar with antagonism and battling for respect.

Ruling the South Node is an 8th house Mars which is conjunct his Gemini Moon. This suggests emotional volatility, anger and a coping pattern of rationalizing feelings. There is a profound need to express his unresolved explosiveness verbally (Gemini), especially in moments of perceived combat (8th house).

Of particular relevance is the square from Pluto in the 11th House to his Mars. This aspect reinforces the notion that McEnroe has extremely combative karma, possibly involved with fighting to the death (Mars/8th House) and feeling wrath from a group or collective body (11th House). The brooding image of him angrily whapping his racket and yelling during a tennis game is a replay of ancient dramas in his soul. For McEnroe, tennis triggered extreme psychological dynamics as well as the need to regain acceptance from the world (Pluto/11th House).

Uranus in Leo in the 10th closely trines the South Node. This describes a public role or career that is extraordinary in performance or talent (Leo) of some variety. Although a great asset (trine), the brilliance (Uranus) of this expression (Leo) also contributed to his unresolved karmic situation. Now he is to use the same virtuosity to ultimately find greater equilibrium.

The North Node is in Libra in the 12th house—an unambiguous statement about the need to find peace (Libra) and let go (12th) of past conditioning. This North Node is perhaps as gentle, serene and loving as you can get. The promise is to partner with the benevolence of Spirit and to learn to appreciate divine beauty.

Ruling the North Node is Venus in Pisces on the cusp of the 6th house—an intention to learn and work on (6th) ways to relate to others (Venus) in compassionate and forgiving ways (Pisces). McEnroe is well known for his tennis exploits which do replicate his spiritual condition quite emphatically, but few are aware of his musical talent and love and appreciation of art. He has developed an impressive collection of paintings and seems to genuinely find solace and meaning through this hobby. He has also learned to poke fun at his reputation and has adapted a disposition that is quite friendly (Libra) and engaging. The more he invests in this direction, the more his inflamed Moon heals.

Kurt Cobain

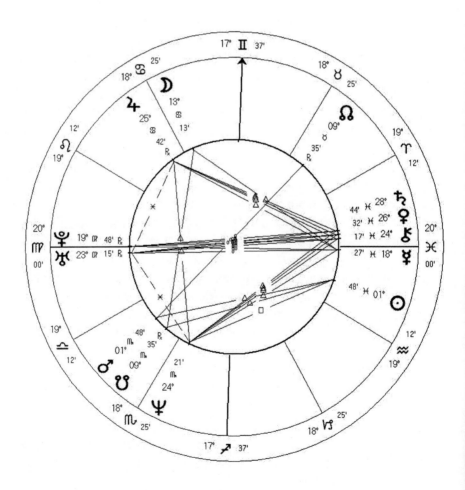

Grunge-rock pioneer Kurt Cobain has a Scorpio South Node in the 2nd House. This equates to lessons regarding a most wounded (Scorpio) self-esteem (2nd House), a simmering intensity (Scorpio) that grounds him (2nd House). He has a reservoir of powerful feelings (Scorpio) as a resource (2nd House) to use in the present life—but certainly healing is necessary.

A raging Mars in Scorpio is conjunct the South Node. This bloody planet in the 2nd House does suggest anger or aggression directed at the self, or a violent nature lurking within. He is clearly here to form a new relationship with the management of painful emotions, one that is less impulsive (Mars) and more secure (healthy 2nd House).

Pluto in Virgo on the Ascendant is the ruler of the South Node. With Pluto conjunct Uranus, the behavior (1st House) is unpredictable (Uranus), passionate to the point of obsessive (Pluto), and obliterating (Pluto/Uranus) the function of decency or modesty (Virgo). Cobain actually feels quite insecure and weak (Virgo), but adapts the persona (Ascendant) of a guitar-smashing, suicidal, screaming maniac (Pluto/Uranus). This Pluto/Uranus conjunction is opposed a stellium of planets around the Descendant (7th House cusp), setting up immense power struggles with others.

A Cancer Moon in the 10th House trines the South Node. An asset in his spiritual journey is a willingness to show his emotions in public. He has a need (Moon) to be seen (10th House) for who he really is inside (Cancer). Ideally, this can be further developed into a demonstration of love, or he can just display his inner contents in a most visible manner.

The North Node is in Taurus in the 8th House. Simply stated, he is here to trust. Cobain has guarded his wounding, and his spiritual growth proceeds by learning how to find comfort (Taurus) by working through issues with others (8th House). Taurus in the 8th House sounds like a mud bath and a deep soulful hug from a loved one. The 8th is a cauldron of transformation, a psychic chamber of sorts. Cobain will find peace (Taurus) if he is willing to connect with others in authentic ways.

Venus in Pisces in the 7th House rules the North Node. Ideally, he finds compassionate (Pisces) others (Venus, 7th) that bring spiritual partnership. A 7th House Venus in Pisces dissolves into the love from a significant companion. Furthermore, this Venus is conjunct both Saturn and Chiron. The type of relationship that benefits him most is enduring (Saturn) and healing (Chiron), a connection that promotes a sense of mystical union (Pisces).

Also note that the Sun in Pisces in the 6th House is loosely trine the South Node. We may conclude that Cobain's soul was beginning to find greater spiritual solace (Pisces) through self-work (6th House), and the present life (Sun) is to continue this program. The exact trine between Sun and Mars indicates that using his powerful (Scorpio) drive (Mars) to serve the solar intention is warranted. The Sun is square Neptune indicating urgency to soften, heal and touch Spirit. Coincidentally, he named his rock band Nirvana. If Cobain had been able to reach closer to nirvana, his Cancer Moon's needs for love would have been satisfied. Sadly, the South Node condition overtook him, resulting in suicide.

Seasons of the Sun

Chapter 6
Sun Flowers: Becoming Whole

There is no mistaking the Sun. All of life is organized by the Earth's rotation and revolution around this magnificent source of light and heat. It nourishes and sustains everything in the entire solar system while holding planets in place through the pull of gravity.

The Sun potentially has the quality of mindfulness, the ability to be fully aware in the moment. The Sun also powers us—it's the center of the solar system and the central powerhouse of the psyche. When we are present, we are aware (light) and vital (heat), focusing attention on whatever tasks are at hand. In contrast, when we are sleeping or not paying attention, the "lights are off."

By observing children, we see an increased awareness and engagement with life. Infants are notoriously unconscious with poor boundaries. They don't know where the self ends and a mother or caretaker begins. Slowly children derive a healthy sense of self or ego and learn to radiate individuality. Older people have more subtleties and nuances to their character because of the accumulation of life experience. Simply stated, we become who we are.

In this presentation of the luminaries, a similar developmental progression is adopted. From a spiritual view, we arrive with the instinctual and unconscious tendencies typified by the Moon—and the Sun indicates what we are becoming. The overall condition of the Sun (sign, house and aspects) in the natal chart elucidates what the soul seeks to become more aware of and radiate into the world. It marks the most central and important of all planetary energies that we are here to express. From many other chart factors, we get a sense of why a particular soul is enrolled in the specific learning program that the Sun illustrates.

The Sun is a central frequency of spiritual growth but it may also be overused to the detriment of other planets. We become blinded when we look directly at the Sun, and too much solar focus leads to perceptual blindness. It is natural for us to want our little internal solar system to have brightness and luminosity. The sense of self wants to shine. Yet, if we are too eager to radiate the self, it is much more difficult to access the other planetary energies.

Like everything in astrology, there is a gift and a challenge in the Sun. We have easy access to the Sun as it's the life force and our quality of awareness. Mastering the potential of the Sun, though, is a life's work. When younger, it is quite common to fumble and become flustered by the Sun's power. A Capricorn may be overly serious as a youngster, only to become the wise elder in later years. A Leo may be showy and self-focused on the way to the charisma and regality that is the birthright—and a Scorpio learns an increasingly more mature fascination with the taboo, dark or unconscious. Children and adolescents are oftentimes caricatures of the Sun sign they embody.

The following are descriptions of the 12 different Sun signs. In contrast to the Moon section, where the signs were explored for their unconscious and protective functions, here we see the signs much more brightly. The soul always intends for a personality to manage the Sun well; therefore, we look to the promise it conveys. Of course, we need to be sensitive to the pitfalls because few are able to proceed unimpeded to its potential.

The Sun through the Signs

After peering through the looking glass at the past (Moon) and its lessons (Nodes) we look to the Sun to learn more about the present. The Sun energizes and connects the life force with the world. When we are fully engaged, we radiate the Sun and come closer to claiming our greatness. Like a light bulb, the more present we become, the more luminosity we give forth. The sign indicates the nature or character of this light and heat.

Aries Sun

Souls that incarnate with an Aries Sun have access to fireworks, and they are here to make explosions of some variety. Traditionally considered exalted in Aries, this Sun placement is the strongest, most outwardly powerful and commanding of all. There is an irrefutable soul intention to take risks, to proceed through life unencumbered toward the mantle of leadership. A call to action, decisiveness and the initiatory spirit are qualities and resources at Aries' disposal.

In the lesser developed form, Aries can be impulsive and imprudent in its behavior. The fledgling Ram is often unaware of the consequences of its decisions and finds itself in the unenviable position of conflict and strife that could have been avoided with foresight. Nevertheless, these experiences are bumps on the road toward learning lessons of unfettered alignment with one's desires and resolute action.

For some reason, which can be clarified by examining the entire chart, the soul was either thwarted in proceeding courageously, crumbled in the face of opposition, was too preoccupied with being diplomatic or simply "chickened out" by adapting a more reserved or passive temperament. There are several other possibilities too. The Moon and South Node (and other factors) would give further information regarding the reasons for needing this powerful Sun placement.

Clearly lessons regarding self-alignment and the accrual of personal power are indicated. It serves Aries to increase its strength by exercise and/or weight training, or possibly the soul is interested in developing emotional or intellectual vigor if the house placement indicates. However Aries wears the armor of the gladiator; the Ram bolsters the personal will to confront battles that need to be fought.

Due to the innate warrior inclinations, it is absolutely essential for Aries to cultivate awareness in order to use its capabilities for the greater good. An unconscious Aries could very well become the enemy of many, stew in thralls of anger or be a selfish, brash nuisance. These outcomes, however unfortunate, would be self-created and rightfully deserved. With successful development of awareness and vitality, the Aries Sun reaches the pinnacle of its birthright—unbounded creative and powerful leadership.

Thomas Jefferson

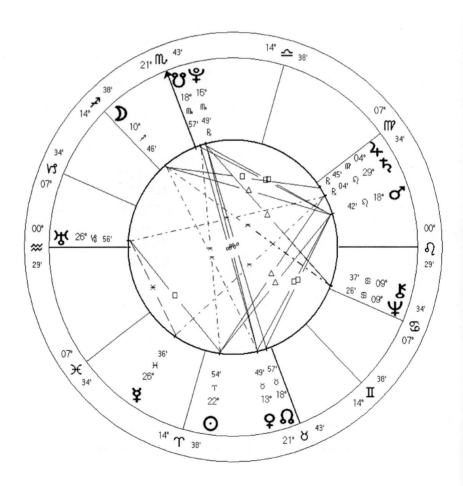

President, revolutionary and Renaissance Man Thomas Jefferson has a leadership-focused Aries Sun in the 3rd House. This is a soul intention to advance by developing his intellect and using his mind as a weapon. The 3rd is a house of perception and cognition but also diversity and absorbing the richness of variety. His fascination with many subjects fits well in this stimulating house.

The Sun is trine Mars in Leo in the 7th, and Mars serves as ruler of the solar force. Mars is willing to fight for its rights, and in the 7th House, that includes inflaming others if necessary. Sun trine Mars in fire signs shows a spirited sense of teamwork in channeling one's passions, to inspire others through one's example.

Saturn in Leo also forms a trine to the Sun. Part of Jefferson's spiritual work (Saturn) regards the development of open-hearted joy (Leo) with others (7th House). This Saturn puts responsibility ahead of fun, and Jefferson is correcting the tendency by making fun his responsibility. With a trine aspect from Saturn to an Aries Sun, his essence takes on more of a noble or stately flavor.

Uranus in the 12th House in Capricorn squares the Sun. Uranus/Sun contacts indicate paradigm shifters, revolutionaries and others who upset the apple cart. There is a soul intention to be a progressive catalyst, to bring in the future, even at the cost of turmoil if need be. This Uranus in Capricorn indicates that the revolutionary process occurs within institutions, social structures including governing bodies, tradition and overthrowing what is old and worn out. The 12th is a house of dissolution and endings.

The promise is to fashion a new (Uranus) kind of structure (Capricorn) that reflects greater compassion, vision and spiritual sustenance (12th House). Perhaps this goes along with "In God We Trust" rather than trusting a king. Capricorn further emphasizes that authoritative energy is brought directly to the life force. Also, Jefferson has an Aquarius Ascendant making Uranus his chart ruler. His Uranus is located toward the end of the 12th House (conjunct the Ascendant) so it is on the verge of rebirth.

However, it still maintains the 12th House themes of dissolution and conceiving a new vision.

The Sun is quincunx the South Node in Scorpio in the 9th House. Jefferson's central lesson is about healing differences in realms of philosophy, religion or world views. Interestingly, the 9th House has connotations with overseas relations, travel and other global issues. Aries takes up arms, and for Jefferson this is against controlling forces (Scorpio) within ideological or foreign realms (9th House). Note that Mars (which is trine the Sun) is tightly square the Nodes—asserting (Mars) his "pursuit of happiness" (Leo) is very much hanging in the balance of his soul's work. Jefferson is declaring (3rd House Sun) his independence (Aries).

Taurus Sun

As a fixed sign, Taurus is enduring, fortified and resourceful. The Bull can be tough, but it prefers to be left alone to enjoy the pleasures of the day—to be an animal in tune with nature. This sign bestows a healthy degree of stamina and strength, delicately balanced with a desire not to have to use it. Taurus is developing the self-worth that informs the optimal ways to use its resources.

The 2nd sign is peaceful, natural and sensual. Souls incarnating with a Taurus Sun are integrating more tranquility and receptivity to the nurturance that the Earth itself provides. In many cases, the soul has been through many trying dramas and circumstances. The current lifetime concerns the development of personal security, safety, repose and inner harmony.

We can look to both the polarity and the preceding sign for clues to what needs to be developed. In the case of Taurus, we have the polarity in Scorpio, and Aries precedes it. These two signs are the bloodiest, most confrontational and downright hostile signs in the system. There is a soul intention to advance from conflict (Aries) and balance intensity (Scorpio) with the development of serenity (Taurus). This is a general guideline, and the overall condition of the Moon and its Nodes would spell out the rationales for why any Sun is needed. Other possibilities, besides the need to settle after a storm, include the soul that has been so overly involved in spiritual pursuits that becoming more grounded is now necessary; or the condition where a soul was too other-focused and is now working on anchoring in the self.

The present lifetime largely concerns bolstering self-efficacy and reaching a sense of personal sanctuary and self-confidence. This disposition can transform into gluttony, passivity to the point of inertia, and simplifying the life at the expense of growth. The trap of excessive materialism and the allure of unnecessary comforts must also be kept in proportion. Taurus can be a power shopper, which is the misguided extension of the soul intention to become valuable to the self.

It is so essential to feel good in a world that continually presents hardships in one form or another. Taurus is learning to reach a state of self-assurance and to appreciate the beautiful. It is a wonderful gift to incarnate with a life force so attuned to pleasure and the ability to take a practical, hands-on approach to living. With successful development, the Bull becomes like Buddha (a famous Taurus), an open, receptive vessel for Spirit.

Saddam Hussein

The former Iraqi dictator has a Taurus Sun in the 12th House. His soul is interested in developing serenity, security and pleasantness (Taurus) in areas of spiritual connection and raising consciousness (12th House). The promise of this Sun is to feel comforted as a member of an interconnected spiritual family.

Uranus conjoins the Sun which suggests that this lifetime is a wholesale reformation of his soul history. Uranus in Taurus portrays a disturbance (Uranus) in arriving at inner peace (Taurus), and the need to strive toward its attainment. Ideally the Sun brings warmth and intention to this process. With a poor response to the higher potentialities of the Sun, Saddam is left acting out stubbornness (Taurus), intractable self-allegiance (Uranus) and overly materialistic tendencies. Residing in the 12th

139

House, furtiveness, confinement and loss are the hazards if a true lifeline to Spirit is not cultivated.

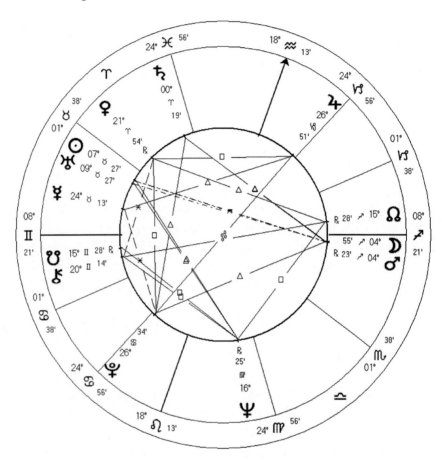

A Moon/Mars conjunction forms a quincunx with the Sun. This highly charged combination is simply hostile and threatening, emotionally reactive, and stems from a deep-seated need (Moon) to be right (Sagittarius) and victorious (Mars). Fighting for an ideology or to spread a doctrine is a strong motivator. Located in the 6th House, this combative combo is familiar with positions of weakness or subservience in relation to his perceived aggressors.

Developing the awareness of the peaceful Sun would calm (Taurus) and revolutionize (Uranus) this emotional temperament. Furthermore, the 12th is an area of cleansing and healing—a bright Sun dispersing energy to this Moon would enable it to grasp the meaning (Sagittarius) of grace (Taurus/12th House). A less than optimal response just brings the obstinate (Taurus) and reckless (Uranus) life energy to the inflamed and belligerent lunar condition.

The Sun forms a loose trine to Neptune in Virgo in the 4th House. Generous orbs of influence are acceptable for the Sun, and the trine from Neptune to Uranus is tighter and clearly a part of the solar profile. The soul intention of Sun/Neptune contacts is to allow greater softness, compassion and surrender to what is spiritually enriching. Neptune in Virgo is humble, service-minded and able to find beauty in the commonplace. The pitfall of this Sun/Neptune trine is identity confusion, loftiness of ego and even messiah complexes.

Hussein is a good example of a dimly lit Sun. We do see the developmental program and the ultimate promise of redemption if he would choose a "higher" path. We also see the unfortunate consequences his chart outlines with poor spiritual growth.

Gemini Sun

Lighten up! Become brilliant! Get busy living! How fun is it to have a Gemini Sun? Ask them and I'm sure they'll let you know all about it. Gemini is curious, quick-minded, versatile and dexterous. A lively sign, it's always on the go in an endless pursuit of information and experience. The Twins actively dialogue, entertain all types of ideas and do not discriminate or judge. A sign of duality, Gemini is bouncing around between polarities, stimulating and designing possibilities. Like an intricate network of firing neurons, Gemini is fantastically alive and eager for input.

Souls that incarnate with the Sun radiating the Gemini archetype are ripe for the next lessons about learning. Of course, we all learn—that's what evolution is about, but the Gemini Sun needs to further open its mind and entertain a cornucopia of input. Perhaps the soul was indoctrinated into limited belief systems in prior lives. Maybe it was too comfortable living a simple existence or much time was spent in some sort of seclusion—spiritual, punitive, or otherwise. Whatever the reason, Gemini is jazzed by the energy of engagement.

Another possibility is psychological heaviness or severe wounding which is being corrected by learning how to lighten up and take part in life more enthusiastically. Certainly the condition of the Moon must be acknowledged and reconciled, but the forward momentum involves an opening to experience. Whatever the situation the rest of the chart suggests, the soul requires more information.

Like all signs, Gemini has a dark side. Here, it takes the form of losing focus in an endless whirlwind of chaos, questioning to the point of unhealthy skepticism or being rendered impotent in decision-making. The most sinister of all is the cold and indifferent heart. Life is fascinating, but it also has depth. Gemini is prone to the radical post-modern belief that quantity trumps quality and nothing should be considered "better." Many times it's necessary to make distinctions between what is moral and what is offensive, what is substantial and what is unnecessary. Gemini may leave the discussion to read the dictionary.

There is a reason why somebody incarnates with a Gemini Sun. Figuring out what that is, and doing the required work in order to claim its zany brilliance, is the program. We all teach what we are learning, and Gemini has tremendous gifts to share. The more they use the light of awareness in illuminating the truth of the soul, the more powerful their lessons become.

Dr. Ruth Westheimer

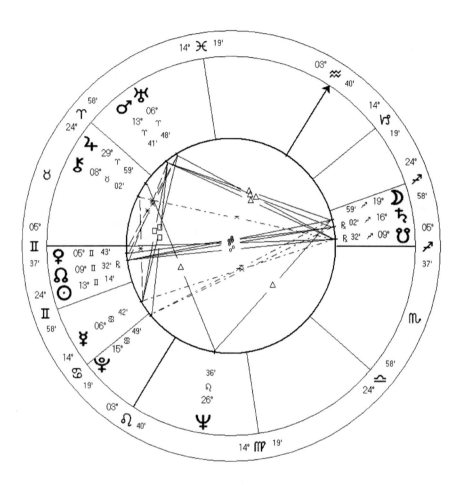

Sexual educator and celebrity Dr. Ruth has a Gemini Sun in the 1st House. She is here to actively (1st House) convey a message (Gemini), as a leader in educational pursuits. This 1st House solar intention is active, witty, versatile—an infectious, almost giddy vibe. The challenge would be restlessness, over-extension and superficiality.

The tightest aspect to the Sun is the sextile from Mars in Aries in the 11th House. Mars brings some forcefulness to the character—the intention is to "go for it" and blaze a unique trail.

Mars also has correlations to libido, passions and the eagerness of sexual expression. The sextile brings even more excitement and greater oomph to this genial Sun.

Venus, sitting directly on the Ascendant, is also conjunct the Sun. This suggests the intention to initiate (1st House) connections (Venus), and involve oneself in a variety (Gemini) of teaching opportunities. Dr. Ruth naturally comes across as friendly (Venus) and fascinating (Gemini). This personality attribute serves the deeper function of facilitating the development of intellectual leadership relevant to the 1st House Sun.

The Sun is opposed to the Moon along the Nodal axis with Saturn also involved. This is a most complex configuration! First, let's discuss the Moon/Saturn/South Node stellium in Sagittarius in the 7th House: there is an emotional need (Moon) to connect with others (7th House) in joint purpose (Sagittarius). Ruth's soul has been used to receiving direction and guidelines from others (Sagittarius in the 7th House), essentially telling her what to do. Moon/Saturn further emphasizes the need for authority figures, stability and structure provided by those she relates with (7th House). It also shows some emotional (Moon) hardships (Saturn) in discovering and feeling free to pursue her chosen path (Sagittarius).

With successful growth, the lunar need is transformed into purposeful (Sagittarius) contacts (7th House) that may even serve her ambition (Saturn). Through the opposition to the Sun, this is connected to the Gemini intention of educational advancement described earlier. Sun opposed Saturn is about bringing in the sturdy energy of accomplishment to the life force, while the Sun/Moon opposition (Full Moon) often makes for a compelling impact on others. The opposition between the luminaries directly brings her emotional intentions (Moon) to a determined dispersal in the present lifetime (Sun).

Let's also consider that Uranus (conjunct Mars, sextile Venus/North Node) is a focal planet. Though not classically sextile the Sun, its connection to Mars (which does sextile the Sun) and linkages to Venus and the Nodes makes it a part of the solar profile. This Uranus in Aries finds personal liberation through leadership and alignment with the self, including sexual expression.

Located in the 11th House, this Uranus is interested in large-scale networking, finding a like-minded group of people, an audience or allies. Its scope includes social issues, particularly in regard to individual passions (Mars). The sextile between Uranus and Venus serves to bring awakening energy (Uranus) to what it means to couple (Venus). Dr. Ruth is an advocate of and educator (1st House) for relational (Venus) progress (Uranus)—this is her gift to the world (11th House).

Cancer Sun

Truly feeling what you're feeling while you're feeling it is often avoided. A soul that incarnates with a Cancer Sun seeks to develop emotional intelligence—the ability to identify, understand and manage the emotions. The 4th sign concerns the development of nurturing abilities, a concern for home, roots and recognizing the importance of attachments.

There are various reasons why a soul would need to learn about the heart—in many cases it was avoided. Being trapped in the head, in one's public responsibilities or in masculine posturing are some examples. There could be a legacy of detachment or the refusal to confront feelings due to wounding that has occurred. Ready or not, souls that incarnate in this Sun season are going to feel who they are or organize the entire life around defensive measures to avoid or control it.

With its hard shell, Cancer is adept at protection. It simply won't allow difficulty in, choosing to deflect and project unwanted emotions onto others. Cancer is also skilled at hiding, which only leads to feeling lonely, misunderstood and hurt. Another strategy is becoming the aggressor. The Crab can use its claws to sneak up and harm its enemies, which catalyzes the conflict it initially wanted to avoid. When emotionally activated we behave irrationally; and this sign is prone to such actions more than most.

These tribulations are lessons on the way to heartfelt centeredness. The Cancer path is not an easy one to travel, for attributes such as receptivity, empathy and vulnerability are not prized in modern life as much as achievement and outward displays of strength. Cancer, though, is learning that the rewards of inner life are just as amazing, and that meaning can be found within (Jupiter is exalted in Cancer).

However much we may deny it, unconditionally loving the self and others remains extraordinarily rare. This has caused pain and anguish for billions. Cancer Suns have the task of helping heal this by getting in touch with themselves and using that emotional power to truly bond with others in satisfying and growth-promoting ways. Love heals the soul.

Tom Cruise

A-list movie star and vocal Scientologist Tom Cruise has a Cancer Sun in the 10th House. This soul's intention is to fashion a career that reflects his inner desires—to display and model his sensitivity in public ways. From his roles in such movies as *Rain Man, Jerry Maguire, Vanilla Sky, The Last Samurai* or *War of the Worlds*, a similar theme is consistent—there is a deepening into his heart, into the importance of roots, family and love.

Of the several aspects to his Sun, the tightest is the trine from Neptune in Scorpio in the 2nd House. This watery combination not only makes an emotional impact on others, but gives the aura of his energy a sense of glamour and intrigue. Being a sex (Scorpio) symbol (Neptune) or taking on iconographic status and glamorous projections comes easily. The purpose of such an aspect is to connect intimately. By so doing, Cruise builds confidence (2nd House) about the spiritual (Neptune) depth (Scorpio) available in this life.

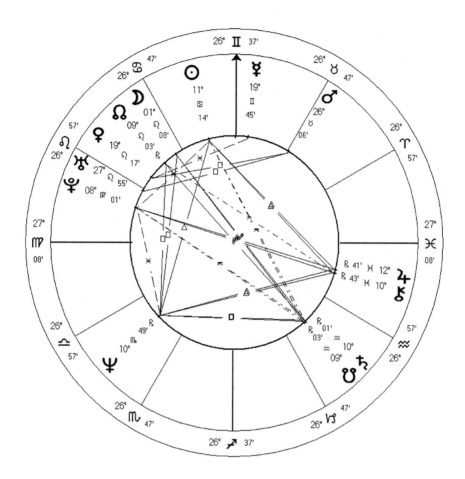

Jupiter/Chiron in Pisces in the 6th House also forms a trine to the Sun. Jupiter in Pisces is a lofty, idealistic energy full of possibilities. However, its residence in the 6th House suggests questioning and doubt or at least the need to work at attaining the soaring promise. The conjunction with Chiron tilts the analysis in the direction of loss or sorrow (Pisces) regarding spiritual direction. Tom is working on (6th House) religious (Jupiter) healing (Chiron) to arrive at greater fluidity, softness and compassion (Pisces). Advancing an agenda unconsciously connected with his spiritual struggles (Jupiter/Chiron) is the hazard.

147

Pluto in Virgo residing in the 12th House forms a sextile to the Sun. This Pluto suggests great loss—a sizable karmic scar regarding compassion and the benevolence of existence. There is suspicion, possibly stemming from hurt and grief. Learning to trust life and to access the power tucked deeply in the unconscious is the program of the Sun/Pluto aspect. Pluto here does indicate an avoidance of the unpleasant.

Tom is becoming more adept at realizing the intensity of his soul, and in using this energy to make an impact on others. This 12th House Pluto requires deep immersion into shamanic or transpersonal realms—without such depth, he would be prone to unconsciously use the power of such a contact for coercive ends. In a sense he would be spreading unresolved psychic pain in an enthusiastic (Jupiter in Pisces), glamorous (Neptune) and commanding (Pluto) way.

Saturn and the South Node are in Aquarius in the 5th House. This suggests a legacy of removal or inaccessibility (Aquarius), restriction and repression (Saturn) of individual expression (5th House). It's as if Tom was an observer (Aquarius) of others creativity (5th House) while a task-master (Saturn) had him sit in a corner. The lesson for the current life is to show himself vividly (North Node in Leo) to an audience (11th House). (Note that ruling the South Node is Uranus in Leo in the 12th—a statement that his creative talents were unable to shine into the world in prior lives).

The Sun forms a quincunx to the South Node/Saturn. As mentioned above, having a career on his own terms is critical for his growth. However, there is unfinished work involved with mastering (Saturn) his own unique (Aquarius) expressive gifts (5th House). The intention is to become a serious and dedicated performer, one who is recognized for his expertise. Pluto is also quincunx to the South Node, and along with the Sun, a yod is formed. All of the power available with the Sun/Pluto sextile is required to bust through the stultifying remnants of the South Node/Saturn limitation.

Leo Sun

Here the Sun is in its home sign, so its strength is amplified. An extraverted and fixed fire sign, Leo is simultaneously joyful and majestic. It entails the development of personality and its unique creative expression into the world. Leo has the gifts of talent, charisma and robust vitality. Souls that incarnate with this glorious placement are called upon to shine into the world.

Why would someone need to show who they are more openly? The first obvious answer is because they resisted doing so in past lives. Now they are more likely to display their colorful characteristics whether intended or not. Leo just wears the personality more vibrantly than others. Some Leo Suns are moving away from themes of retreat or seclusion illustrated in their charts, others show strong affiliation with group identification and others cling to safety, modesty and/or decorum. Leo wants to throw caution to the lions and truly indulge the appetite for living.

Similar to Gemini, there may be significant wounding in the karmic profile and Leos are given a spiritual license to have a good time—simply because they deserve it. The soul is learning to reengage with an uninhibited and joyful disposition toward the goodness of life. For some Leo Suns, it's necessary and appropriate spiritual practice to perform in a theatrical group, play a musical instrument or tell silly jokes. These activities help secure or restore a greater sense of trust, openness and delight— inviting the inner child to come forward.

Such a powerful Sun can be misused, and it may easily become unbalanced. Leo struggles include narcissism, pride, childishness, a lack of accountability and the discarding of reason. "My way or the highway," is what the struggling Lion might say. Leo's brightness may overshadow others and there may be no awareness whatsoever of the impact they are making. Another pitfall to negotiate is the tendency to oversimplify matters or keep everything bright and friendly—and this may impede deeper levels of processing.

Leo Suns are developing into the people who reflect the glory of life back to us through their panache and creativity. They are to be noticed for their impressive sense of style and character for they can show us the purity and generosity of Spirit. It is the spiritual path of Leo to grow into the promise of radiating beneficent kindness that warms our souls.

Madonna

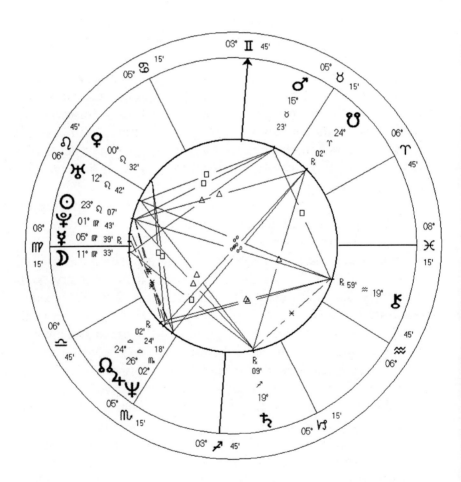

Megastar celebrity Madonna has a Leo Sun in the 12th House—a soul intention to find joy and exuberance (Leo) in release and surrender to spiritual development (12th House). Applying the performance-oriented and dramatic solar force as a vehicle to inspire and feel connected to something larger than the self fits with the 12th House. Madonna is here to display positivity and compassion.

Pluto in early Virgo is conjunct the Sun. In the 12th House, Pluto sits in the soul cage of unresolved wounding and avoided hurt. It conveys a sense of intense grief while Virgo indicates that the nature of the struggle is likely to involve guilt, shame or other "I could have been better" feelings. Madonna is bringing awareness to this part of her soul and is learning how to transform it into power—to have a life of great impact. Mercury is also close by to Pluto, so learning and speaking about spiritual issues (12th House) is appropriate. She likely was taught damaging (Pluto) messages (Mercury) in her soul's past, and in this lifetime she is to be an advocate for her own sense of Spirit.

The Sun also conjuncts Uranus—a combination that points to reinvention. This may take the form of shocking others, breaking through limitations and challenging the norms of society. Her soul is interested in pushing the envelope, a focus on progress and change. She is enormously famous and plays this role on a global scale, to assist in the development of the collective consciousness (12th House).

Jupiter in Libra in the 2nd House sextiles the Sun. Madonna is becoming more confident (Jupiter), strong, rooted (2nd House) and peaceful (Libra) in herself. This aspect connects the Sun from the contemplative arena (12th House) into enterprising and business contexts. Jupiter in the 2nd is fortuitous for financial success, but the deeper purpose is for her to feel secure and comfortable on her own terms, within her skin. Nevertheless, this is a highly-spirited aspect that gives great buoyancy to the character.

At her roots (4th House) Madonna has a heavy-handed (Saturn) disciplinarian telling her how to live her life (Sagittarius) and what to believe. Instead of being controlled, she is now taking charge and developing her own philosophical or religious convictions. Sun trine Saturn gives an aura of authority, ambition and direction—in Sagittarius this entails discovery, and in the 4th, of a private and emotional nature.

The Sun trines the Aries South Node in the 8th House. This South Node speaks of battle and a feisty nature with others (8th House). There is a familiarity with passionate exchanges including sex or aggression (Aries). The North Node conveys the lesson of finding greater interpersonal peace (Libra) and feeling secure in herself (2nd House). The Sun is building upon the passion of the South Node and bringing spiritual joy (Leo Sun in the 12th) to a new way of relating.

Mars is the ruler of the important South Node and it is square the Sun. Part of the drama of the South Node is around feeling stuck (Mars in Taurus) in religious proclamations (9th House). Her anger (Mars) is turned within (Taurus) and simmers. This square suggests once again that she is to find comfort (Taurus) in her own spiritual path (9th House), to actively pursue (Mars) her truth. Along with aspects to Saturn, Pluto, Uranus and Jupiter, this Sun is quite a go-getter! Mars adds even more intensity and drive.

The final aspect this busy Sun forms is an opposition to Chiron, which rounds out a T-square with Mars. Chiron in Aquarius in the 6th House conveys a wound regarding being true to herself (Aquarius). Her soul has likely accepted subservient positions and modesty and was chastised (6th House) for any hint of rebellion (Aquarius). This is also echoed by her Virgo Moon on the Ascendant —she was told to be a good girl and did so. Chiron's opposition to the Sun suggests the intention to get in touch with that rebellious (Aquarius) spirit and work at (6th House) healing (Chiron) it. Considering the aspects the Sun makes, especially the conjunction with Uranus, it is fully appropriate for Madonna to be as unique and expressive as she desires. This is a lifetime of breakthrough.

Virgo Sun

This earth sign is concerned with self-improvement, attaining tangible results, craftsmanship, improving health and performing hands-on tasks that assist in making life more workable. An engineer, an acupuncturist, or a volunteer at a soup kitchen are all faces of Virgo. The 6th sign is focused on precision, thoughtfulness and a willingness to do one's share. This is also the sign of unequal relationships such as mentor/apprentice or guru/disciple—any hierarchical situation where the student may eventually become a teacher someday.

There is a theme of maturation and modesty. Souls that incarnate with the Sun in Virgo are here to spend a lifetime more engaged in activities that promote personal growth than most others. The reasons for this vary. An honest self-assessment of one's development may have been avoided in past-lives. Perhaps the soul is of a domineering or aggressive nature and humility and restraint are being cultivated. There also may be a legacy of impediment to working on the heart's desire, and now is the time to get to task. Some Virgos are correcting an imbalance in the direction of religious or spiritual endeavors at the expense of fully showing up in the mundane, everyday world.

For whatever reason we may deduce from the rest of the chart, Virgo finds itself in the position of service to the self and humankind. The present life involves taking a real honest look at what can be realistically accomplished—and the energy they embody compels a daily regimen of productivity. Many Virgos become the untold heroes who donate blood, clothe the needy or perform the unrewarding job without complaint.

The central struggle of the Virgo Sun is to feel satisfied. If they become workaholics or perfectionists, lost in details or overly skeptical, contentment is impossible. If they choose not to rise to the occasion and do the work on the table (whatever they perceive it to be), they become extraordinarily self-critical, shamed and ineffectual. This can potentially lead to poor health practices, anxiety and a miserable disposition around others.

Being a Virgo Sun has rich nobility for those who can radiate its proactive inclinations. The soul is becoming more healthy and viable. Upon successful maturation, Virgo Suns become our mentors, teachers and role models. They are indispensable for spiritual evolution.

Stephen King

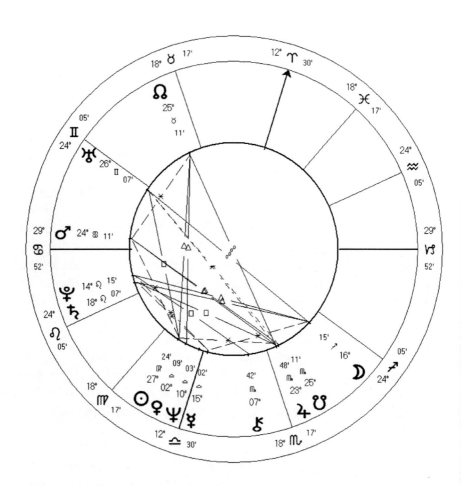

Popular horror and fantasy writer Stephen King has a methodical Virgo Sun in the 3rd House of writing, perception and communications. He is keenly attuned to the nuances of his environment and uses them for study and rumination. Virgo wants to craft a body of work. One possibility of this combination is a soul intention to be a prolific writer, and that's exactly what he has become.

The Sun connects to 3 other planets as part of a stellium—with Venus in Libra the closest. Venus concerns

154

socialization, artistry and money. In the 3rd, this goes along with the literary arts, while in Libra, there is the study of human behavior. King is becoming more learned about how people find peace and rely on each other. He is adapting a more graceful disposition himself.

Next in line is Neptune, also in Libra in the 3rd House. This portrays a longing (Neptune) in his soul to give the poetic quality of his mind greater expression. The form of his communication (3rd House) has a fantastic, other-worldly scope (Neptune) but it's presented in a way that is pleasing (Libra). Sun/Neptune also sacrifices for a cause. Considering King's voluminous output, some have accused him of being a slave to his work (Virgo).

Finally, Mercury is also a part of the stellium. It is in the 4th House, but connected to the solar force through Venus and Neptune. This Mercury suggests that intellectual pursuits are deeply rooted (4th House) in his soul and bring him a sense of beauty and harmony (Libra). Mercury next to Neptune speaks of a limitless creative mind.

Jupiter/South Node in Scorpio in the 5th House forms a sextile to the Sun. This shows a familiarity with (South Node) and adventurous appetite (Jupiter) for exploring realms of the dark (Scorpio) as a hobby or creative outlet (5th House). It is fun (5th House) for him to entertain the taboo (Scorpio) and consider all the possibilities (Jupiter) lurking in the shadows.

As the Nodes pertain to lessons, he is learning to be less caught up in the dark and to adopt a broader perspective (11th House)—to arrive at greater comfort within (Taurus). At some level, his obsession (Jupiter in Scorpio) has impacted his nerves. The North Node invites him to be more entrepreneurial and worldly (Taurus, 11th House). The Virgo Sun in the 3rd indicates that his perceptual faculties and literary craftsmanship are the mediums to bring the gifts of the South Node into the fruition the North Node promises.

Finally, 2 planets from the 12th House form aspects to the Sun. Uranus is square, and Mars is sextile the solar energy. The 12th is our connection to another world, to endless consciousness, to the great mysteries. When asked where he gets his ideas, King has answered that they're really not his—it's like an archaeological dig and he just discovers them. His 12th House planets explain his tremendous imagination.

Mars in Cancer does indicate energy directed towards "digging" in the depths (Cancer). It is quite possible that King arrives in this lifetime with a frustrated emotional (Cancer) will (Mars) that was barred from complete expression (12th House). As a result, he directs his energy (Mars) inward (Cancer) and ends up in the collective consciousness (12th House). The sextile to the Sun suggests that he may connect this forceful energy to the methodical (Virgo) life force (Sun). Sun/Mars is a go-getter, which releases the thwarted drive in his soul.

Last, and certainly far from least, is the tight square from Uranus in Gemini in the 12th House to the Sun. This Uranus portends intellectual (Gemini) brilliance and perspective (Uranus)—to connect one's awareness with the larger matrix of divine intelligence. It also infuses the ego structure (Sun) with zany, wild and unpredictable energy. King's very essence is of awakening, to shock and to stimulate a consideration of the ineffable. He is an agent of the mysterious (12th House), but also the fascinating (Gemini). The purpose of having such an aspect is to help bring jazzy and fresh energy to a spiritual legacy preoccupied with investigating what could be under his bed.

Libra Sun

The 7th sign is perhaps the most pleasing, refined and easy to get along with. Libra concerns the development of grace and tact, to excel in the art of socialization and to appreciate the finer things in life. Noted for its balance, artistic sensibilities, and knack of diplomacy, this cardinal air sign assists us in the civilization of culture through its message of justice and equality.

A soul that incarnates with the Sun in Libra needs to learn the next lessons about relating. It is time to become engaged and active to achieve a sense of equal sharing in intimate relationships, as well as in friendships and business partnerships.

Libra Suns have a sense of style, an attunement to social cues and an interest in building alliances.

Why would a soul require the experience of a Libra Sun? Some examples are: self-preoccupation, a coarseness of character or the inability to attain successful relationships (prevented by one's responsibilities, isolation, confinement, or simply choosing un-involvement), or a prevailing disregard for justice.

The major reason a soul chooses to incarnate with a Libra Sun is to work through wounding in the relationship arena. Many souls have been let down, abused, betrayed or treated poorly in some way. Instead of the reasonable defensive strategy of retreat, Spirit is guiding them to get back on the horse that threw them. By embodying this social, giving, and generally sweet energy, others are naturally drawn to the Libra charm, and relationship work becomes possible.

Mismanagement of this energy manifests as codependency or losing oneself in others, slickness and superficiality or an exaggerated insistence on fairness or justice. Sometimes Libras cannot be alone and end up staying in unhealthy relationships. Balance requires attending to self needs. Walking the Libra path adeptly requires self-definition (polarity in Aries) and learning how to do self work (Virgo is the preceding sign).

Libra is about the cultivation of balance, beauty and gracefulness in all areas of socialization, and many Libras have an artistic talent to share. Those that incarnate with this most pleasing Sun are learning about aesthetics and they're here to teach the rest of us as well. By cultivating a greater sense of civility in their own lives, they help civilize the planet.

Jimmy Carter

Former President and international humanitarian Jimmy Carter has a Libra Sun in the 12th House. His soul is interested in receiving spiritual sustenance and connection to humanity (12th House) through developing diplomatic skills designed for peace.

Carter finds meaning in life by radiating a compassionate temperament that brings about spiritual cleansing.

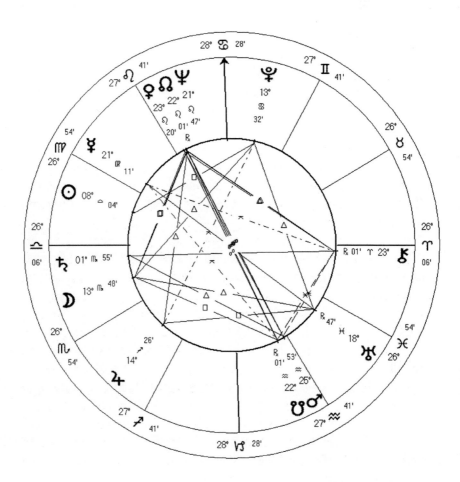

The lone aspect this Sun makes is a square to Pluto in Cancer in the 9th House. This most sensitive Pluto seems hurt (Cancer) by dogmatic proclamations within religious or political settings (9th House). It indicates concern about the state of the world and how people find a sense of purpose or meaning for their existence. Carter has been wounded by rigidity and narrow-perspectives. He has likely lost some faith (9th House) in the sweetness and innate loving potentials (Cancer) of humanity.

Connecting the brightness of a cooperative (Libra) and inspired (12th House) Sun with this Pluto is the central spiritual work. The otherwise contemplative Sun enters worldly domains through the 9th House linkage. Politics is certainly included in this far-reaching house of cosmopolitan understandings. Carter is learning how to get into his heart despite the hurt, and transform the power there into a constructive contribution. He is able to make an impact (Pluto) as an international (9th House) advocate of love (Cancer) and greater sensitivity to others. Note that his 1st House Scorpio Moon is in mutual reception with Pluto, bringing this challenge directly into his persona and behaviors.

The other chart factor to consider is the Sun's connection with a Leo stellium in the 10th House. Venus is in mutual reception with the Sun, while the North Node and Neptune are very close and ruled by the Libran solar force. As we note in the square to Pluto, this unassuming Sun is again brought to worldly domains. Carter is tapped into the source of spiritual kindness, and he disseminates it from leadership positions.

As the North Node pertains to current lessons and soul aspirations, a Leo North Node in the 10th House is a dramatic statement about creating a public persona (10th House) to promote openness and the goodness of life (Leo). Leo denotes regality or nobility and gives Carter greater strength. Instead of the more dominating facets of power, the inclusion of Venus and Neptune soften this intention to include diplomacy, togetherness, perspective and transpersonal love. Carter is here to model spiritual kindness, to help connect people together as members of the family of humanity.

Scorpio Sun

Are you afraid of the dark? If so, perhaps you'll return as a Scorpio Sun to become more familiar with it. The 8th sign concerns all things scary, taboo, psychologically complex, wounding and darkly fascinating like an operation, plane accident or horror flick. Ruled by Pluto, Scorpio involves regenerative power, the process of delving into the deepest interpersonal terrain and the exchange of radical truths with others. Scorpio, a fixed water sign, involves many of the processes that happen behind closed doors—and we usually don't speak of them in polite conversation.

What happens behind closed doors? Let's have a look. We gaze into each others' souls and sometimes we act incredibly unconsciously and end up hurting one another. We share our hearts and bodies and blend material and other resources. We make deals, exchange intimate gifts and, unfortunately, also brutality. Scorpio experiences are the truly unforgettable moments of the human drama. Those with the Sun in this sign are plugged into a lifetime of plumbing the soul in order to evolve from a condition that was less seasoned and wise.

There are many reasons why someone becomes a Scorpio—and they all have to do with learning to manage intensity adeptly. Besides being afraid of the literal and proverbial dark, some souls are ready to confront their own wounding more seriously. Others have been averse to risk or have been complacent living a more comfortable existence and it's time now to get more psychological and complicated. Some souls are accustomed to "living a lie," have been criminal or unethical, lacking integrity—and this is the season of accountability. Scorpio calls for a relentless confrontation with honesty. Ultimately, the lesson that "lying wastes time" is understood and practiced.

Due to the difficulty of this terrain, no wonder many are squeamish! Those who choose to avoid embracing Scorpio's power often face it outside the self. They can't avoid conflict, marry someone who is severely wounded or become an "expert" at healing others. All of this is really a part of healing oneself. When Scorpio behaves unconsciously, it is manipulative, controlling, morbid, depressed or even suicidal. Some choose to shut down from emotions completely and wear a cool, detached mask that covers the volatility underneath.

Scorpio Suns are becoming a shaman, an explorer, a truth detective or a genuine psychological/spiritual healer. They have tremendous insight into the human condition and teach us how to navigate the labyrinth of the unconscious until it reunites with our spiritual source. There are few (if any) paths more noble and important for the survival, deepening and furthering of evolution because Scorpio saves us from ourselves. With their own successful development, they have access to a love and power only dreamt of in more common moments. The sign of the highest emotional highs and the lowest lows, Scorpio's extremes reach into the alchemical power of Spirit.

Hillary Clinton

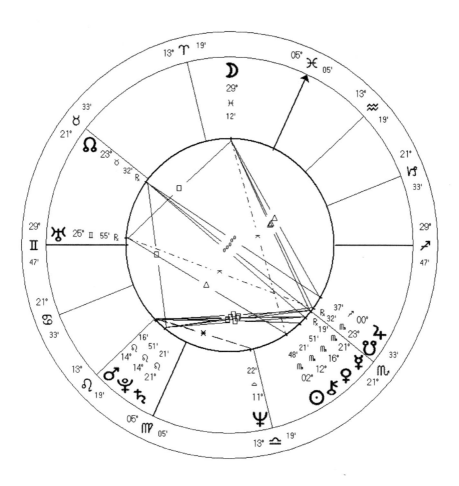

Senator and former First Lady Hillary Clinton has a Scorpio Sun in the 5th House. Her solar intention is to radiate power, determination and passion into realms of personal sharing. This profile suggests risk-taking to present one's truth—she is learning to show her true colors, regardless of how others receive her.

The Sun is conjunct Chiron in Scorpio. A very deep psychic (Scorpio) injury (Chiron) in her soul involves free-flowing articulation (5th)—having a sense of spontaneity in her presentation. Chiron is conjunct Venus, with classically feminine connotations—in Scorpio, there is a theme of control in relationships. Having the Sun appear here suggests that she is to assume power and to align with the wounded (Chiron) feminine (Venus) with a renewed sense of determination (Scorpio). Being a champion and example of "the powerful woman" is part of this astrological configuration.

Uranus in Gemini in the 12th House trines the Sun. The life force is able to connect smoothly with her intellectual (Gemini) self-alignment (Uranus). The natal position of Uranus in the 12th, and square the Moon, suggests that her need to express this has previously met struggle and loss. The present (Sun) lifetime aims to correct this unfinished work.

A Pisces Moon in the 10th House forms a quincunx to the Sun. Hillary has an emotional need (Moon) to have a compassionate (Pisces) public role (10th) interested in building something visionary. Under her more brazen exterior (Scorpio) is a kind and soft heart that wants to assist in our collective evolution. The aspect between Moon and Sun suggests that in order to fulfill the need now, she must build upon her softer foundation by integrating more boldness and risk into her life. The gentle Pisces Moon is easy prey to more aggressive adversaries. With her powerful Sun, she is able to strongly meet interpersonal challenges head-on.

Sagittarius Sun

Some need familiarity with the depths, and others, the heights. Sagittarius is the sign of expansion, travel, broadening horizons, a search for answers and the attainment of perspective. It covers all things foreign, what is just beyond one's reach, and invites discovery. The 9th sign has a large appetite for life—like a Viking wielding a flagon of ale after a stormy day at sea, life is an endless series of adventures. Sometimes our greatest lessons come by pushing our edges out into the open spaces of the unknown.

With a broader perspective comes an understanding of morality, of making sound choices that are in accordance with "right" living, however that becomes personally defined. The link between Sagittarius and philosophy stems from this ability to stand back from the large mural and take in its entirety. A Sagittarius Sun learns to see the "big picture" and then teaches the rest of us how to see it.

The Sagittarius experience is needed for souls that have been limited in some way: by logic or reason, a sheltered existence, being overly humble and self-effacing, introspective, or averse to ascension due to a fear of heights. Some souls have been so damaged by organized religion or other philosophical systems that they are here to discover a truth that works for them. Others have lost faith in living, in wonder, in Spirit. Some souls just need to broaden their experience.

The challenge is over-extension at the expense of focus, the know-it-all syndrome and the tendency to preach and persuade others that the Sagittarian's individual truth should be shared by all. The extremist, the fanatic and the ill-equipped, unsafe adventurer are faces of Sagittarius to avoid. A fire sign, Sagittarius can burn others or take imprudent risks and end up in tatters or embers.

The Sagittarius Sun travels a road of boundless questing. What does an astronaut feel when looking down at the Earth? What does an explorer feel when discovering a hidden vista? What does the philosopher think of her latest breakthrough?

These souls have much opportunity to explore great adventures if they can muster the bravado to pursue them. By so doing, they inspire us to similarly aim high.

Ludwig van Beethoven

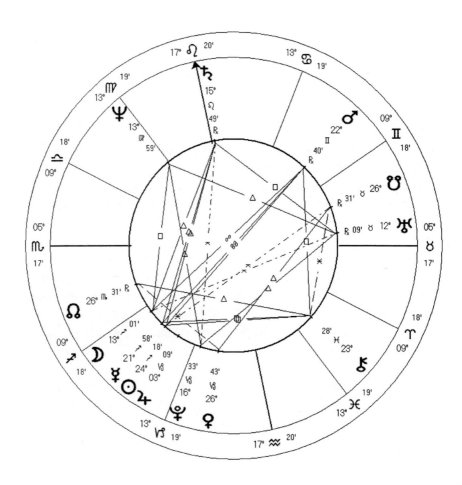

Classical composer extraordinaire Beethoven has a Sagittarius Sun in the 2nd House. He is more fully developing (Sun) an inner foundation (2nd House) of purpose and the ability to inspire (Sagittarius). A 2nd House Sun is attempting to prove to the self that it is viable and efficacious—for Beethoven it involves channeling the life force into a mission (Sagittarius).

Another Sagittarian signature is clearly evident in the Sun's conjunction with Jupiter (ruler of Sagittarius) in early Capricorn. This Jupiter is interested in sculpting a solid career contribution and making a lasting mark. Capricorn provides an earthy vessel for the broad aspirations of the Sun. Together this hard-working combination desires large-scale (Sagittarius) results (Capricorn).

Mercury in Sagittarius closely conjoins the Sun suggesting that communication (Mercury) of a rousing and spirited nature (Sagittarius) is active. Furthermore, Mercury is the ruler of Mars in Gemini, a prominent planet in the chart since it directly opposes the Sun. The Sun/Mars opposition is made even more pronounced by the addition of Chiron in Pisces, which makes it a T-square.

Mars in Gemini in the 8th House is driven (Mars) to learn and communicate (Gemini) about the depths of the unconscious and what moves us most intensely (8th House). It is curious (Gemini) about ecstasy (8th House), eager to experience transformative states of consciousness and to unite with mystery and intrigue. Rising to the solar challenge, Beethoven needs to courageously (Mars) enter realms of darkness and fascination while feeling anchored (2nd House Sun) and able to be constructive from these forays of discovery (Sagittarius). With Gemini and Mercury involved, the need is to give voice (or sound) to what one finds.

Chiron in Pisces in the 5th shows great creative sensitivity, but difficulty in achieving satisfaction. Beethoven's soul is likely to be upset or dejected—there's a yearning to finish the intention. With the Sun and Mars injecting bravado, this Chiron is dramatically challenged to develop a talent (5th House) that is fluid, poetic and perhaps even mesmerizing (Pisces). The development of this talent may involve the overcoming of impairment (Chiron)—this of course is borne out by his eventual deafness.

It is also appropriate to comment upon Beethoven's Saturn in Leo since the Sun serves as its ruler. This Saturn is quite close to the commanding and creative Leo Midheaven, indicating that much of his work is performance-related (Leo), albeit serious and measured (Saturn). This Saturn is trine to his communicative Mercury and his Moon.

Something quite extraordinary is also present, which is fascinating to discuss. Beethoven has the rare Grand Trine of the 3 outermost planets in his chart. This alignment will only occur once every 500 years or so. This harmonious flow of energy among the collectively-oriented planets potentially has great impact on the world if used with clear intention. It promises genius and a staggering sense of historical significance for Beethoven: his Venus is conjunct Pluto, an artistry of epic proportions, and his Saturn (great works) connects by forming tight aspects with Uranus (square) and Pluto (quincunx). Since the Sun is only indirectly linked to the Grand Trine, the thrust of the life force is more immediately involved in the Mercury, Mars and Chiron formations. The Grand Trine is the backdrop and has affirmed his legacy as a man whose works have significantly shaped our collective consciousness.

Capricorn Sun

A cardinal earth sign, Capricorn is organized, managerial, initiatory, pragmatic and serious. The Sea Goat endures through whatever trials and tribulations it must in order to reach the summit of its intentions. Concerned with contributing to society, and the preservation of tried and tested methods, the 10th sign oversees the maintenance of integrity. Somebody has to be in charge, and Capricorn is not at all shy about accepting this important responsibility.

Some souls are ready to exercise ambition and ascend to the pinnacle of a chosen profession. This trajectory of accomplishment certainly bolsters self-interests, but ideally Capricorn is sculpting tangible gifts for our collective advancement. This soul path concerns the development of will to slog through difficulty and master the very things that previously served as obstacles. It is not an easy task to carry on in lieu of few immediate rewards, but Capricorns are becoming our elders beneficently guiding us along.

Prior soul history may have included themes of laziness, retreat, thwarted attempts at achievement, dreaming without results, a lack of public focus or a commitment to family responsibilities and nurturance of the young. Some may have played subservient roles and are now ready for greater authority. Others may have been overly engaged in frivolous matters and are learning to become more steadfast with their time.

On the way toward discipline and wisdom, Capricorn has several challenges to negotiate. It can become domineering, rigid and cold—refusing to compromise or change and unable to admit its failings. The heaviness may transform into depression: then lightening up becomes a chore! Capricorn may become so concerned with status and reputation that ambition swells into self-promotion neglecting the collective contribution that is part of this Sun season.

Souls that incarnate with Capricorn Suns are here to further evolution through their inherent understanding that society is built upon pillars of solidity and integrity. They are keenly aware that life is hard, and are developing the fortitude to serve as models of endurance and strength. These souls are involved in the process of maturation that emboldens the entire collective toward a similar state of wisdom.

Dolly Parton

Country music star Dolly Parton has a Capricorn Sun in the 5th House. She has the soul intention to radiate greater authority—to work diligently with a creative talent (5th House) and increase her influence and stature (Capricorn). The 10th sign concerns the preservation of tradition, and working within established structures. Indeed, her career path has included deep respect for the country stars that came before her, while country music itself is rooted to certain stylistic norms and traditions.

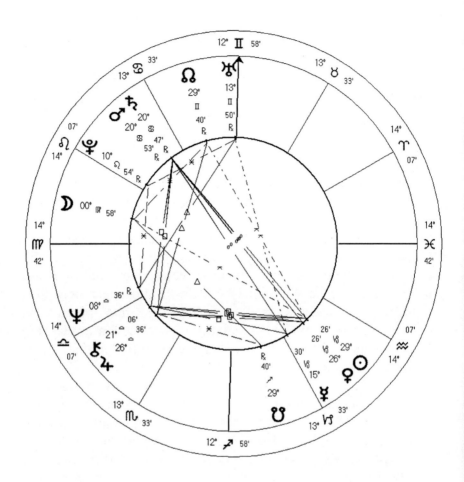

Venus in Capricorn is conjunct the Sun, adding artistic and relational flavoring to her essence. In the 5th House and in Capricorn, this is a friendly and courteous demeanor. The hard-working quality of Capricorn is responsible for Dolly's incredibly prolific career spanning many decades and literally thousands of original songs.

Jupiter/Chiron in Libra in the 2nd House squares the Sun. This aspect speaks of the development of confidence and material abundance to overcome lack or restriction (Chiron) that hobbles artistic or social (Libra) aspirations (Jupiter). Jupiter square Sun challenges Dolly to take bold risks, to think on a large scale and display a grand presence. The addition of Chiron to the mix

168

allows her to remember her vulnerabilities and not lose sight of her soul's fragile roots.

Saturn/Mars in Cancer opposes the Sun from the 11th House. The 5/11 axis involves the relationship between performer and audience, and Dolly is particularly attuned to this dynamic. This Saturn/Mars conjunction is exceptionally close, suggesting that karmic hardship (Saturn) involving her drive (Mars) toward reaching an audience or receiving acclaim from a chosen group (11th) has been difficult to achieve. Saturn/Mars in Cancer is a frustrated temperament with no effective outlet. There is emotional limitation or responsibility that hinders advancement—and this is supported by the Moon's (rules Cancer) residence in Virgo in the 12th House.

Bridging this central opposition in Dolly's chart involves a determined (Saturn) effort (Mars) to bring her interior life (Cancer) to an audience (11th) through the development of the 5th House artistic and personable Sun/Venus. Jupiter is at the pivot point of the T-square, a cheerleader of purpose and a reminder of the rewards made possible through perseverance.

The Sun is also involved in a yod—it's the focal point of the Moon sextile the North Node, both quincunx and pointing to it. Referenced earlier, the 12th House Moon is humble and sacrificial, behind the scenes and dutiful. The treasures in those qualities are made vibrant and manifest through the linkage with the solar energy. The 10th House North Node in Gemini repeats the message of public visibility—to have a variety of experiences (Gemini) as a communicator.

Aquarius Sun

The Water Bearer is concerned with humanity as a whole with its collective focus and desire for progress. Unlike Capricorn that seeks to preserve working traditions, Aquarius looks for ways to bring the future into the present. The 11th sign is fixed and airy in nature—intellectually obstinate and true to its ideals. Its progressive mindset is willing to be an outsider or maverick in order to confront the status quo.

The gifts of the Aquarian include an ability to potentially intuit the mind of Spirit, or however else the intelligence of nature can be construed. There is an electric and sometimes erratic quality to Aquarius stemming from energy awakened by the potential for revolution. Aquarius is excited to form alliances and join with other souls in the grip of new possibilities. They are motivated by *agape*—the love of all humanity.

Aquarian Suns are here to align themselves with a greater sense of individuality, one that is simultaneously unconcerned with reputation and oriented toward evolution. Aquarius is about freedom and liberty. Indeed, many Aquarians have a soul legacy of restriction, the drudgery of routine, confining societal roles and codes of behavior, imprisonment or the adherence to others' expectations.

This lifelong process of individuation and transpersonal focus may be sidetracked by losing the human touch. Aquarius can embrace detached, cold and impersonal patterns that alienate others and thus short-circuit their aims. Some identify with upheaval or revolution to an extent that becomes unwarranted or harmful. The personal style may be eccentric and anti-social—the rebel without a clue. Aquarius must guard against aloofness and be present and available to share their good intentions.

Aquarius is jazzy and unique, innovative and brilliant. Those that incarnate with the Sun here are developing self-alignment to help bring all of humanity in alignment with forward evolution. They have the ability to awaken and guide others to a more holistic and sane vision of humanity. The Aquarius Sun is learning to bust through any self-imposed limitations to arrive at freedom.

Oprah Winfrey

Talk show host, actress, and media mogul Oprah has an Aquarian Sun on the cusp of the 6th House. This solar intention is to shine humanitarian and liberating energy (Aquarius) into areas geared for refinement and improvement (6th House). She is working on (6th House) her own personal freedom (Aquarius)—

and by so doing, she helps (6th House) advance the state of the world (Aquarius).

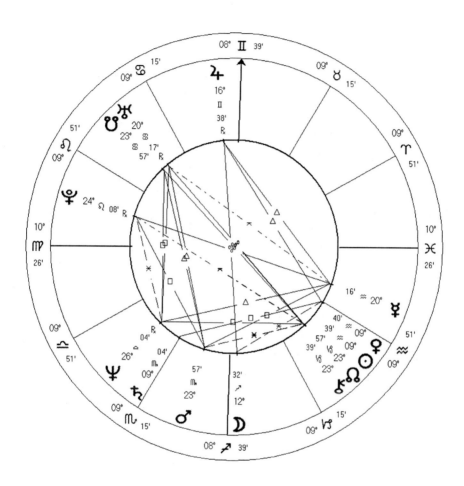

   Oprah's Sun is especially close to Venus: only a minute (1/60th of a degree) separates the two planets. Her awareness is fused with socialization—in the 6th House, this is directed toward assisting others with their growth. Sun/Venus brings an engaging personality. In Aquarius it awakens and challenges preconceptions. Millions (Aquarius) find Oprah extremely personable (Venus).

Saturn in Scorpio squares the Sun from the 3rd House cusp, and once again the tightness of the aspect is remarkable. This Saturn is embroiled with buried psychic turmoil (Scorpio), issues of power and control applied to communication and learning (3rd House). Soul lessons include the development of a strong voice (Scorpio/3rd House) previously muffled (Saturn) and an intellect previously coerced (Scorpio). Oprah assumes the very power that defeated her in past lives—to speak determinedly as an agent for liberation. This Sun/Saturn connection assumes stature and makes an impact on others.

Jupiter in Gemini in the 10th House trines the Sun. This brings Oprah's essence straight up to public and leadership arenas (10th House) in a grand (Jupiter) but versatile manner (Gemini). Oprah benefits by simply "going for it," by taking risks and aiming high. A bountiful (Jupiter) career (10th House) in broadcasting, communications and journalism (Gemini) is within her reach. Gemini has its finger in many pies, and Jupiter brings an international or cosmopolitan flavor. Speaking to large audiences fits this aspect. The connection to the 6th House Aquarian Sun is that the message delivered (Gemini) is for self-improvement, greater health and busting through limitation.

The Sun is also sextile the Moon in Sagittarius in the 4th House. Deep within (4th House) she is a woman on a mission (Sagittarius)—an emotional alignment (Moon) with her convictions (Sagittarius). This Moon is quite private in the 4th House and sits in tension with the 10th House Jupiter. The Sun mediates the exchange by being in supportive aspect to both planets. The present life involves delivering the lunar intention to a visible career—which enables her Aquarian Sun to reach its liberation.

Pisces Sun

The 12th and final sign is closest to experiencing the other-worldly or mystical essence of Spirit. When all is said and done, we return home. Water and mutable in nature, Pisces dissolves the apparent membrane between worlds and embodies

172

the compassionate and loving essence of divinity. Attuned to inspiration, the gifts of the Fishes include poetic or artistic ability, caring for the welfare of humanity, access to transpersonal levels of consciousness and an almost psychedelic vision of the reality of Spirit.

Becoming a Pisces Sun is not at all easy because it entails reaching advanced states of consciousness. Ultimately, the soul intention is to find stillness and peace, to be a vessel of spiritual love to share with others. In a world where there are gangs, terrorists, and gratuitous violence, Pisces arms itself with love. Meditation, dream work, hypnosis or other transpersonal methods to connect with heightened states of consciousness are important to cultivate in order to assist in the spiritual work.

A soul might need to become a Pisces Sun in order to realize Spirit more fully or engage a process of grieving. Some may have a pattern of workaholism, perfectionism, skepticism, detachment or lack of feeling, aggressiveness, rigidity or a pompous and egocentric personality. The soul is developing gentleness and compassion—the ability to merge with other souls to unify in Spirit.

With this serene and often sacrificial disposition, the Piscean may lose itself to addiction, escapist tendencies or larger causes. They may become ineffectual, out of touch with the realities around them. Some prefer to travel the astral layers of consciousness, endlessly surf the Internet or swim in a bottle of spirits rather than use the hands of Spirit to heal this world. The struggling Pisces may develop mental illness or become imprisoned by their own dissatisfaction with the world.

The sensitivity of Pisces is an incredible gift but it does take effort and maturity to use it effectively. Those that incarnate as Pisces Suns are intimately involved in healing the collective, and often that begins with the self. By learning to identify both as an individual and as part of Spirit, they can channel love like an artery from the larger heart. They teach us that there is far more to this mystery than what we are currently seeing. A Pisces Sun is to be a clear vessel of Spirit, once they rid themselves of anything that holds them back.

Ansel Adams

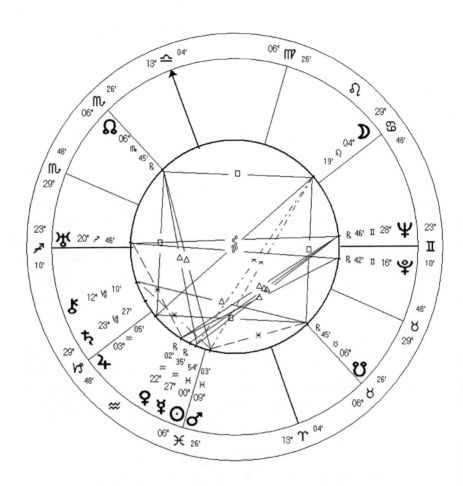

Photographer and environmentalist Ansel Adams has a Pisces Sun in the 2nd House. Present is an intention to embody (2nd House) more of the poetic and ethereal nature of Spirit (Pisces). Adams is learning how to be comfortable engaging in, and conveying, transcendent modes of perception and awareness. He is an agent that dissolves the barriers (Pisces) between subject and object, self and nature, and by so doing he becomes more confident and stronger within himself (2nd House). He stated,

"The only things that compatibly exist in this grand universe are the creative works of the human spirit."

The Pisces Sun is in the middle of a 4 planet stellium which includes Venus and Mercury in late Aquarius (2nd House), as well as Mars in Pisces located in the 3rd House. The 2nd House relates to feeling solid, able to endure in life from a position of self-assurance and self-preservation. His Aquarian attunement gives a global context. Mercury in Aquarius is interested in learning about the interconnectedness of humanity and nature while Venus wants to join with others in the pursuit of worldly causes. The Sun's proximity to these planets suggests that his biography would likely include a personal investment (2nd House) in humanitarian causes such as his conservation interests.

Mars in the 3rd House in Pisces correlates to his continual movement and perspicacity. He actively (Mars) merges (Pisces) with his immediate environment through perception and study (3rd House). Adams is driven (Mars) to find poeticism around him—to be a leader (Sun/Mars) in discovering spiritual beauty (Pisces). A conjunction of Sun and Mars does yield a strong presence, though in Pisces, the power is lyrical.

Neptune in Gemini in the 7th House trines the Sun. Being a Pisces, Neptune rules his Sun. This further emphasizes the connection to this metaphysical archetype. Neptune in Gemini also echoes the 3rd House focus previously discussed. There is an intention to perceive and learn about spiritual beauty and to communicate this to others (7th House). Neptune in the 7th also speaks of a yearning for partnership—this may certainly be personal, but with Neptune, there are also transpersonal dimensions. Neptune in Gemini in the 7th House is an I—Thou relationship in understanding Spirit. Adams is metaphorically married to (7th House) perceiving (Gemini) the transcendent (Neptune).

The final solar aspect is the quincunx to the Moon in Leo in the 8th House. This Moon needs joy, exuberance (Leo) and a vital exchange with others (8th House). Adams finds great aliveness by delving deeply into his passions. Although this Moon does relate to interpersonal scenarios, it is brought to the more transcendent ambition of his Pisces Sun. He is bringing his established (Moon) passions into greater contemplative (Pisces) light (Sun). Ansel Adams' life is characterized by his immersion in transformative experiences with the oneness of the natural world.

Chapter 7
The Sun in the Astrology Chart

Housing the Sun

The Sun sign is one of several factors to consider when examining the major soul intentions. The Sun's house conveys what the primary area of realization should ideally be. There is a desire to become more conscious within the jurisdiction of the house, to get to know its workings and strive toward mastery. A positive response to one's Sun would gradually illuminate the area and claim the gifts that reside there. It is essential for soul development to spend the lifetime understanding the scope of the house.

A Sun in the 1st House is learning to embody solar characteristics as part of the persona. The attributes of the Sun sign need to be active. One's presence and will must be aligned to achieve one's destiny. The path to discover the authentic self requires taking conscious and intentional steps that reflect the inherent message of the chart. The gift is to have maximum control of the life force; the challenge is to accept responsibility for improving usage of one's energy. It is quite possible that impulsive desires become the greatest obstacle to overcome.

In the 2nd House, the soul is learning to become more confident and self-assured. The intention is to be sturdy—to make the solar power a source of strength. The soul wants to apply the solar nature in tangible and practical ways. Investing in the Sun brings greater durability and potency to bear on one's goals. The challenge is rigidity, overcompensation, insecurity and excessive need to prove oneself through the accumulation of resources. The lesson is that the self is the greatest source of wealth.

With a Sun in the 3rd House, personal power is used for learning about the world. One must maximize Sun sign experiences to gain understanding. The soul wants to strengthen its ability to perceive how the mind works and direct this knowledge toward a goal. The danger is to lose focus or become intellectually self-satisfied. One can rely on the self for guidance all the way to disaster. The goal is to trust one's own thinking and approach the world on one's own terms.

A Sun in the 4th House intends to direct energy inward. Finding one's heart, the truth of one's lineage, becoming rooted to family or accepting a more settled way of being are some examples. The soul wants to experience love and attachments, both to others and to the self. Learning to center, tune in and feel the self deeply will further growth. Self-realization is challenging because the journey is inward. Refusing to make that journey will replay karmic tendencies until one learns that sustenance comes from within.

In the 5th House, the solar qualities are active and animated. The Sun needs to radiate through a talent, social connections, having children, or having fun. It's appropriate, and spiritually important to learn how to engage fully in creative realms because there is a contribution to make to the greater whole. Self-realization occurs through self-demonstrations. The challenge is becoming defined through the results of one's efforts or reviews from others. A 5th House Sun is vulnerable to rejection and misunderstandings. The gift is to find one's uniqueness and share.

A 6th House Sun is in a training program to learn greater mastery of the solar energy. It is necessary to receive guidance and to work on the self in methodical ways to gain the promise of the Sun. Process is required to craft the self over a period of time. Ultimately, one becomes the mentor or example of how to embody the solar profile and use it advantageously. The struggle is not to give up, accept failure or stay an eternal "wanna be."

This house challenges a person to overcome hesitation, doubt and insecurities.

A Sun positioned in the 7th House is learning the next lessons about relating to others. There is a marked social intention because other people are essential tools to catalyze self-awareness. It is important to learn the art of cooperation and how to merge with others in joint endeavors including, but not limited to, personal relationships. The obvious challenge is not to define the self in relation to others or to incessantly follow another's lead. The goal is to learn equality rather than orbiting around the other. As the 7th is above the horizon, one should radiate out into the world and mix socially.

The 8th brings more focus to deeper levels of intimacy and soul contact. The intention is to be able to work through psychologically loaded scenarios and achieve greater success about sharing and exchanging truths. The draw toward bonding may produce opportunities to confront one's intimate injuries. The soul is ready to enter the darker realms. Power is derived through honesty; the challenge is not to become overwhelmed.

A 9th House Sun finds its vitality through following a spiritual path, however that is personally defined. Aligning with purpose and taking steps to realize a soul mission is being developed. Cross-cultural experiences, all forms of higher learning and entering a variety of boundary-stretching experiences are of great assistance. One challenge to negotiate is the tendency to disperse energy haphazardly or to prematurely follow an uninformed path. The 9th House is quite advanced and requires a steadfast effort to understand its reach. The soul seeks adventure and new vistas to explore. Making sound choices is critical.

The 10th House is the pinnacle of the chart, the most visible area. The soul intention is to be seen as a contributing member of society. Making one's mark professionally, accepting leadership roles, building a reputation or serving as an example for others are included. It's easy to get caught up in appearances or compromise integrity for reward in this house. One could over-extend in vocational pursuits and neglect other facets of life.

As the Sun denotes a process of becoming, there is also the chance of never finding a calling and thus never feeling completely alive and engaged.

The 11th House is about taking part in global, communal or group endeavors. Finding natural allies for a collective purpose help heal the planet. Entering public spheres of influence or serving as a networker brings people and resources together. As the 11th is far along in the astrological cycle, oftentimes people with the Sun here do not discover how to contribute until later in life. This is where one receives acclaim from peers for work done well. Never reaching this endpoint renders one an anonymous face in the crowd.

Finally, in the 12th, the soul seeks to experience Spirit directly. There is likely a need to work through unresolved karmic business through raising consciousness and dissolving ancient psychic remnants that hinder renewal. Here, the life force naturally gravitates toward stillness and privacy. This enables inner work to be completed. A person with a 12th House Sun may face great obstacles in life, which serve to reorient consciousness toward contemplation. Managed wisely, there is great potential for spiritual growth and the finishing of necessary work. One must guard against becoming overly secretive or ineffectual. The soul is learning to find solace and compassion.

Sign/House Integration

Combining a Sun sign and a house yields more specific information about soul intention. The Sun is learning to bring presence and awareness to a general evolutionary process (sign) and to apply it intentionally into a particular area of life (house).

Let's consider a Scorpio Sun in the 10th House. The soul intention is to become and embody greater power, complexity, adeptness with psychological processing and risk-taking in a visible way. The calling is possibly to perform tasks that others would be squeamish about, impatient with or unable to perform because of the demands of intense focus. Working as a therapist with crisis populations, mortician, private detective, researcher, surgeon or hypnotist are some examples. Performing such a job familiarizes the soul with edgy and transformative experiences that also serve an important collective need. Even if a person shies away from such careers, there is still a disposition that can make others uncomfortable. With this combination, one may develop an aura of danger, promiscuity, anger or even madness.

A Gemini Sun in the 7th House is learning about communication and other relationship skills. A diversity of contacts provides opportunities to do so. The Sun is increasing its scope of understanding life and requires a generous portion of data (Gemini). Since the prime area of application is the relational 7th House, it is appropriate to observe and sample how others choose to live. The hazard is to be non-committal in intimate relationships. Getting to know another deeply would provide substantial experience and data, so Gemini here is not necessarily flighty. Nevertheless, even in marriage, this soul will want a diversity of input from others. A less than optimal response to this Sun would be to shy away from social interaction. The Moon, South Node or other indicators may show guardedness or wounds that prevent this.

A Virgo Sun in the 11th House is industrious about humanitarian projects. The soul desires to take an active role to improve the world. Applying the focus and discriminating qualities of Virgo in a broad context yields a wizard at technological, scientific and other ways that connect us and propel us forward. Anything from astrologer to rocket scientist to Peace Corps coordinator would fit here. This combination ideally produces an expert at something innovative. The challenge is the difficulty one encounters in refining one's skills (Virgo) and connecting with the right people (11th House). One pitfall is feeling lost and defeated by a great big world. A poor response to this Sun would position someone as well-intentioned but anonymous and cynical.

Aspects to the Sun

The planets that form aspects to the Sun support its development. They are central allies or resources for the developing life force and are also part of what we are becoming. Joining in partnership with the aspected planets, the Sun channels its energy into other domains and processes. These planets impart the most flowing (soft aspects) and challenging (hard aspects) lessons and opportunities. The biography of the life force is wedded to this process of assimilation.

One's sense of health and vitality is contingent upon working with these planets in a collaborative way. If we struggle accepting the solar program and developing it, the unconsciousness of the Moon tends to drive behavior. However, we still hold the life force (Sun), and the manifestation of the Sun and its aspected allies becomes unbalanced if not distorted. There is a double-edged sword of gift and/or challenge to everything in the astrological system. A less than optimal response to the Sun renders its aspected planets less effective and intentional.

About orbs: If you were to take *everything* in the solar system and put it together, the collection of mass would fit inside the Sun with room to spare. Also, all other planets and objects are revolving around the massive star. The Sun is the center— physically and astrologically. Thus, we must allow greater aspectual orbs than for other planets.

The most powerful aspect is the conjunction. The standard orb for a conjunction to the Sun is about 10 degrees. Due to the reasons stated above, it is prudent to extend this orb to 15 degrees. Furthermore, any planet in the same sign as the Sun is working with the same process and is inherently linked to the Sun. Any planet in the same house as the Sun is functioning in the same realm. The Sun is generous with its energy, and we must be generous in interpreting its scope.

In the pecking order of aspects, the opposition is usually second in strength. Any planet within 15 degrees of a direct opposition is connected to the solar force. With the square or trine a 10 degree orb is appropriate, and 6 degrees for the sextile or quincunx will show an affect. Some like to also look at minor aspects, and here is an incredibly rich area hardly explored. By extending the traditionally tiny orbs of minor aspects to allow greater impact from the Sun, most any chart immediately shows another aspect or two from the Sun to the other planets. The scope of the Sun is that large.

By allowing greater orbs of influence, rarely do we see an unaspected Sun. With Mercury and Venus always close by, there is less of a chance for the Sun to be without companions compared to the other planets. The Sun usually makes a few or several aspects.

A note on combust: It is traditionally thought that any planet within about 8 degrees of a conjunction with the Sun experiences combust—being consumed or overpowered by the solar force. The planet conjunct the Sun is considered weakened and has difficulty finding expression. Although there is much truth to the Sun overpowering other planets (in any aspect) there is also a gift. Planets close to the Sun receive great light (awareness) and heat (vitality) and with *intentional* use their scope is broadened. Oprah Winfrey's example of the Sun tightly conjunct Venus is testament to the power available under combust. She certainly has abundant wealth and popularity (Venus). The key is cultivating consciousness and presence— without it, the Sun very well may overwhelm and suppress the planetary function.

Sun/Mercury

Mercury is always close to the Sun—ranging from exact conjunction to just shy of one zodiac sign (about 28 degrees) behind or ahead. Awareness (Sun) seems to be continually accompanied by that little verbal string of commentary (Mercury) in most of what we do. (The only possible major aspect these planets can make is the conjunction). It's necessary to distinguish between these functions to not become so totally identified with the intellect at the exclusion of other planetary frequencies.

Nevertheless, Mercury is always a side-kick—we do approach the world in verbal and rational ways.

The issue is to what extent the Sun and Mercury are aligned. Much of the time the Sun and Mercury occupy the same sign (or house) so they're working with the same developmental program (or area of life). Considering the large orb we allow for the Sun, it would be conjunct Mercury in a great percentage of cases. Differences between Mercury and Sun are evident when Mercury is far enough away to make aspects to other planets independently from the Sun. Therefore, when Mercury has its own sense of autonomy and a unique profile unto itself these functions are separated somewhat.

The Sun and Mercury in adjacent signs does point to a substantial difference. This difference may result in bringing in more angles and variation to the Sun/Mercury relationship or conversely, there could be a fragmentation and diffusion of focus.

Some examples of the gifts of having the Sun closely aligned with Mercury are: A strong and willful intellect, great awareness and focus with verbal skills and communication, the ability to perceive and assimilate information well. Challenges include the subjugation of the intellect to ego impulses, increased subjectivity to cognitive processing and over-identification with one's thoughts.

The gifts of having the Sun distanced from Mercury are: detaching from busy cogitation, tending toward greater objectivity, incorporating other planetary functions to the Sun/Mercury dyad and having a multi-faceted rather than sharply focused approach to perception. Challenges include miscommunication and poor integration, separate agendas and dispositions, the inability to clarify and formulate precise intentions and poor awareness of and attention to intellectual matters.

Sun/Venus

As is the case with Mercury, Venus is always near the Sun. Here there is greater latitude—these two planets are always no more than 2 zodiac signs apart, falling just short of the 60 degree sextile aspect at the furthest point. Therefore, the only aspect possible between Sun and Venus is a conjunction. Having Venus tied to the Sun increases our relational and sensual orientation. However, the Sun concerns the self, and its connection with Venus is about how social and bodily issues pertain to one's development.

The greater degrees of freedom that Venus potentially has in relation to the Sun allow for more differentiation in Sun/Venus partnering. Whereas Mercury never moves too far away from a conjunction, Venus enjoys more elbow room. It is common to find Venus with a unique profile of sign, house and aspects. Since Venus moves quickly near the Sun and slows for its stations while furthest away, having the Sun closely conjunct Venus is the exception, not the norm.

If they are conjunct, the soul intention is to develop and radiate a pleasing and harmonious disposition (modified in deference to the sign). Venus brings a social and engaging quality to the life force. When aligned with the Sun itself, the soul is interested in taking the lead in forming connections.

Gifts of having the Sun in conjunction with Venus are: likeability, alignment between one's energy and social needs, aesthetic appreciation/talent, an attention to style and innate diplomatic skills. Challenges include the over-absorption of the self into social behaviors—having relationships be all about "me," the tendency to sell oneself, acting as a mirror for others rather than authentically connecting, and an over-attachment to pleasure.

With greater autonomy between the Sun and Venus, the gifts include: a more diverse planetary layout potentially adding to a variety of experiences, greater objectivity and less attachment to social needs and less interference in the development of other solar intentions. Challenges include a gulf between the life force and attaining what is supportive and desirable, less awareness on relating leading to loneliness, less innate charm and appeal—which may in fact be advantageous, to allow focus on other matters.

Sun/Mars

When the Sun is in major aspect to Mars, the soul needs to develop greater force, leadership skills, drive, and to become aware of and partner with one's passions. This is perhaps the most active of all planetary pairings: decisive action and courage are called for.

In the spiritual past, one has avoided such power. Being brave and bold is not historically championed among some segments of society. Sun/Mars aims to bolster the life force, to emerge strongly from past subservience, weakness, ineffectuality or an over-identification with softer or more nurturing qualities.

The conjunction indicates the intention to become more charismatic, daring and adventuresome—to lead with one's desires. Developing leadership ability and learning to forge ahead unencumbered are being sought. Sometimes one needs to develop more confidence in expressing sexuality.

The sextile suggests a teaming with Mars rather than embodying it. Learning to "go for it" and exercise assertiveness is appropriate. With the square, there is a need for balance and reconciliation between the energies. The Sun is urgently developing greater force, so aggressiveness must be checked. The life force is edgy. Successful growth transforms this is into power and clarity.

The trine eases the interchange through harmony. The Sun uses Mars as a resource, but must invest energy to claim the gift. The opposition requires working through Martial issues with others. Confronting assertive or aggressive energy from others supports the development of personal power. It is necessary to learn how to manage conflict.

Sun/Jupiter

Bringing the bountiful and spirited planet Jupiter to the Sun makes for a fruitful merger. Both of these fiery planets are robust and generous. The life force assumes a larger presence— these individuals make an impact. The intent is to develop a sense of mission and serve as our life teachers and sources of inspiration.

Many souls have been lethargic, confused, misguided or impeded in finding a sense of purpose. Some are wounded from religion or have had the life force squashed by misfortune. Connecting the Sun with Jupiter helps these souls to enthusiastically get back on the horse that threw them. A new chapter of limitless opportunity is being offered.

Jupiter conjunct the Sun would be the clearest example of the near mythic proportions of presence possible with such a combination. The energy of these people is infectious and they leave large footprints wherever they go. The soul is ready to take on big roles and begin substantial projects. Leadership is likely—motivation is fueled by purpose.

The sextile shows some distance between the planets so the effect is not so much fusion but cooperation. Ideally the Sun shines with clear intent, backed by a sense of what is possible. The soul is eager to see new horizons. With the square, there is pressure to take risks and adventure. The hazard is imprudent or thoughtless behavior. Learning to forge ahead confidently requires wisdom and temperance.

Jupiter trine the Sun is a natural and smooth relationship—easy to take for granted. It is likely that the soul has earned such a reward but now must actually take advantage of it. With focus, there is power available for spirited action. A person likely confronts Jupiter themes, people and situations with the opposition. This combination urges risk-taking, putting oneself out there to actively engage in experiences that expand boundaries.

Sun/Saturn

Saturn concerns maturation, solidification, integrity, endurance and ultimately wisdom. Pairing the Sun with this energy speaks of a soul desire to advance seriously in a deliberate manner and to incorporate unshakable strength through the accumulation of experience. This combination often requires

187

solitude and the uncovering of resources in order to blossom into the steady force it promises. Durability and seasoning are called for.

The karmic legacy may be fraught with complacency, ease, luxury, adolescent themes or any condition that avoided the responsibilities of becoming an elder. The soul wants serious accomplishments. To avoid this challenge results in heaviness, limitation, blockage and even depression. A person with this combination is ready to embrace the school of life head-on and make something tangible in the process.

The conjunction illustrates the soul desire to wed the life force with fortitude and perhaps austerity. These souls are becoming our elders—and on the way face challenges designed to force the maturity necessary to claim the part. The gift is the sense of accomplishment and self-respect.

The sextile aspect between these planets positions Saturn as a benevolent anchor that guides the life force in practical ways. Directing intent to fashion some form of collective contribution is warranted. Saturn square the Sun is saying, "Get serious! Get grounded and make something of yourself!" Within the unfolding spiritual growth, this is a crisis point where it's crucial to take measures in sculpting a mature life work. One must assume more authority and responsibility and negotiate challenges.

Saturn trine the Sun gives a person ample reserves of energetic clout to focus the life into productive channels. The reserves are there when needed, but do not weigh down the vitality like the more challenging aspects do. The opposition, however, presents a real test of integration. There may be situations where one must take command and use authority. Gradually one becomes influential and respected. This may occur after a period of deflecting or assigning power to others in the formative years.

Sun/Uranus

Both of these planets concern individuation and becoming. This highly dynamic pairing unequivocally calls for a strong alliance between the self and the higher self (or innate potential). We may speculate that in past life scenarios, the path of lesser resistance was taken and now greater gusto is required. Perhaps there was too much conformity, playing it safe or conservative thinking.

This combination does lead to positions, lifestyles or proclivities that are counter to what is mainstream or traditional. The willingness to be true to the self, no matter how unpopular, brings the soul closer to itself. One is then positioned to assist the greater progress of humanity.

Sun conjunct Uranus should completely immerse the self in radically new and exciting ways. There is a readiness to latch on and accept a role in changing the conditions of the present to become closer to a utopian vision. This combination is excitable, jazzy and brimming with energy ready to overthrow worn-out structures. The soul is in a stage of complete reinvention.

The sextile emphasizes the enthusiastic spirit of this interchange. Personal growth is accelerated by channeling Uranian energy into progressive projects. The square puts on more pressure to take risks for the sake of self-alignment. The soul is becoming more familiar with maverick or outsider status but must guard against displaying erratic behavior. This mixture is like a wild horse that needs taming.

The trine expresses the exchange in more collaborative ways. The integration between these planets is more natural. These people happily take on unusual or highly individualistic roles. The opposition portends a continual confrontation with the archetype of Uranus throughout the life in order to understand and integrate its potential. The soul needs to welcome individuation and face people and circumstances that require new responses.

Sun/Neptune

At first glance, this seems like an impossible task of integration. Neptune dissolves, while the Sun energizes. Neptune is selfless and the Sun is about the self. Neptune aims to transcend ego limitations and the Sun concerns the development of ego functions. Here the program is to infuse the life force with mystical wonder and cosmic perspective. The soul is becoming more contemplative.

There is a need to live in the transpersonal. Perhaps there was religious ideology without the accompanying spiritual experience. Another possibility is a soul too attached to outcomes, ambition, personality or earthly pleasure. This lifetime is in the hallway between this world and the next. The gift is to discover what is behind the veil and share it with others. The struggle is in getting lost and losing potency and clear intention.

With Neptune conjunct the Sun, the fusion is direct. These souls have the special assignment to be devoted to spiritual practice and model the integration of higher levels of consciousness to others. The danger here is in the dissolution of the self through destructive means (addictions, martyr tendencies, etc).

The sextile is less intense. The soul seeks the more lively side of Neptune as in spiritual seeking adventures. The square encourages softening, receptivity and trusting life. Lessons about compassion and surrender are urgent to develop.

Neptune trine the Sun is interactive and seeks affiliation. The task is to help spread the wisdom of Neptune through collaboration with others and the sharing of insight. The opposition provides the opportunity to work through confusion and deception with other people—to learn how to merge in relationships.

Sun/Pluto

The Sun and Pluto both concern power. The soul intention is to be more daring and passionate about life. This combination necessitates the development of Plutonian qualities (psychological depth, intensity and impact) in the biographical life. For better or for worse, the soul has signed up to wrestle with the darker side of life to catalyze a new frontier of spiritual potential.

Plutonian material was avoided or problematic in past incarnations (note the soul condition of Bruce Lee, who has Sun trine Pluto in the present life). Considering how unappetizing Pluto often is, who could blame souls for ignoring or struggling with it? The current season of the Sun requires meeting it head-on. What unfolds can be dark—but it can also be magical, like deep intimacy or emotional regeneration.

The conjunction portends the immersion in crisis or other experiences that stretch or rip apart one's comfort zone. Eventually, one learns mastery of such realities, which positions the soul to make a compelling impact on others and the world at large. Those with this conjunction are agents of evolutionary change.

The Sun sextile Pluto will give the life force poignancy but there is also a spirited and active quality. One may learn how to use Pluto as a tool for discovery. The square is a statement of the need to confront, often wildly or forcefully, the darkness inside oneself and out in the world. One will dance with the metaphorical devil now and learn that it is safe to enter the dark. Furthermore, there is enormous power to be claimed there.

The trine aspect is about powerful collaborations. The life force has seeds that may blossom into a commanding presence upon the involvement with edgy or purposeful projects and others. The opposition tells of the need to perform the alchemical fusion of light (Sun) and dark (Pluto). Managing initial resistance and eventual integration with psychologically complex and frightening material is a part of the soul path.

Chapter 8
Bridging Old and New

Spiritual growth involves an integration of Spirit, the vast all-encompassing energetic field of life infused with endless awareness and vitality, into the life force. The more we can embody the promise of our Suns, the more we may potentially fulfill the soul intentions. Beyond the perimeter of our mundane consciousness is a "higher" understanding of our purpose and spiritual character. Developing consciousness is the key to growing toward the soul's purpose.

Of course we are connected to life. As long as we have a pulse, we're alive. However, we must not sleepwalk through life. There are many levels of conscious engagement or mindfulness. There are always new ways to stretch ourselves and discover unlived potential. As it's been said, "life is not a dress rehearsal." The more we "show up," the more strength we accrue. As the Sun is linked to the sign Leo, self-revelation can be endless joy. The clearest map available is the condition of the natal Sun. Its sign, house and aspects yield a specific profile of soul intention.

Integrating Sun into Moon

Partnering Moon with Sun brings the past into the present for healing and integration. The overarching theme of this book is that through increasing awareness of the unconscious, we understand who we really are and can proceed though life with conscious intent. If we do not venture in the Moon's depths, the unconscious will subtly or overtly control behavior.

193

The Moon clutches to its familiar feelings. It holds onto its pain as well as its happiness—all of life is absorbed. It's curious when someone habitually makes poor health or relationship choices. "Don't they know better?" is the head-scratching question. At the intellectual level, one can be aware of healthy choices, but at the emotional level, work needs to be done.

There are emotional coping reasons why someone finds comfort in cigarettes, food or sex. When the emotions are allowed expression, the Moon is given release. Then, one can choose new and creative behaviors. This work can proceed rather quickly or may take many years, depending on how deeply the emotions are buried. Ultimately, the Moon opens from its protective hold and may be receptive to new input. Engaging openly with life (Sun) offers many new opportunities.

So, we are born freely expressing the condition of our Moons as we gradually develop awareness throughout the lifetime in a never-ending quest for wholeness. As unfinished works in progress, most of what we encounter can stimulate awakening. We are unconsciously drawn to catalysts that foster emotional completion. The psyche has invisible threads, ancient and enduring, from our spiritual past. These threads connect with the present in ways that enable closure.

We may take notice of how the environment brings up a feeling state and follow the thread. We are often too caught up in the immediate drama to understand that the feelings aroused reflect more complexity than just what's unfolding in the current moment. This is especially true when the intensity of an emotional response is out of proportion to the situation.

Developing consciousness involves pursuing the threads, seeing events as gifts to stimulate growth. For example, a pet may be killed by a car. This is no doubt tragic and it's appropriate to grieve. The failure to do so will only cause further pain. What if *prior* tragic events were never fully grieved? Then, we draw grief-laden events to us until we're through grieving the initial one(s).

The death of the pet brings the past into the present. In some mysterious way, the pet serves as a spiritual catalyst designed to get the owner in touch with unresolved feelings of grief and loss. A thread into the unconscious triggers an archeological dig where we dredge up emotional artifacts. These artifacts can finally be embraced, honored and released.

Emotions are energy in motion. When the Moon holds them tightly, they become stagnant. Awareness and presence stimulate motion—partnering Sun with Moon allows the present to heal the past.

Transmuting the Past

The Moon is like a great sponge holding the remnants of the spiritual journey that have made the greatest impact. As we are all approaching greater wholeness, the need to resolve the past is universal. The relationship between Moon and Sun is the central partnership for this spiritual work. The emotional stimulation that vexes us is the buried treasure that enhances us. Each of the astrological energies is a double-edged sword that can simultaneously cause problems and promote well-being. The following is a listing of the 12 themes. The struggle becomes the gift when we have processed our emotions effectively.

Sign (related planet)	Emotional challenge	Empowered gift
Aries (Mars)	anger	direction, assertion
Taurus (Venus)	stagnation	comfort, security
Gemini (Mercury)	disorganization	knowledge, curiosity
Cancer (Moon)	upset, hurt feelings	heartfelt receptiveness
Leo (Sun)	egocentricity	warmth, expression
Virgo (Mercury)	shame, guilt	competence, diligence
Libra (Venus)	co-dependence	interdependence
Scorpio (Pluto)	intense wounding	power, impact
Sagittarius (Jupiter)	dogmatism, grandiosity	spiritual direction
Capricorn (Saturn)	coldness, fear	mastery, wisdom
Aquarius (Uranus)	detachment	perspective
Pisces (Neptune)	sadness, grief	compassionate love

It is essential to really *feel* who we are, and channel the feelings consciously. This sounds like a relatively simple program, but the reasons why the material has gone unconscious need to be attended to and negotiated. Most of us do a handy job of avoiding or suppressing difficult emotions. This just postpones an inevitable confrontation. We have the choice to "clear it out, or play it out." Either way, one's biography will be strongly affected by the unconscious.

Living with tumultuous emotions is unpleasant. Who wants to sit and stew in anger, sadness or pain? No wonder most of us avoid it, but it doesn't go away. By embracing all of ourselves, the energy is able to transmute into its gift. This normally entails some form of catharsis.

There are many times when we employ emotional survival tactics. When catastrophe strikes we may rationalize it rather than actually feel the appropriate emotion(s). When violated, we may conclude we did something "wrong" to deserve such treatment rather than feel the appropriate pain or anger. When acting without concern for others, we may feel justified rather than empathize with them. A multitude of circumstances catch us up in the moment and we do not take the time to allow the impact to be felt.

When we do allow emotions to be felt, the process is no longer put on hold—it's able to reach its necessary conclusion. Short-term pain leads to long-term gain. The buried treasure emerges. Sadness transmutes to compassion, anger to direction. We equip ourselves with previously buried treasures. The grave mistake is to build the momentum of the growing Sun without integrating it with the Moon. Some believe we should just "grow up" and out of our limitations, while the truth may be that we actually mature by also growing *in*to who we really are inside.

The benevolent Sun is warm and sustaining. As emotional material is embraced and processed, solar energy accesses its most positive facets. This is the reward for doing the often difficult, if not outright painful, work most of us have hanging in the balance to perform. The Sun renews our hope and allows us to externalize who we are for both personal and collective reasons.

Keeping unconscious defensive measures in place takes a lot of energy. How much healthier to use energy proactively! When the past is resolved we can be in the present. The Sun indicates how we may thrive with newfound strength once the past is successfully reconciled.

The Sun and the Past

From the perspective of soul growth, we are picking up where we left off in past lives. We arrive with strengths and challenges, lessons of great variety. As has been discussed, the Sun involves the energy of the present—the life force and awareness of the immediate environment. How the Sun is configured into the rest of the chart gives clues about how the past is brought into the present.

Those with the Sun in aspect to the Nodes are re-experiencing similar themes from the past in order to increase consciousness and integration. The case of Helen Keller reviewed earlier is one such example. The life path will encounter familiar dynamics again to radiate the Sun in new creative ways.

Even if the Sun has no connection (by aspect or rulership) to the Nodes, the drama depicted by the Nodes will still be active and relevant. The difference is that the focus and attention of the present life is eager to take on new challenges for personal evolution that will complement the prior growth attained. It is less necessary to "relive" some sort of circumstance.

There are a few ways the Sun may connect to the South Node. It may be in aspect to it or serve as its ruler. Approximately one out of every 12 people has a Leo South Node, which suggests that the Sun (ruler of this South Node) has been significantly developed in prior lives.

If the Sun is conjunct a Gemini South Node, we can deduce that the soul embodied Gemini characteristics (writer, speaker, scientist, youthful disposition) carried forth into the present for a continuation with this theme. The Dalai Lama has

197

his Cancer Sun conjunct his Cancer South Node. He is the 14th reincarnation of a particular soul legacy and is picking up where he left off.

With the Sun square the Nodes, the biography (Sun) was in sharp friction with the style and lessons the South Node portrays. The soul is at cross-purposes, with conflicting impulses, and completing the work is needed. An Aquarius Sun square a Scorpio South Node serves as an example. The South Node points to familiarity with scenarios of emotional volatility or conflict. One possibility is that the soul decided to detach, analyze or dissociate (Aquarius). Through embodying the Aquarian disposition again, the soul intends to individuate and learn to live a new way, liberated from crisis and striving to reach the serenity and stability of the Taurus North Node.

When the Sun makes an aspect to the Moon, greater attention to the feeling nature is important in the current life. The unconsciousness of the Moon requires illumination in the current lifetime—possibly to correct the tendency to act unconsciously. With challenging aspects (square, opposition) there is urgency to touch in and use the lunar condition constructively. With the supportive aspects (sextile, trine), there is greater accord between the luminaries. Present evolution (Sun) requires sharing the inner contents (Moon) in immediate ways.

Some people have the Sun and Moon in the same sign. Keep in mind that there is a spectrum of growth that ranges from clumsiness to mastery. If a soul has worked significantly with a particular sign, there may be more work to do. For the present incarnation, a continuation with a specific process (sign) is needed for growth.

The Sun is always new. Even in the cases cited above where the Sun has strong links to the past, the soul intention is always to grow and develop it further in novel ways. If the Sun has connection to the past, it is like renewing a book from the library. We have the chance to learn more about it, another time period to fully live it in original and innovative ways.

Claiming the Future

The Sun has a special relationship with Uranus. As mentioned in Chapter 1, these planets are linked through the sign rulership polarity they make (Leo/Aquarius). Both concern individuality, reaching upward toward possibilities and the eternal process of becoming. The essential difference is that the Sun is immediate and personal while Uranus is transpersonal in nature and often removed from consciousness.

Regardless of whether the Sun forms an aspect to Uranus in a particular chart, these planets have a relationship to one another as both are part of the psyche. Connecting the personal to the transpersonal is a process we can learn. What may unfold is an alignment with a higher sense of perspective, to partner with the components of us that are less invested in personal concerns. Each of us is an amazing amalgam of both personal and impersonal parts.

Due to its investment in developing personality, the Sun must strive to reach the transpersonal. Attunement to Uranus connects the awareness to the over-arching intelligence of nature. Since it is a transpersonal planet, reaching this promise requires the releasing of focus from the personal and toward this macro-intelligence. Since the energy of Uranus (and all planets) is part of the psyche, we only need consciously to access it. Each of us has an enormous reservoir of untapped brilliance. This may be part of the reason why scientists claim that most people use only a small portion of the brain.

With Uranus accessed, the Sun's ego function takes on an entirely new role. Instead of being caught up in personal matters such as getting noticed or maintaining a sense of viability, the life force is influenced by more global or universal concerns. We may observe (Uranus) ourselves like we're a character in a story. We can maintain the identification with the self (Sun), but also see that what's unfolding has broader implications outside the boundaries of ego. From the Uranian perspective, the Sun is a vehicle to help drive evolution.

With *too much* detachment, the Sun is in thrall to the future. This happens when the life force is put into positions of danger or takes on risks and challenges that are imprudent or grossly premature. If a person faces difficult consequences as a result of these risks, then the partnership between Sun and Uranus is thwarted. An impotent Sun is blocked from embodying and maximizing potentials for reformation.

Balance between Solar and Uranian components is a delicate operation. Until one becomes aware of the transpersonal facets of Uranus, it is difficult to bring them to the personality. There is always a calibration process needed. If successful integration is attained, the vitality and exuberance of the Sun is preserved but complemented by the impetus to use one's essence as an instrument for progressive evolution. We engage personally with life while paradoxically not taking everything personally. The ego can simultaneously be passionate in its quest, while honoring the neutrality of the Uranian perspective.

Familial Roots

It was mentioned in Chapter 1 that psychological astrology tends to equate the Moon with the mother and the Sun with the father. The rationale is that mothers traditionally spend more time rearing children and a baby, of course, is incubated in the womb. The father's role is often to encourage individual expansion and uniqueness.

Life today is not so black-and-white. In a 1950s traditional marriage, these clear lines of division make greater sense. In modern times, many fathers rear children equally, and in many cases, more so than mothers. There are adoptions, sperm and egg donors, step-parents, children raised by relatives, homosexual pairings and communal parenting arrangements. All of these situations confuse who in fact is the mother or father indicated by the luminaries.

The approach here is to view the Moon broadly—an overarching statement about the soul history with nurturing issues. It encapsulates all influences within the developmental

200

years. If, for some reason, a soul needs to experience an unconventional upbringing for its spiritual growth, the Moon may be in challenging aspect to Uranus. We cannot assume the biological mother to be distant or erratic—this is only one possibility of many.

The Sun is about becoming who we are, free of any regressive or limiting influences conveyed by the Moon. Oftentimes, this entails individuating from the family rather than being more like the father. It is possible that the father has characteristics of his child's Sun, but many times this isn't the case.

Viewed from a spiritual perspective, the luminaries extend to broader themes: the Moon relates to the unconscious, including emotional and nurturing issues, while the Sun indicates who we can become with successful growth. The Moon covers the issue of our roots: parenting, conditions of the early home life and nurturing issues.

My own personal research supports the idea that the connection between the Sun and father is unfounded. In fact, emotional/nurturing issues with the father can be found within the Moon, 4th House and Cancer theme. (As a son and father myself, my experience is that father/child connections are extraordinarily emotional). This runs counter to most astrological teaching, especially approaches that ignore, or are skeptical of, the soul-growth view. I encourage the reader to conduct similar research to arrive at the most informed conclusion.

Patterns of Light

Chapter 9
The Lunar Cycle

One of the more obvious ways that the Sun and Moon are linked is the lunar cycle. In this monthly dance between the luminaries, there is a continual reminder of the cyclical nature of life. 12 times every year, we witness the full emergence of Luna into dazzling manifestation only to then gradually recede and go dark.

The Moon's position in the cycle is indicative of a particular developmental stage. We can look at the natal relationship between the luminaries for information about tasks a soul attempts. The progressed lunar cycle is also relevant, pointing more to the temporal focus within the lifespan. The application to the monthly cycle we observe in the sky is also suitable.

Many astrologers have written and taught about the phases of the Moon, but they are not used frequently in practice and have become a secondary or forgotten variable. Why is this? Perhaps it has to do with a general undervaluing of a cyclical perspective in astrological study. Understanding life in an evolutionary context including death and rebirth is analogous to the ebb and flow of the Moon. In the current astrological climate, the metaphysical is often marginalized in favor of more practical, predictive or personality emphasis that disregards or ignores a spiritual viewpoint.

The first task to consider is just how to divide up the lunar cycle. Many astrologers use 8 phases—4 in the waxing half (new, crescent, first quarter, gibbous) and 4 in the waning (full, disseminating, last quarter, balsamic). The 4-fold division of new, first quarter, full and last quarter is frequently used on the weather page in the newspaper and is the usual notation on calendars. Since the zodiac is based on the number 12, it is logical to similarly use 12 phases. Some have extended it to 28 phases which roughly matches the number of days in the cycle. There are many ways to slice a pie, and who's to say which is best? There are many approaches to astrology, and even different zodiacs, so we leave room for a variety of methods.

The divisional technique discussed here uses 12 phases. Each of the 12 phases corresponds to an aspect as well as an astrology sign. One problem with the more common 8 phases is that they each cover 45 degrees of the zodiac and the beginning of the phase has a far different feel compared to the latter stages. For example the first quarter phase (spanning 90-135 degrees) carries the energy of the square, but the latter part (120 on) is more like the trine. 12 lunar phases may seem laborious at first, but it's no different from having 12 signs or houses and follows the exact same logic.

The spatial relationship between the luminaries (noted in the natal chart) illustrates how the present lifetime builds upon past dynamics. During the waxing half of the cycle, the Moon has greater distance to travel to reach the promise of the Sun. The upsurge of energy in this hemicycle positions the Moon for eager pursuit of a goal. The emotional resources accrued in prior lives actively meet the world. There is great possibility that the Moon will play out its condition (both strengths and folly) so the native may further learn of its nature.

The waning half is more contemplative. Here, the lunar condition requires release and distribution. The potential of the Sun is maximized through cleansing and developing consciousness of the lunar condition. Waning Moons are more invested in social or universal themes—the resources and wisdom the Moon has developed is ideally channeled into collective endeavors.

It's important to note that the phases flow from one to the next. The beginning of a phase picks up where the prior one leaves off. Rather than rigid, defined boundaries there is a smooth trajectory as the cycle proceeds. What changes is the amount of light becomes a bit greater (waxing) or lesser (waning).

1) New Moon

A cycle begins. As the Moon starts its journey there is darkness with unlimited creative potential. There is a sense of trepidation and uncertainty. Many paths are available, but how to choose? Like day 1 of an expedition, what does the trip have in store? The newly born Moon is like a fawn standing on shaky legs. The accumulation and integration of experience gives strength and confidence. Gradually awareness of the lunar condition becomes sharper, but at the New Moon there is a mix of hope and naiveté.

In the New Moon phase, the Moon is 0 to 30 degrees ahead of the Sun. The related aspect is the conjunction and the associated sign is Aries. The Moon is initiatory and bold in its desires. The temptation is to rush ahead unconsciously and thereby recreate a past drama situation. Nevertheless, the universe provides many opportunities to design a new masterwork if the moment is seized. Setting a course of clear intention is the task now. Trusting that clarity will gradually unfold helps realize the intent.

As witnessed in a natal chart, the Sun and Moon are usually in the same zodiac sign. The soul is working with a process it knows well. However, there is more work to do with a particular sign. This phase compels action, so greater awareness of the sign's core meaning can be understood and made manifest in one's behavior.

If the New Moon is in Gemini, the soul plays out a drama of intellectualizing emotions in order to reach the embodiment of emotional intelligence (positive quality of this Moon). One eventual goal is to share its knowledge in a radiant fashion through teaching, writing or some other type of active communication. Spirit says, "Yes, you're witty and smart—now learn about your feelings. Then you'll be able to truly teach anything and everything!"

205

The Moon may also be in the sign ahead of the Sun. There is less of a "redo" quality, but a similar program of venturing into the unknown. Something about the current Sun sign was missed in past life dynamics and that omission needs to be enlivened and integrated. Each sign builds on the previous. Here, the lesson of the preceding sign was not learned well, so there is a need to become aware of its teaching.

The Sun may be in Capricorn and the Moon in Aquarius, with 30 degrees (or less) separating the luminaries. Here the feeling nature has a quality of detachment, rebelliousness or possibly emotional aloofness. Through the waxing quality of this position, the Moon is assertively venturing out, equipped with its self-allegiance to achieve the earthy strength and discipline of Capricorn. The soul may have an emotional need to be contrary. Now the lesson is to work within structures and institutions productively. Instead of being an outcast, the soul is interested in becoming a leader willing to work within the boundaries of the status quo.

2) Waxing Crescent

At this phase, the Moon is 30 to 60 degrees (one or two signs) ahead of the Sun. The related aspect is the semisextile and Taurus is the associated sign. The waxing semisextile has a nourishing energy that compels forward momentum while the Taurus association brings an emphasis on resources and commitment, feeling secure in one's efforts.

The waxing crescent phase requires a firm commitment to proceed with confidence and security. The focus is on abundance and the creation of resources for the trek. Light is beginning to accrue on the Moon's surface and intentions are changing into effort. Trusting one's direction is the theme.

If the course was initially set without strong intention, adjustments are necessary. There's still time to make changes— in fact, it is essential in this building phase. The eager energy is given a "hands-on" treatment to develop the ways and means to successful completion. Potentially there is some frustration if one realizes the chosen direction was uninformed. To stubbornly forge ahead anyway, without making necessary adjustments, locks in folly for the entire cycle. This phase is to solidify dedication and cement intention.

A Libra Sun with a Scorpio Moon is learning to embody and radiate greater peace and harmony. A waxing crescent Scorpio Moon is eager to form connections and work out emotional relating with others. This allows for chances to exercise the developing solar force, which wants contentment in interpersonal relationships. A Scorpio Moon has formerly been upset in relationships. This is now to be corrected by the development of grace and harmony (Libra Sun).

Some in this phase have the Moon two signs ahead of the Sun. Compared to adjacent signs, there is a greater alliance between Sun and Moon here (natural sextile) and the luminaries nourish each other for substantial forward momentum. The lessons of the waxing crescent phase pertain, but here the luminaries are working in agreement.

A chart with a Cancer Sun and a Virgo Moon serves as an example. This soul has good intentions, but may be restricted or controlled in its feeling nature or demonstrate other Virgo defensive postures such as perfectionism, over-analysis or self-criticism. The Sun in Cancer's soul intention is to soften and emotionalize, to develop the capacity to freely form attachments.

The Virgoan emotional need to "be good" is learning to radiate love (Cancer). Throughout the life journey, this soul is combining the need for productivity (Virgo) with the solar power of the emotions (Cancer) in a healthy and cooperative way. Lively energy engages doing works that come from a heart-centered place. A poor response is to play out the Virgo defensive strategies in openly needy or emotionally struggling ways (Cancer).

3) Waxing Sextile

The waxing sextile phase positions the Moon 60 to 90 degrees ahead (two or three signs) of the Sun; the corresponding sign is Gemini. The Moon appears in plain view for a longer period in the sky after sunset. Unlike the first two phases, the Moon has a greater degree of freedom from the Sun because the momentum is now separating from the enormous solar influence. The result is a sense of lightness and excitement.

The theme of this phase is stimulation, versatility and the continuation of energetic advancement. After a commitment to the process is cemented, there is an almost wild sense of discovery and excitement. The more unconscious version has a frenetic energy that doesn't stem from an intentional place— therefore, we see an unruly display of emotional material. Managed well, the security gained in the prior phase enters greater complexity. The advancing light on the Moon is beginning to reveal more of the developing story.

With the Sun in Libra and the Moon in Sagittarius, the soul is learning to complement the need for truth, being right or having freedom, with a greater sense of fairness and the acknowledgment of other people's needs. Sagittarius can be dogmatic while Libra is diplomatic. Here, the fiery Moon, fueled by the energetic waxing sextile phase, thrusts out into the world to pursue greater harmony, peace and the radiance of beauty. The soul is learning to have meaningful (Sagittarius) relationships (Libra).

With poor development of Libra awareness, the challenge is a disposition that is *unconsciously* drawn to relationships (Libra) to satisfy an underlying need for righteous entitlement and "knowing what's best." An un-evolved expression of this pairing is constantly telling people what to do.

The Moon may also be three signs ahead of the Sun, but not yet configured in a square relationship. Being 3 signs away, there is friction, but since the degree hasn't reached the crisis point of 90, there is still some of the sextile enthusiasm. This "blending" is not so different from an out-of-sign aspect, which is quite common. Again, the Moon is flowing and soft, rather than rigid and defined.

The Sun may be in Capricorn and the Moon in Aries. Here, the soul has a fighting spirit and an emotional need for conflict or self-assertion. The soul wants to transmute anger and/or a competitive drive (Aries) into a structured and disciplined effort (Capricorn). It desires to become seasoned and to make a definite impact on the world through its integrity and mastery. The Aries spirit driven by the waxing sextile is able to thrust forward unimpeded to support the solar wisdom and leadership. The pitfall is to lead with a spear or a dagger— unaware of the piercing effect—and assume positions of power from a fearful, rather than a confident, place.

4) First Quarter

The first quarter phase is between 90 and 120 degrees (three and four signs). The corresponding aspect is the square and the associated sign is Cancer. Here we have a crisis point, an urgent need for resolute action. At this phase, there is no going back; we must find the inner strength to fulfill our aims. The Moon is gathering more light than darkness and the shift is to an interpersonal focus. The more light shed upon the Moon, the more one's inner life and unconscious tendencies are out in the open.

The square quality of this phase brings about significant friction. Since the "point of no return" has been passed—the seeds planted at the New Moon have sprouted. This phase requires endurance, often in the face of strife. Since the Sun and Moon are square, there is a natural discordance between the luminaries that either promotes breakthrough or the renewal of unfortunate struggle. Either way, this phase is more emotional.

A Scorpio Sun square an Aquarius Moon serves as an example. The soul is familiar with emotional detachment, trauma or self-alignment designed for protection. Scorpio, the most emotionally daring and intense sign, is in stark friction with the Aquarian aloofness. So, these luminaries square off to reconcile emotional issues. The present incarnation is to become more interpersonally engaged (Scorpio), and the waxing quality of this lunar phase places the person actively into the human drama. The Aquarian tendency is played out openly in order for the soul to identify the disposition and learn to use the solar radiance for intimate bonding. There is always the choice to run into a series of relational calamities regarding emotional investment or distance.

In the first quarter, the Moon may also be four signs ahead of the Sun but not far enough to reach the trine aspect of 120 degrees. Here, the Sun may be in late Sagittarius and the Moon in early Aries. Although signs of the same element are naturally supportive, there are also ways that conflict occurs. Here, the soul has a self-focus, and perhaps an emotional need for competition and conflict (Aries). This is the heart of a warrior who is now learning to channel energy into loftier and more universal aims such as higher education, spiritual direction and a more reasoned grasp on morality (Sagittarius). The hazard to avoid is an unconscious need to tussle with others, further bolstered by the Sagittarian sense of entitlement and certainty. The intent is to learn perspective and contribute something meaningful that stems from the ample inner passion.

5) Waxing Trine

The waxing trine is between 120 and 150 degrees—the Moon is four or five signs ahead of the Sun. The associated sign is Leo and the corresponding aspect is the trine. The nature of the waxing trine phase is liveliness, connection and spirited engagement with life. This phase has a social quality that emerges from the trials of the first quarter with fiery intent. The luminaries are in a favorable and flowing aspect pattern that allows for smooth acceleration of effort. The struggle is having little urgency to act—either expecting reward or others' support to see the venture through.

Unlike the frictional nature of the square, the trine's sunny and optimistic nature does make for an easy partnership between the luminaries. However, this could lead to misuse of the energies as well. Nevertheless, the gifts of such a configuration are to be relished. The Leonine association adds a zesty and colorful component to this phase. Overconfidence is the pitfall to be avoided.

The Sun may be in Gemini and the Moon in Libra. The soul, interested in developing communication skills, increasing the knowledge base and entering a diversity of experience (Gemini), can naturally rely upon its familiar emotional disposition of socialization and concern for others (Libra). Although the relationship between the luminaries naturally supports growth by allowing the graceful temperament (Libra) to achieve maximal data input (Gemini), we must always see the Sun as a process of becoming. This soul is learning to realign with its own thinking and perceptions and not so much on the directives of others. Managed poorly, this combination produces a chatterbox looking randomly to chew another's ear off while neglecting its own soul lesson of becoming learned and intellectually dexterous.

There is also the chance that the Moon is five signs ahead of the Sun—as the case with a late Aquarius Sun and an early Cancer Moon. This sensitive Moon has ample light and is a "natural" at forming connections. The solar intention is to learn detachment and to orient oneself to larger societal frameworks. Managed well, the lunar understanding of love can inform the solar function in its pursuit of greater individuation and a worldly focus. A poorly evolved expression of this combination would be a split between the need for closeness and a cooler exterior. The message "I love you, now go away," is sent to intimate others.

6) Waxing Quincunx

The waxing quincunx phase occurs when the Moon is between 150 and 180 degrees ahead of the Sun—corresponding to either five or six zodiacal signs. It has qualities similar to Virgo and the quincunx. The hallmark of this phase is adaptation, maneuvering and strategizing in order to reach the eventual climax of the Full Moon phase that follows. There is a natural tendency to work with others in the pursuit of a goal. This Moon is dutiful and persistent as it learns to overcome obstacles.

The Moon is approaching its maximal light and the lunar qualities are seen strongly. Naturally an industrious Moon in this phase, there are major resources available to tap the solar potential. However, like the quincunx, there is a push-pull feeling here—something naturally supportive and something to work through. The waxing quincunx Moon labors toward fullness, refining its emotional tendencies in interpersonal settings.

Consider the Sun in Libra and the Moon in Pisces. The soul may feel sadness or be familiar with issues of loss, worldly compassion or mystical experience (Pisces). Now there is an intention to become more social and engaged in relationships. The lunar disposition is thrown into experiences resulting in either interpersonal connections based on a spiritual ideal or the replaying of an unconscious pattern of being let down by others. Since the tenderness of the inner life is worn so openly, others may find this Libra Sun to be quite sensitive and endearing. This is a soul hard at work (waxing quincunx) in the pursuit of interpersonal peace. The hazard is an unconscious resignation (Pisces) to settle for unfulfilling relationships.

The Sun and Moon may also be in opposite signs, but falling short of a Full Moon. A Taurus Sun with a Scorpio Moon is one example. Here there is an intention to soften, to become more comfortable with the self (Taurus) and to channel the inner emotional intensity (Scorpio Moon) into practical projects. The waxing quincunx quality to this Moon can assist productivity, but working with others from an unconscious place potentially results in exhausting drama. The Scorpio Moon is projected out to others and prickly relations may thwart the soul intention to become more solid and peaceful (Taurus). Managed well, this is a powerful and earthy combination that will reach abundance and satisfaction.

7) Full Moon

The climax of the cycle occurs at the Full Moon. Like the New Moon and first quarter, the Full Moon phase denotes a turning point. Similar to an "angle" on a chart, this begins a new

212

quadrant of experience. What was initiated at the New Moon has reached manifestation—for better or for worse. This phase brings the consequences or rewards for the work taken on in the cycle. The Moon begins its waning hemicycle from the position of maximum illumination.

The Full Moon phase has the Moon 180–210 degrees (six or seven signs) ahead of the Sun. The related sign and aspect are Libra and the opposition. Here, the Moon hides nothing and reaches out toward others. The resolution of tension within relationships and the exchange of emotional truths are emphasized. As folklore has it, people do tend to get a bit frenzied or "loony" around the Full Moon because the inner feelings are naturally displayed.

Those born under this phase tend to make an emotional impact on others, although much of the time it's unconscious. Since we're instinctually more like the Moon, when Full Moon people get involved in relationships they have a mirror into their own unconscious. They need others to show them who they really are and to catalyze growth toward the conscious Sun.

A person with a Capricorn Moon and a Cancer Sun is learning to be more heartfelt and open in relationships. The feeling component is restricted, heavy or authoritative (Capricorn). The intention is to soften and find strength in vulnerability (Cancer). Regardless of gender, Cancer is an overseer of family roots, the link to the next generation, and a natural parent or guardian. Managed well, this soul is loving (Cancer) but firm (Capricorn), and comfortably collaborates with a partner (Full Moon). A poor response is to dominate others (Capricorn) and unconsciously act in a highly reactive or emotionally effusive manner (Cancer).

A Scorpio Sun opposite a Gemini Moon may also be configured as a Full Moon. Here there is an intention to be less cerebral and more intensely engaged in personal connections. This soul may be drawn to intellectual situations only to find that to be less than energizing. In order to maintain vitality, the Scorpio solar energy will deepen and catalyze experiences that provide psychic depth and learning. Managed well, this is somebody who uses the instinctual ability to fascinate and communicate (Gemini) as a springboard to more authentic bonding (Scorpio). A less optimal response would be to intellectualize emotions while unconsciously emanating highly charged Scorpio energy, which creates dramatic scenarios and conflict.

8) Waning Quincunx

The waning quincunx phase positions the Moon 210–240 degrees (seven or eight signs) ahead of the Sun with the related sign being Scorpio. The Moon is slowly shedding light, but at this stage it is still highly visible and notably intense. The quincunx does add a quality of conflict resolution, here for emotional processing and completion. Managed well, this phase is ripe with power, a commanding effect in the world. These people can become agents for interpersonal growth—in themselves and in others.

This phase then has much to do with absorption—how emotional experience is assimilated. What lessons can be gleaned? How can wisdom become processed? As the Moon is now beginning to rejoin the Sun once more, the impact we make upon others tends to come back to us. If the journey has been navigated well, the world will bring back the fruits of our labor. This bolsters personal strength and resources, be it financial or emotional. If the cycle has not been pursued consciously, a painful confrontation with futility is openly displayed.

A Pisces Sun and a Libra Moon serves as an example. The intention is to move away from the unconscious need for placation or taking the lead from others (Libra), and toward an awareness of Spirit as the guiding light (Pisces). The Libra Moon indicates an instinctual focus on others—in the waning quincunx, the social components are emphasized. This person is likely to be popular and the recipient of much good will from others for their pleasing and thoughtful demeanor. The soul is learning to see the interconnectedness of consciousness activated through socialization—and to behave in ways that reflect a compassionate or transcendent calling (Pisces). By working with others, greater compassion may be made visible and the Pisces Sun becomes energized.

Consider the Sun in Virgo with the Moon in Taurus. Here the soul may be interested in working harder than in the past. This Moon desires comfort, security and a need for peace but to energize the Sun, precise and methodical work is required. Learning comes in the form of emotional catalysts or associations that have the waning quincunx (Scorpio) quality of deep processing. The path toward the Virgo Sun is likely to be challenging; this stimulates the Taurus Moon to take risks.

9) Waning Trine

At the waning trine, the Moon is between 240 and 270 degrees ahead of the Sun (eight to nine signs). The associated sign is Sagittarius which seeks meaning and perspective, and the phase is in pursuit of advancement and discovery. The waning trine is positive and gregarious, but is now focused more on the world and less on others. The Moon still has a healthy amount of light, though the knowledge that it's leaving puts an emphasis on maximizing the gifts that the cycle yields. If the journey has been navigated skillfully, there is great abundance and reward in this phase. Many worldly opportunities are available to connect in ways that disseminates the acquired wisdom. If the cycle has been poorly managed, a sense of relief from the more difficult waning quincunx is felt—we know what went wrong and the dissolving Moon brings some comfort.

Having the Sun and Moon trine one another is advantageous, but there are always ways to mismanage this. The luminaries may easily collaborate in *not* growing. In a sense, they serve as cheerleaders for adventure but not necessarily for those that bring learning. Due to their inherent compatibility, the challenge is to become motivated to use the gift wisely and channel the experience toward some collective goal. With the waning light, one may slip too easily into complacency.

215

A Scorpio Sun with a Cancer Moon shows the development of consciousness in an emotional way. Here the soul intends to be less protective and inward and more daring and engaged with others. The ample emotional reserves are ready to assist in ways that trigger greater insight. The waning trine between the luminaries provides a most spirited emotional disposition. Others may feel this power as mesmerizing or invasive. Either way, this configuration is geared toward recognizing emotional truths with an eye toward discovery and self-revelation.

Having the Sun in Sagittarius and the Moon in Virgo (but shy of 270 degrees apart) shows another evolutionary program. This is clearly an intention to let go and trust life, to develop an ability to release into the unknown on the proverbial quest (Sagittarius). The waning trine naturally supports this process and emphasizes the accumulation of experience in pursuit of a well-rounded understanding of life. The struggle is a clenched Virgo disposition colliding with Sagittarian righteous behavior. This may alienate others and result in a dogmatic and controlling temperament.

10) Last Quarter

This phase finds the Moon 270–300 degrees ahead of the Sun, corresponding to 9 or 10 zodiac signs. The related aspect is the waning square, and the sign is Capricorn. The last quarter brings a turning point in the illumination of the Moon. From this point on, the Moon has more darkness than light and is approaching its eventual dissolution. If one clings to the Moon's light and fights the inevitable release, this futile attempt to delay closure will bring cold reality. One feels fear if the cycle hasn't been handled adequately. When lessons are acknowledged, one develops integrity and accepts reality.

The gift is to offer what has been learned out into the world. By distributing the wisdom acquired, one can become a pillar of strength or an elder who teaches others. The retiree who founds a school before dying is an example. If too much emphasis is on preserving a legacy, the final lunar phases will be painful. Those born with this natal phase spend a lifetime making a contribution to humanity.

An Aquarius Sun backed by a Scorpio Moon is one illustration of this lunar phase. The soul intention is to release wounding and turmoil and look toward future possibilities. It is a critical stage in the spiritual history of the soul to find a new way of behaving (Aquarius) and to accept (last quarter) the painful lessons (Scorpio Moon) in the unconscious. Handled adeptly, this person can become a powerful agent for change, a skillful provocateur of growth. A less optimal response results in an intense cauldron of emotion, an unwillingness to honestly connect with others and a temperament of fear and repression.

Another example would be a late Aries Sun partnered with an early Aquarius Moon. The soul wants to develop courage and leadership skills confidently and to resolve a removed emotional disposition. There is a thirst for action and engagement (Aries) to correct the tendency to rebel or move away from the events in the moment (Aquarius). The last quarter quality speaks to the need for the resolution of fear. Ultimately the soul is integrating a sense of solidity and acceptance of the tribulations that brought about emotional removal (Aquarius). An unconscious response to this configuration could result in a fighter (Aries) with a sizable chip on the shoulder (Aquarius) scared of defeat and emotionally stoic (waning square).

11) Waning Sextile

At this lunar phase, the Moon is between 300 and 330 degrees ahead of the Sun, corresponding to either 10 or 11 zodiac signs. The associated sign is Aquarius, and the waning sextile is excited about future potentials. This Moon is only visible in the early morning, a few hours before sunrise. At this time, most are asleep and only a few are awakening. The focus is on preparation, and a new vision is crafted here. However, the current cycle isn't quite finished so the future must be brought into the present.

There is an increased involvement with collective issues, and one ideally experiences the fulfillment of the goals and aspirations that launched the cycle. If the cycle was handled less adroitly, the waning sextile provides some support to begin preparations for the next. There is an acknowledgement that "what's done is done." Since there's no going back, it's wise to honor the closing moments of the current cycle by integrating the lessons into consciousness and learning to see the broader evolutionary purpose.

A Pisces Sun paired with a Capricorn Moon is one example. The soul is interested in softening, developing compassion and exercising creativity and intuitive functions. The often rigid or shut-down emotional temperament of a Capricorn Moon is challenged to dissolve (waning phase) and discover broader truths (waning sextile). Managed well, this is someone able to work diligently on spiritual matters that potentially benefit humanity. A poor response is a depressed and confused person prone to escapist tendencies, unwilling to see the wisdom of letting go.

A Gemini Sun with a Taurus Moon is another possibility. To achieve the solar radiance of variety, spontaneity, and intelligence, the lunar attachment to stability and safety is challenged to dissolve and envision new possibilities. An optimal response is the storyteller who inspires others. The weaker manifestation is where the personality scrambles about in pursuit of material resources, a power shopper always in need of more.

12) Waning Crescent

The final phase has the Moon 330 to 360 degrees ahead of the Sun. It's either in the sign preceding the Sun or sharing the same sign. The related aspect is the waning semisextile and Pisces is the sign associated with this phase. Often called the balsamic phase, this is the darkest and quietest position, and involves finishing and letting go. There is something about the lunar condition that needs to be shed in order for growth to be renewed. As the Moon returns to the Sun, we do not see it at all

218

in the sky. If resolution isn't completed, unfinished work is brought into a new cycle. The waning semisextile provides a sense of supporting dissolution with its quality of nourishment.

This is an emotional phase because saying goodbye is often difficult. The gift is to honor experiences and absorb their wisdom. In the previous phase (waning sextile), the lessons of the cycle are intellectually understood. In this phase they are felt, honored and hopefully absorbed.

A Libra Sun with a Virgo Moon illustrates the condition where the soul intends to release feelings of guilt, self-criticism or an emotional need for subservience (Virgo), and to develop greater peace and a more gregarious social nature (Libra). This soul is seeking relationships of equality—and it must let go of feeling unprepared. With successful release, one can have pleasant relationships (Libra) supported by responsible and accountable behavior (Virgo) that are spiritually enriching (waning crescent). A less optimal response is someone who prefers to hide (waning crescent) and wallow in self-doubt and skepticism (Virgo) while adopting a superficial persona (Libra).

The Moon and Sun may also be in the same sign, with the Moon behind and approaching the Sun. This is very different from a New Moon. A New Moon is action-oriented, spirited and has the Aries quality of assertion. The waning crescent is contemplative, softer and more interested in realms of consciousness. However, both of these phases are "do over" ones. There is something about the zodiac sign that is familiar to the soul, but more work needs to be done. The difference is that with the waning crescent, the lower qualities of the sign are in need of release while in the New Moon they are intended to be played out behaviorally to trigger greater insight and integration.

Let's use Cancer as an example. The soul is aligned with its feeling nature and vulnerability on an instinctual level. Now it's time to bring the emotional unconscious nature to greater awareness and then be able to radiate (Sun) a loving disposition as part of the life force. Since a Cancer Moon is often hidden and this lunar phase requires contemplative moments, there is a risk of projecting a protective and defensive disposition. An introverted style is appropriate, but the pitfall is a full-fledged aversion to showing the self (Sun) to others. A better way to express this phase is to relate to others from an emotionally honest place.

Chapter 10
Eclipses: Exposing the Gap

Eclipses are either at the New Moon (solar eclipse) or Full Moon (lunar eclipse), which herald the initiation and climax points in the lunar cycle. Since they always occur near the Moon's Nodal axis, we may deduce that they are major harbingers of spiritual lessons. The luminaries are positioned in intense aspect formations (conjunction, opposition) and activate the Nodal dynamics. Eclipses expose the gap between the past and the present.

Eclipses foretell a confrontation with the unconscious. What exactly is needed in order to bring the unconscious into awareness? Is it confrontation, consequences or a moment of brilliant clarity? These events tend to catalyze major shifts. They are emotional events that often stimulate breakdown and potential breakthrough.

The opportunity to make quantum leaps in one's spiritual growth is possible. Since the energy is so concentrated at these times, sudden realizations or peak experiences that lead to immediate changes are frequent. Eclipses correlate to such things as breakthroughs in therapy, cessation of smoking or finding a soul partner.

At the other end is breakdown, when issues come to a head and can't be ignored. Unfortunately, people may become overwhelmed around eclipse times and act in imprudent ways: adultery, suicide, dangerous behaviors, break-ups or unpacking and trying on previously unconscious parts of the psyche.

Gathering research from current events and hearing personal anecdotes of occurrences around eclipses has convinced me that these unique times are indeed major crisis points. The volume of life is turned up. The purpose of this amplification is to jump-start evolution. Even trying or painful moments serve to increase awareness of buried tendencies.

At a solar eclipse, the Moon moves between the Earth and Sun, temporarily blocking our view of the Sun. Unconscious material from the past (Moon) is obscuring, or taking over the present (Sun) moment. The potential to behave irrationally or be overwhelmed by unresolved needs is probable. At these times, the past is brought directly into the present.

With a lunar eclipse, the Earth is positioned between the Sun and Moon. The shadow of the Earth hides the Full Moon— we see it disappear for a couple of hours. The Full Moon is a time when emotional material from the past is at its greatest strength. Lessons are brought to evolutionary focus or even crisis. The difference between the lunar and solar eclipses is that lunar eclipses tend to be played out more relationally.

Picture the Moon's temporary disappearing act. The gift is to resolve emotional material (the Moon's disappearance) and then to fashion a new relationship (reappearance) with it. With such resolution, we may align clearly with the present reality, free of replaying unconscious patterns. The struggle is to avoid renewing historical emotional patterns that are seeking healing and completion. There is a dramatic confrontation with the past, and we may deepen the very patterns that limit growth and cause interpersonal challenge.

We observe just how dramatic eclipses are. When an eclipse is visible, we lift our chins toward the sky and gawk in wonder. It is an astounding sight to see these familiar spheres disappear, only to reemerge again. These times serve as turning points in the shifting dance of the luminaries. We may note the degree of the eclipse and see what it impacts in our charts.

Solar Eclipses

The Moon swallows the Sun! It gets eerily dark for a little while; what are the gods doing? It's madness, or is it wonder? Could it be both?

Solar eclipses occur at the New Moon. At this phase of the lunar cycle, the Moon is hidden—lurking around as potential, waiting to journey into manifestation. The Moon is just finishing one cycle as it prepares for another. Like a celestial announcement, the coming cycle of a solar eclipse has great import.

A New Moon is a time to set intentions, which may follow a process toward maturation or more tangible materialization. Like any beginning, there is a sense of unlimited possibility. Ideally, we team emotion (Moon) with awareness and presence (Sun) in order to approach life with clarity and purpose.

With a solar eclipse, unconscious needs surface and emotion may overwhelm our awareness. The Sun is obscured by what is irrational and protective, so a regressive course is often set. What potentially occurs is a complete reliving of emotional struggle. This is actually important to do as the pattern can come into illumination for greater integration. As the cycle progresses, more light is shed upon the emotional stratagem.

Solar eclipses have an ominous reputation. This reflects how difficult and even painful it is for most of us to come into greater awareness and vitality. It is the central process of spiritual growth, so these semiannual events are truly markers of crisis and potential breakthrough. When we see a solar eclipse approaching, we must respect rather than fear it, for we have advance knowledge that a period of unconsciousness is foretold, and there is something we can do about it.

There are collective and personal levels to eclipses. At the collective level, the sign and aspects of the eclipse are energetically activated. An eclipse in Aries may heighten issues of war, independence or self-alignment. If it also squares Neptune, a challenge to develop compassion for one's enemies is thematically relevant. The purpose is to merge together (Neptune) while maintaining autonomy (Aries).

At the more personal level, the eclipse degree may be noted in the natal chart for its house placement and any aspects it makes to planets. If a solar eclipse falls in the first House, unconscious behavior is likely—in the 4th, a period of introspection is warranted and in the 7th, an interpersonal component is coming into play.

For example, a solar eclipse may conjunct a person's Jupiter in Pisces. This natal placement of Jupiter is a visionary and a traveler of the inner terrain. It likes to explore dreams or hypnosis and designs a compassionate philosophy or generous disposition toward the welfare of others. A less refined expression is the person existentially lost or troubled. The onset of the solar eclipse would stimulate this Jupiter either to regress into a more infantile expression or just act out to see where the struggle is.

Some possibilities would be to take foolish risks (Jupiter) in Piscean endeavors (using dangerous or illegal mind-altering substances) or following an ill-advised spiritual discipline that alienates rather than merges. Pisces tends to be gullible and when Jupiter acts unconsciously dire consequences can result. There's potential to be drawn into a scam, of a spiritual, intellectual or emotional nature.

The purpose of the solar eclipse is to get awareness and momentum on the right track. This event may trigger the Jupiter in Pisces to discover how to explore consciousness. Compassion may come to fuller expression; the existentially lost may have that elusive once-in-a-lifetime breakthrough. The outcome of any astrological event is pro-growth and delightfully positive if we can rise to the occasion with humility and perspective.

Another example: A solar eclipse may square a person's Mercury in Capricorn. This planet is developing mastery of the intellectual and communicative functions. The eclipse may bring lessons or opportunities to speak with more authority and banish fear regarding cognitive capabilities. Perhaps a situation unfolds where more responsibilities are given at work, which potentially leads to more visibility as an "ideas person" or communicator. Maybe consequences of being intellectually rigid become clear and catalyze efforts to be well-informed.

Half of the time solar eclipses occur near the South Node of the Moon, and the other half, near the North. Those that occur near the South are more indicative of re-experiencing patterns or dramas from past lives. This may be much to the disadvantage of someone trying to move away from restrictive or habitual patterns or it actually may uncover a buried treasure from the past. The South Node is not inherently malevolent; it merely holds what is natural, familiar or second-nature to the soul. At any rate, a solar eclipse conjunct the South Node tends to be more past-oriented.

When falling close to the North Node, there is emphasis on the development of new skills and abilities. However, this is always a stretch and the unconscious may create a formidable barrier to overcome. With clear intention and decisive action this is an opportunity for a giant leap forward.

It is important to keep in mind that when one of the Nodes is activated the other is too, for they are always configured as an opposition. Therefore, for all solar and lunar eclipses, both Nodes are stimulated. Making the distinctions of where the luminaries actually fall is secondary since both are always involved. It is more important to note what houses and planets are contacted.

Lunar Eclipses

The Moon vanishes before our eyes! We may glimpse her through the shadows—sometimes with a reddish hue, she appears distorted or mysterious. Clearly something is going on with her, for she displays a most unusual temper. What is the *feeling*?

The Moon embodies the past, our habitual and instinctive emotional reactions—and a lunar eclipse is a time of potential breakthrough or frenzied unconsciousness with these patterns. The gift is the opportunity to eradicate unnecessary emotional strategies that no longer serve us. As the Moon disappears, we too can flush away fragments of the past that are losing their purpose. The Moon emerges from the shadows anew, cleansed and illuminated for its beauty to shine forth.

The struggle is to behave unconsciously and face the resulting consequences. The literal disappearance of the Moon represents the figurative disappearance of awareness that shines on our lunar predilections (note the folklore of werewolves; our animalistic tendencies may be in full bloom). As a result, the lessons applicable to the lunar coping mechanisms play out in some way. Oppositions frequently pertain to relationships, and the Full Moon is the time when emotions are most pronounced and evident. It is common to have highly emotional exchanges with others around a lunar eclipse.

These are moments of great volatility, potentially cataclysmic in some way. It is more than folklore that people tend to become "lunatics" at the Full Moon, and studies of admissions to psychiatric facilities at this time confirm it. The alcoholic who "falls of the wagon" or the repressed introvert who finally lashes out, are examples of issues coming to a head.

Lunar eclipses, and Full Moons in general, balance with the polarity indicated by the Sun. The more evolved expression of the Sun works as a beacon for clarifying and resolving worn out emotional patterns. The potential for integrating lunar and solar functions is at the peak—this is true for both types of eclipses.

If a lunar eclipse falls in Aquarius, the Sun is in Leo. In a global sense, we are all being faced with the challenge of releasing any emotional detachment tendencies we may have. If there is a history of aloofness, dissociation from feeling due to trauma or perhaps the inheritance of a cooler emotional disposition from the parents—this eclipse will stir it up. It is likely to be addressed via interpersonal exchanges, either consciously or not. The eclipse holds the potential to do significant work in clearing away emotional protective strategies and opening to the radiance, warmth and "in the moment" awareness that Leo offers.

The eclipse is more significant when it forms tight aspects to natal planets. The 4th harmonic aspects (conjunction, opposition, square) tend to have more strength and urgency. However, I have found that trines, sextiles and minor aspects with tight orbs also have relevance. If a lunar eclipse is at 7 degrees Aquarius (Moon) and 7 Leo (Sun) impacting a person's natal Venus positioned at 7 Aquarius, that planet is summoned to mature in some way. To get a sense of what the lessons are, we must first examine the planet on its own.

Venus in Aquarius is quite social, friendly and good-natured, but possibly not comfortable with emotionally close connections. This Venus enjoys groups or communities and likes to be part of something that makes a difference, such as Habitat For Humanity or the Peace Corps. Venus in Aquarius may also be drawn to relationships with the odd, the eccentric or those that live contrary to mainstream values. The lunar eclipse will exaggerate these tendencies so that the owner of the Venus may *feel* the longing for group affiliation, or bohemian connections, and behave in these ways. It also may trigger a sense of imbalance in these directions in order to stimulate integration with the Leonine qualities of warmth and presence—the ability to share openly and from the heart.

If the Moon contacts a natal planet as part of a lunar eclipse, we will feel it strongly and possibly act it out in an exaggerated way. We may learn of possible imbalances and foster a more mature relationship by valuing qualities at both ends of the polarity. If the eclipse doesn't make any contacts with natal planets, it still is activating a house—and lessons pertinent to that area will be illuminated for greater integration.

Another wrinkle to consider is whether the Moon is near the North or South Node as part of the eclipse configuration. If the Moon is near the North Node, there is more emphasis on moving toward greater feeling or inward depth. The Sun near the North Node indicates that greater awareness and outward reach is appropriate. Also, the two rulers of the Nodes give further information about the impact of the eclipse and how the lessons may be best used.

Timing of Eclipses

There is some debate as to how long the effect of an eclipse lasts. Some say they are relevant for weeks, even months, before and after the actual eclipse occurs. Others are more conservative and limit the impact to the surrounding days.

I have come to view eclipses as chapters in an ongoing story of evolution. A solar eclipse (at a New Moon) signifies a beginning. The solar eclipse six months later will signal another new beginning. The eclipses build from one to the next. Since a solar eclipse is always about six months ahead of the last one, it will usually correspond to six zodiac signs. If a solar eclipse is in Aries, the next one is likely to be in Libra—unless the initial one was in early Aries, the following may be in late Virgo, as eclipses gradually move backwards through the zodiac. This backward motion provides the metaphor of retrieving from the past.

At any rate, six months after an eclipse is broadly analogous to the Full Moon time, when the seeds planted at the prior New Moon have ripened—similar to how the waxing lunar phase eventually reaches fullness. The lessons activated at a solar eclipse have reached a climax, right at the time of another eclipse. There is sort of a hand-off from one eclipse to the next. Then the eclipse that falls around the same time the following year signifies yet another new beginning. This, of course, would be the half way point of the previous set of eclipses.

So, eclipses can be thought of as overlapping chapters of evolution. Since the eclipses that are six months apart (the ones immediately before and after any given set of eclipses) are in some proximity to one another, there is a sense of continuity. For example on 4/19/04 the solar eclipse was at 29 Aries, followed by the next on 10/14/04 at 21 Libra. On 4/8/05 the solar eclipse was at 19 Aries, on 10/3/05 it was at 10 Libra, followed by 3/29/06 at 8 Aries. On 9/22/06 it slid back to 29 Virgo. The Aries/Libra axis was active for about two years before moving on to Virgo/Pisces. (The Nodes shift signs every 1.5 years, so eclipses occupy a sign polarity for roughly the same duration.)

The actual eclipse times are when the energy is most active. These are the "hot" moments, when lessons come to a head. The number of days or weeks surrounding the eclipse when we feel its maximal impact is speculative. Similar to the orb we allow for natal aspects, there is no cut-and-dry answer. What we do know is that eclipses are dramatic, and open (as well as continue) a (overlapping) chapter of spiritual growth. It is useful to examine the eclipse chart for the six month chapter, as well as for an additional six months during the "waning" phase when another eclipse is "waxing." Therefore, a set of eclipses (both solar and lunar) occurs every six months and are active for about a year. The actual days surrounding the events tend to have the most impact.

Eclipse examples:

Solar Eclipse: June 21, 2001 preceding September 11, 2001.

This is the chart of the solar eclipse before September 11th, 2001. The eclipse occurred at 0 degrees Cancer, at the summer solstice. Many astrologers believe that 0 degrees of the cardinal signs are important points on the zodiac, just as the angles indicate new sectors of activity. The beginning of cardinal signs fall on the solstices and equinoxes, which do correspond to major turning points. We may conclude that this particular eclipse packs more of a punch than others.

Cast for New York City, the eclipse is in the 12th House, and rules the chart since Leo is on the Ascendant. What is most striking about this chart is the connection the luminaries have with a series of oppositions. The Sun and Moon are not far from Jupiter and Mercury in late Gemini, which oppose Chiron, Mars and Pluto in Sagittarius. Saturn is also in Gemini, albeit earlier, but is linked in through its opposition to Pluto. So, many planets in the chart are connected to the eclipse, most tellingly the Saturn/Pluto opposition which reached greater exactitude on 9/11.

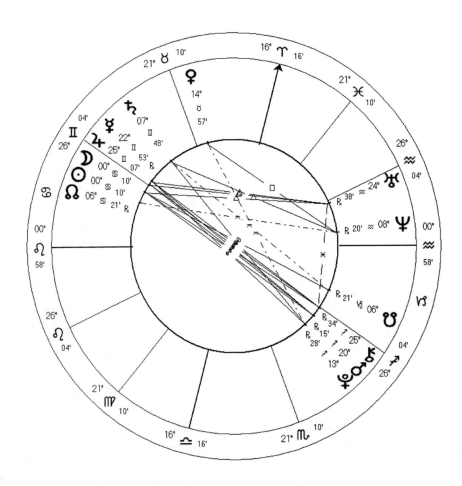

The opposition of Jupiter/Mercury (Gemini) with Chiron/Mars/Pluto (Sagittarius) shows a dramatic conflict between ideas and belief systems with explosive and wounding responses. Jupiter opposed Mars in itself speaks of amplified aggression and polarized opinions. Connected to the Saturn/Pluto opposition it brings cataclysmic impact (Pluto) to structures (Saturn). The tension between world views is accentuated, and brought to violent confrontation.

Aries is on the Midheaven, so Mars, the "God of War," rules the most obvious and public sector of the chart. This Mars is embroiled in philosophical or religious (Sagittarius) conflict. Interestingly, Venus in Taurus sits in the 10th, but is unaspected except for a quincunx to Pluto. The yearning for peace and tranquility (Venus in Taurus) is being called to work through (quincunx) the darker realities of religious fanaticism (Pluto in Sagittarius).

The eclipse in the 12th House pertains to great sorrow, loss, and emotional (Cancer) pain. The challenge is to remain connected to the heart (Cancer) and find sustenance through Spirit (12th). All eclipses involve working through emotional material, and this particular eclipse exaggerates this theme by both the Cancer and 12th House signatures.

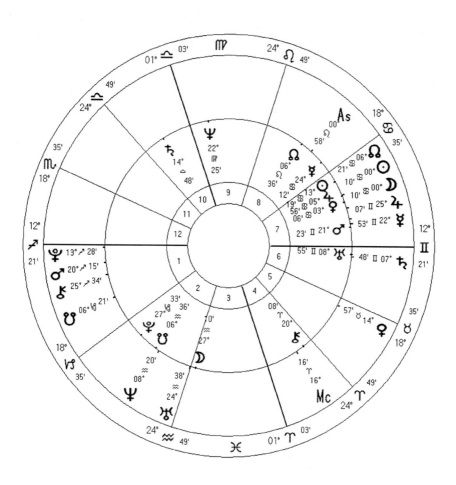

231

This biwheel shows the pre-9/11 solar eclipse (outer wheel) in relation to the U.S. Sibley chart (inner wheel), which is widely used as the birthchart for the country. The solar eclipse falls in the U.S. 7th House, traditionally termed "the house of open enemies," but it more broadly concerns all types of relations. It is conjunct both Venus (relations) and Jupiter (belief systems) in emotional Cancer, intensifying conflict between U.S. family and religious values and those of others (7th).

Most compellingly, Pluto sits on the U.S. Ascendant in Sagittarius. It is conjunct Mars which is tightly opposed the U.S. 7th House Mars. In fact, the whole series of oppositions that typify this powerful eclipse (described above) is activating the U.S. Mars. This points overwhelmingly to conflict and aggression. Also of note is the U.S. Neptune in the 9th House, in Virgo. This Neptune has pious aspirations (Virgo) that it wishes to spread internationally (9th). Flavored by a square to Mars, this otherwise humble (Virgo) Neptune incorporates war-like connotations. The struggle resulting from Neptune is existential despair and loss, which occurred on 9/11.

The eclipse chart's Saturn is conjunct the U.S. Uranus, illustrating the crystallization (Saturn) of chaos (Uranus)— difficult realities (Saturn) are brought to unpredictable outcomes (Uranus) triggering an honest self-assessment (6th) of our worldly perceptions (Gemini). This Uranus is also the ruler of the U.S. Aquarian South Node. The main lessons of the country have to do with revolution and upheaval. Uranus tends to be stubborn in pursuit of its truth—transiting Saturn brings consequence to this brand of intellectual (Gemini) self-alignment (Uranus).

The Aquarius South Node is met by the eclipse chart Neptune. The country is being challenged to release (Neptune) its rebellious gusto that tends to alienate others. The country was founded by revolution (Aquarius), which it no longer needs to employ. The Nodal movement toward the North indicates that connecting joyfully with others through trust and openness is being developed.

Indeed, the U.S. Moon is also in Aquarius—this need for self-alignment to what is perceived to be "truth" is an integral part of the American character. At the time of the eclipse, Uranus was about 2.5 degrees away from an exact conjunction with the U.S. Moon, close enough to vigorously initiate drastic change. Uranus wants to update matters, while the Moon is concerned with holding on to patterns. This combination speaks of collective emotional turmoil in order to have a new way of feeling rooted to our country—perhaps one that is more humanitarian (Aquarian) in outlook instead of just being fixed or rebellious. Also, note that the Moon rules the Sibley 8th House, which includes death and transformation.

The interaction between the pre-9/11 eclipse chart and the U.S. Sibley chart is striking. It clearly spells out the themes that were at play and what lessons the tragic event brings to the American psyche. For a lunar eclipse example, let's shift to something less intense…baseball.

Lunar Eclipse: October 27, 2004
The Boston Red Sox win the World Series

One of the most dramatic examples of eclipses in recent times occurred in autumn 2004, when the Boston Red Sox finally won the World Series after a lengthy history of heartbreaking defeats and close calls. The eclipse was occurring precisely *at the time the clinching game was being played.* For this analysis, we'll first explore the chart for the Boston Red Sox then we'll see the impact from the eclipse.

The Boston Red Sox first took the field (with a different nickname) on April 26, 1901 in Baltimore, MD, to play the Orioles. I was unable to find the time that the game began, so this chart is cast for 1pm, as day games were the norm then. Here are some of the highlights.

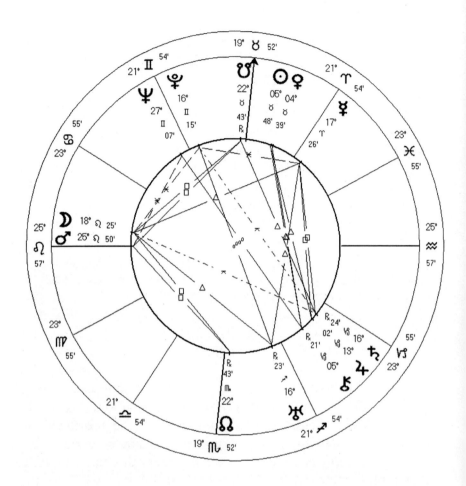

The chart has Mars conjunct Moon rising in Leo. There is an emotional hunger for competition and entertainment. This combination is colorful yet makes a fierce impact. The Red Sox have always been known for their personalities, charisma and drive.

The Sun is conjunct Venus in Taurus in the 9th House. Taurus speaks of the determination that typifies the team, while the 9th shows the continual travel. It's also noteworthy that the Red Sox have been like a religion (9th House) to some—the term "Red Sox Nation," shows a broad unity of purpose in the fan base.

234

Sun/Venus is trine Chiron/Jupiter/Saturn in the 5th House. This connects the life of the team with a tradition (Capricorn) of performance (5th) which includes an Achilles Heel (Chiron) or wound within the history. This Chiron hobbles through adversity, perhaps like Bill Buckner's error or Curt Schilling's wounded ankle. Jupiter/Saturn in Capricorn equates to the big business facets of the organization.

The South Node is in Taurus in the 10th House. This combines to yield a legacy of money and business and high expectations for success. Venus rules the South Node, which is tied into a history (trine to Chiron in Capricorn) of performance related struggle. Nevertheless, this is a strong profile that matches the Red Sox visibility and power as an organization.

Pluto resides in Gemini in the 10th House. This too indicates power, but also the psychological dynamics of ambition. Through the years of *almost* succeeding, this Pluto became more intense, wounded and ruthless. Located in Gemini, Red Sox Nation did become notorious for the verbal vitriol it unleashed on its opponents. This has been directed most notably at the rival New York Yankees with the frequent harangues ending with the declaration that the "Yankees Suck!"

Pluto is tightly opposed Uranus, which suggests the suddenness with which victory has been snatched from their grasp. So many times, unexpected heroics from opposing teams have crushed their dreams. This Uranus in the 4th also supports the deep-seated (4th) faith (Sagittarius) and alignment (Uranus) with the team despite its turmoil.

The North Node in Scorpio in the 4th House suggests that the optimal way to proceed is by continuing to stay rooted (4th) to the passion (Scorpio) and to heal the 10th House Pluto (which rules the North Node). Residing in Gemini, the Pluto puzzle is solved by intelligence and youth.

Boston hired Theo Epstein, who became the youngest general manager of a baseball team in history at the age of 28. He is known for his brilliance, hard work and fresh ideas. His chart (not shown) has quite an affinity with the Red Sox as his Sun

(Capricorn)/Mars (Taurus) trine sits directly on the Red Sox trines in the earth signs.

Most tellingly, this wonder kid has Jupiter/Venus in Aquarius trining the Red Sox Pluto in Gemini. His innovative managerial ideas enhanced and helped to overcome the wounded legacy of defeat. Jupiter/Venus brings a winning edge, as well as the gumption to try new blood. The trades and changes Epstein made to the team's roster put them over the top.

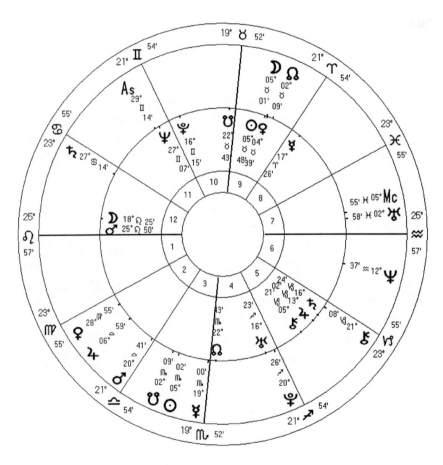

On the night of October 27th, 2004, there was a lunar eclipse during the clinching game of Boston's triumph. The biwheel shows the interplay of the eclipse with the Red Sox

236

chart. The eclipse was at 5 degrees Taurus, right on the Red Sox Sun/Venus. The Moon (past) disappeared to be reborn into the present, voiding the years of struggle to emerge victorious. The drama of the team reached an emotional climax, and faith (9th House) was finally rewarded.

The eclipse chart Mercury was conjunct the Red Sox's North Node suggesting that it was youthful brains and intellectual risks (Scorpio) that brought them the ultimate victory. Neptune is applying to a trine to the Red Sox 10th House Pluto, giving a boost of inspiration to the passion. At this time, Neptune was hitting Epstein's Jupiter/Venus conjunction in Aquarius.

The eclipse chart Pluto is within range of the Red Sox Pluto/Uranus opposition, allowing the metaphorical phoenix to rise from the ashes. Breakthrough was catalyzed by this Pluto as well as by the eclipse chart Uranus, which is sextile to the Red Sox Sun/Venus. This Uranus is in excellent condition in the Red Sox 7th House of "open enemies."

The eclipse chart Jupiter in Libra sits in the Red Sox's 2nd House, bringing good cheer, comfort and benefit. It also forms a square to Chiron's legacy of hobbling, stretching it to work hard (Capricorn) to realize success (Jupiter) and overcome adversity. The Red Sox were down 3 games to 0 to the Yankees and won the next 4 games of the playoffs, then won 4 straight games in the World Series. This was arguably the greatest comeback and winning streak in sports history. Finally, it was the Sox who snatched victory from the jaws of defeat.

Also note the eclipse chart Saturn occupying the Red Sox's 12th House. This Saturn in Cancer shows the emotional difficulties that are being dissolved and released (12th). This Saturn makes no aspects to the Red Sox chart and subsequently loses its hold.

The rest of the planets support the story, but the lunar eclipse sitting directly on the Red Sox's Sun was enough power to end the notorious and even celebrated "curse" that plagued the team. This is compelling testimony to how eclipses portend potential breakthrough from past inhibition and dramatic leaps into the present.

Chapter 11
Summation & Chart Examples

Understanding an astrology chart can be overwhelming. It's difficult to decide what level of importance to ascribe to all of the various factors. The focus of this book is to illustrate an astrological approach that addresses the major chart factors as a point of entry. The Sun, Moon and its Nodes all pertain to the luminaries, the lights in astrology and central players. After these factors are sufficiently grasped (including their aspects and house position), seeing the dispersal of energy through the angles and understanding the rest of the planets gives supporting information.

The Moon is how the soul feels. More than any other planet it conveys the inherent disposition of the soul. Understanding the Moon as a starting point provides the advantage of knowing where someone is coming from. What does the soul *need*? How has the spiritual journey been absorbed? How have emotional and attachment issues been handled? Getting a sense of a soul's vulnerability and unconscious survival strategies provides a foundation.

The condition of the Nodal axis reveals the spiritual or evolutionary lessons being addressed. The South Node points to habitual behavior patterns, natural inclinations, what is familiar and known. The overall condition of this symbol depicts a host of issues and circumstances which were pressing on the soul in its development. It provides a window into what has been.

The North Node is the antithesis. All of us have incarnated to grow and evolve, and by working toward the North

Node we complement and heal the reflexive pull of the more familiar South Node. The North Node points to the cutting edge of further development—in a sense, what the soul is striving to integrate to reach greater wholeness. Upon successful navigation of the Nodal lessons, the Moon becomes healed and integrated.

The Sun is the agent of awareness (light) and vitality (heat). It is a vehicle used by the soul in the current lifetime to energize the entire chart and serve as its centerpiece. By developing the Sun, we become who our souls intend for us to be. Souls are continually striving to reach greater levels of awareness and potency.

Both the North Node and the Sun do point to qualities that promote greater development. The difference is that the North Node is involved with the reconciliation of lessons connected with the drama of the South Node circumstances, while the Sun is a far broader statement of spiritual growth. Being the life force itself, it is the essence of what the incarnation intends to become. Similarly, both the South Node and the Moon are related to the past. The essential difference is that the Moon is pure feeling and pertains to contents in the emotional unconscious, while the South Node is far easier to apply language to, for it conveys situational factors and familiar ways the soul has approached the world.

The following chart examples will not be exhaustive; rather analyses will focus on the luminaries and the Nodal axis in the model described.

Paul McCartney

Former Beatle Sir Paul McCartney has a Leo Moon, quite fitting for an entertainer. His Moon resides in the 11th House, which is where we receive acclaim for our talents and recognition from a community or society. The 11th has a global focus, and those with the Moon here have a need to make a mark on the world. Paul is emotionally invested in doing this through performance and self-expression (Leo).

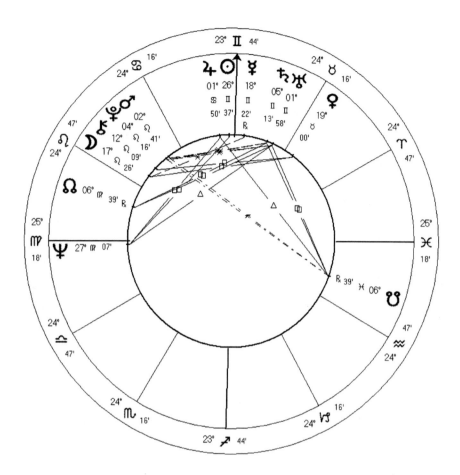

This Leo Moon is not altogether happy and contented. In
fact, there is reason to believe that great frustration is part of the
emotional unconscious. Chiron in Leo conjuncts the Moon
suggesting that a wound related to performance has been
experienced. The proximity of Chiron to both Pluto and Mars
provides additional information regarding the nature of the
wound. Pluto conjunct Mars in Leo shows tremendous frustration
and even anger—a thwarted will in the area of Leo pursuits. The
performer (Leo) was unable to reach an audience (Pluto, Chiron
in 11th) and feels great angst (Mars) and determination to fulfill
the lunar need.

241

Another facet to the lunar nature is the square to Venus in Taurus in the 8th House. The need for performance is challenged by relationship realities—possibly concerning money and security (Taurus) issues. Finding an audience is in stark conflict with the psychological dynamics (8th House) of relationships. Torn between self and other, the soul feels unresolved and restrained about achieving performance-related goals.

The Pisces South Node in the 6th House conveys more of the lessons and possible storyline. Pisces is sacrificial, impotent and dreams rather than manifests. It is soft, compassionate and connected to a vision of what could be. The 6th House pertains to work, service, hands-on tasks and feelings of subservience. This South Node depicts a profile of sacrifice and service—lots of long work days that likely took precedence over other pursuits. The soul is left only dreaming of a life devoid of such grueling responsibilities, and maybe gave up (Pisces) trying to break free of the restraints.

Saturn tightly squares the Nodal axis in the 9th House in Gemini. Both the 9th and Gemini are eager for freedom and a variety of experience, but Saturn is like a 600-pound weight of responsibility squashing the intention. Gemini wants to communicate, perhaps to teach—it also wants to sample life elsewhere on the planet (9th House). Paul's soul was probably stuck in a working-class (6th House South Node) predicament and Saturn's square to the Nodes indicates that striving toward expansion hangs in the balance of spiritual completion.

Uranus is conjunct Saturn and also involved. This leads one to believe that the soul was unable to reach its aspirations and feels unaligned with its truth. Besides the desire to see the world, there are education correlates here. It is quite possible that within the history of Paul's soul, there was blockage (Saturn) and removal (Uranus) from scholarly advancement—perhaps due to the sacrificial necessity to make ends meet. Pluto, and to a lesser extent, Mars, forms a quincunx to the South Node. This emphasizes the inability to successfully fulfill the aspirations of performing (Leo) and reaching an audience (11th). The Nodal dynamic is one of obligation preventing expansion.

Neptune in Virgo in the 1st House is the ruler of the South Node. It clearly supports the story derived by stating that the soul needed to act (1st House) in a sacrificial capacity (Neptune) with the processes of work, responsibility and humility (Virgo). Furthermore, Neptune squares Jupiter in Cancer in the 10th House. The sacrificial nature is connected with a moral imperative (Jupiter) to hold a position (10th) that serves the needs of the family (Cancer). The square speaks to the frustration the soul has with such a responsibility. Also note that this Jupiter forms a trine to the South Node, further indicating its centrality to the lessons being addressed. The trine suggests that the soul has this family-centered ethic well-established.

The North Node is in Virgo in the 12th House—a statement that the work is to now apply effort (Virgo) in the direction of release (12th), to sculpt the vision into something tangible. Paul's soul is interested in applying considerable effort (Virgo) to uplifting, inspirational and transcendent processes (12th House). Achieving the aims of this industrious yet transcendent North Node assists in healing the pent-up lunar disposition.

The ruler of the North Node is Mercury in Gemini in the 9th House—the method is to learn from all quarters of the globe, to sample many types of experiences, people and culture. If Paul can reclaim the Saturn and Uranus in Gemini, he then is able to be a teacher, writer or messenger of some type. This Mercury is conjunct the Gemini Sun in the 10th House, further bringing this intention to his biographical life and role in society.

What a gift to have a Gemini Sun conjunct Jupiter in the 10th House! This is a major intention to become visible, a personality larger than life, one with a message and a cheerful, buoyant spirit. Based on what has been discussed, there's no doubt that Paul has earned it. The present Sun is perfectly positioned to remedy the trials of the past. This is the life intention for leadership instead of servitude, travel instead of inertia, education and experience instead of lack, and diversity instead of drudgery.

The Sun is square to Neptune, which ideally brings the already established ability to sacrifice and work diligently to the present desire for expansion. There is also a sense of collective purpose when an outer planet is connected with public issues. Channeling a message (Gemini Sun) fueled by the loving and uplifting energy of Neptune ("All you need is love") is part of McCartney's contribution toward healing the collective. The challenge is not to lose oneself in a public role—not to allow others to define who he is.

Perhaps most importantly, actualizing the Sun remedies the frustrated lunar needs—it brings purpose and freshness to the present life. The performer (Leo Moon) can now reach a wide audience and spread a message (Gemini) of inspiration and good feeling (Jupiter in Cancer). The position in the lunar cycle is the waxing crescent, indicating that there is an upsurge of creative energy chomping at the bit. The related sign of the waxing crescent is Taurus, so Sun and Moon optimally partner by never giving up, staying committed with an eye toward the resources and abundance available.

Maya Angelou

Poet, inspiration and civil rights champion Maya Angelou has a Libra Moon in the 2nd House—part of her very constitution, her essential resource, is a desire for peace. What is most striking about this benevolent Moon is the slew of challenges it faces in feeling that level of contentment. This is a peaceful flower on the field of a raging battle.

Most striking is the square to the Moon from Pluto in the 11th in Cancer. This Pluto relates to clan (Cancer) and communal (11th) membership conditions that were intense and harmful to her heart and sense of stability. Just being who she was resulted in deleterious assaults from the world family. Dealing with racial discrimination is a leading possibility. Furthermore, Jupiter in Aries in the 8th House opposing her Moon suggests warlike themes that antagonize her tenderness. This Jupiter will fight (Aries) to the death (8th) for a purpose.

244

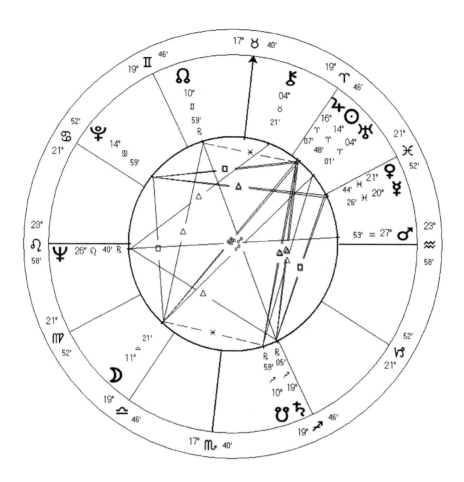

Uranus in Aries, also in the 8th House, is similarly opposed the Moon. This indicates that hostile (Aries) conditions beyond her control (Uranus) caused much wounding and psychological turmoil (8th House). On the list of possibilities is sexual trauma, emotional abuse or being in a setting of warfare.

The South Node suggests that the conflict endured was within the home or clan. It is in the 4th House and in Sagittarius, stating that the soul is familiar with a sense of righteousness or alignment with a particular set of beliefs to guide what is considered to be proper behavior. In fact, with Saturn in Sagittarius conjunct the South Node, the soul has been some sort

245

of religious authority or, at the minimum, it's used to having firm control within the family setting.

This Saturn is square both Venus and Mercury in Pisces in the 7th House (8th House cusp) indicating that relations and communication with a partner or others were filled with difficulty and trying lessons. (Having Mars also in the 7th speaks to lively conflict—in Aquarius it is erratic, unpredictable.) The Piscean quality to the Venus and Mercury suggests a proclivity for selflessness or surrender to the partner, being let down by others and a longing for a greater sense of intimate equality. There is sorrow in this area.

Jupiter rules the South Node and trines both the Saturn and the South Node from the 8th House. This suggests the willingness to fight for what she believes in. Her sense of passionate purpose has been an asset for the soul—however, it has caused much emotional strife as seen in its opposition to the Moon. The Saturn in Sagittarius is a compelling indication of rigidity in the face of conflict—the soul becomes walled in its own fortress of protection (4th). There is heaviness, repression and a legacy of tight-fisted control in hopes of weathering a storm.

The North Node is in Gemini in the 10th House. This is a soul intention to emerge from the fortress and assume the mantle of leadership in the world. Gemini is a sign of lightness and variety, desiring to branch out in new directions. This soul has undoubtedly seen its share of difficult experiences and is now interested in teaching and communicating its wisdom. Also, the emotional wounding and severity of themes displayed in this chart would lead us to think that the soul craves to rediscover the curiosity and fascination of youth (Gemini). Maya is learning to have a sense of wonder again.

The ruler of the North Node is the 7th House Mercury in Pisces, which is conjunct Venus and quite close to the 8th House cusp. The intention is to connect with others in a fluid, peaceful and spiritual fashion. Maya is teaching lessons of inspiration in a creative and imaginative style. On a personal level, she is also learning to forgive those who have harmed her, including the world itself, and to gain a clearer perspective.

The Sun pulls it all together. She is becoming bold, decisive and courageous (Aries), with a strong sense of mission (Sun conjunct Jupiter) and willing to enter her own darkness and challenge those who have wronged her (8th House). She is a physically as well as psychologically formidable adversary to anyone who seeks to inflict harm. Maya incarnates as a warrior, which may conflict with the peaceful Libra need, but done right it is the method to ultimately satisfy it. This soul has signed up to live fully and uncompromisingly.

The Moon is almost full in this chart, just about 3 degrees shy. It is abundantly displayed in all its emotional ripeness, and Maya is bound to make an impact on others. It is a waxing quincunx Moon, which is associated with Virgo. Working diligently with others to reach a state of completion and peace (Libra Moon) is part of this phase. She is to be industrious and active in managing emotional dynamics. This is a Moon of accountability. The Warrior (Aries Sun) fulfills the need for peace (Libra Moon) by tackling emotional dynamics in a responsible and thorough manner.

Salvador Dali

The surrealist, avant-garde artist has an Aries Moon one degree shy of the Midheaven. This is a most public Moon that is finishing up matters pertinent to the 9th House. Dali feels angry (Aries) about religious themes (9th) and how they have impacted his reputation and role in society (approaching the Midheaven). Having the Moon at the pinnacle of the chart often indicates early recognition and visibility, and in this case it somehow led to an emotional need to fight.

The Moon rules Neptune in Cancer in the 12th and is closely square to it. This indicates emotional loss, quite possibly of a familial nature. The appropriate nurturing from parental figures is likely missing, which has resulted in emotional desolation and abandonment issues. There is great sorrow along with the anger discussed earlier.

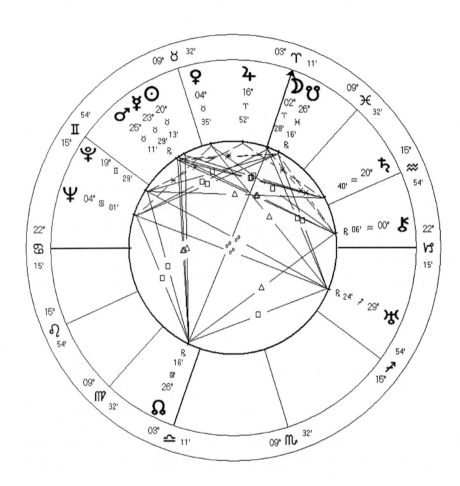

The Moon is also square Uranus in Sagittarius in the 6th House and, together with Neptune, forms a T-square. Uranus/Moon contacts classically equate to shock or trauma which sets up a frenzied and wild emotional structure. The inner life is wired, erratic and unstable. Here, the nature of the trauma is linked to dogmatic prescriptions (Sagittarius) of how young Salvador can improve himself (6th House). One possibility is feeling disempowered by religious intolerance.

The Moon is conjunct the South Node in the 9th House. This signals that religious themes are indeed a part of the karmic struggle. Dali *needed* (Moon) to be taken care of by religious authority, and his soul was convinced to give away its power (Pisces South Node) and make sacrifices for some philosophical/religious (9th) system. There is a highly developed sensitivity and receptivity to strict teachings. The indoctrination happened quite early in life and the result was abuse of some kind which has left his soul in an alarming state of anger and shock.

The severity of the dilemma is confirmed by Pluto's square to the Nodal axis. It is in the 12th House and in Gemini indicating that something secretive (12th House) and dark (Pluto) happened in his youth (Gemini) and wounded his innocence. Since the Moon is in Aries, which is ruled by Mars, a violation of a sexual nature is a possibility, but we can only speculate what form the abuse took. What is clear is that Dali's soul has a profound distrust of the world (Pluto in the 12th) and is likely to abandon faith altogether and react in unpredictable (Uranus) and dissociating ways (Neptune)—indeed, both are part of his biography. Neptune is the ruler of his South Node implying that the issue was played out in secret, perhaps at an institution or in some other place of confinement (12th House).

Dali is the lost soul who behaves as if there is nothing to lose, because everything is already gone. This did manifest as mental illness for his soul's present life. The link between sexual abuse and dissociation is well-founded. It is also not uncommon that such a scenario was delivered under the guise of a protective religion, which understandably leads to a complete rejection of faith and hope in the world.

The North Node is in Virgo in the 3rd House. The soul benefits by taking a hands-on and discerning (Virgo) look at what it has been taught (3rd). Instead of dissociation, Dali is to be grounded, precise and methodical about discovering a more informed understanding of reality. Dali is being sent back to school—his soul wants him to be an open and eager student (3rd House).

The ruler of the North Node is Mercury in Taurus in the 11th House—a most paradoxical statement. Clearly, Dali needs to be more grounded (Virgo North Node with ruler in Taurus). That established, he then applies the solid, secure and aesthetic (Taurus) curiosity into themes of a global and futuristic nature (11th) that provide a larger container for his reality.

Mercury is closely conjunct both the Sun and Mars indicating that tremendous energy and focus is on this goal. His very life force (Sun) and drive (Mars) are dedicated to grounding and giving color (Taurus) to the invisible realms that connect us all (11th). Since the Sun and Mars are so connected to the North Node ruler, it is natural for Dali to become involved in such pursuits. Without the stabilizing forces of earth (Taurus) he would likely succumb to further psychic obliteration. It is also noteworthy that Dali has Venus in Taurus in the 10th House—his "cosmic job description" is clearly within artistry. Connecting the past to the present would result in capturing the contents of religious iconography, disturbing psychic material, and all sorts of perplexing and baffling material into an artistic expression. The 11th House is also where we find our allies and sources of support—Dali is to find a new crowd.

The Sun (as well as Mercury) is tightly square Saturn in Aquarius in the 8th. This is another anchor (Saturn) to the life force and indicates an intention to apply effort and ingenuity (Aquarius) to probe the psychological and often dark territory of the 8th House. His work (Saturn) is to enter the mysterious and taboo (8th), discover brilliance there (Aquarius), and connect it back into his awareness and energy (Sun) to finally become comfortable (Taurus Sun) again. The pitfall is becoming a controlling authority, and eccentrically mad (Aquarius in the 8th). Dali's energy has the ability to frighten us like that of a maniacal clown—the higher intention is to portray the psyche in fascinating ways.

The lunar phase is the waning sextile, associated with Aquarius. This further emphasizes the Aquarian nature but also the necessity to dissolve the angry, upset and wounded Moon (Aries) to embrace the energy of comfort and serenity (Taurus).

The waning sextile encourages one to imagine the future and see that a new start is just ahead. It supports one to just "hang in there" and see the greater truth of the magnificently interconnected and intelligent universe that hosts us.

Princess Diana

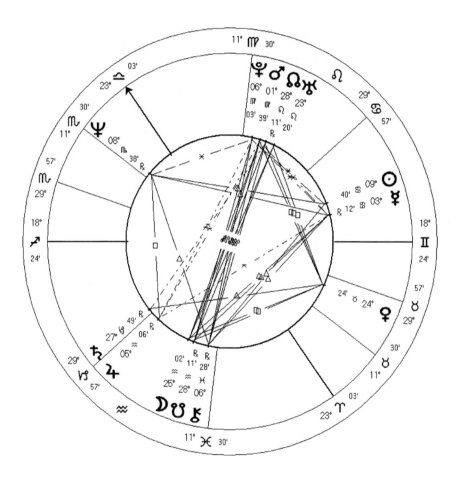

The Princess of Wales has an Aquarius Moon in the 2nd House. There is a legacy of emotional trauma or detachment (Aquarius)—a distancing from the inner self which likely resulted in an over-developed sense of caring for the collective.

251

The 2nd House pertains to issues of confidence, self-esteem and the resources we rely upon to assist us in feeling potent. It is ideally an area of stability, but the Aquarius Moon leads one to conclude that great instability, insecurity and likely trauma is evident in her soul—and the aspects to the Moon only emphasize this profile.

Most tellingly, her Uranus in Leo (which rules the Moon) forms a tight opposition to the Moon from the 8th House. A shock to her emotional system was delivered from the realm of deep intimacy and engagement with other souls. Uranus orbits beyond the parameters of Saturn, the status quo of operations. This suggests that attaining Leo qualities (openness, joy, spontaneity, trusting in life) was problematic and out of reach. Furthermore, the 8th is a house of power—and having an opposition to the tender Moon from this area evokes an image of struggle and conflict in feeling nurtured or respected by intimates.

Assuming positions of weakness or even subservience is further emphasized by the Moon's opposition to Mars (also in the 8th) and its conjunction with Chiron. Assertive, if not aggressive, energy opposed and threatened her. She has great sensitivity for the vulnerable and oppressed (Chiron in Pisces) since her own biography is one of dealing with harshness. Having Pluto also tied in with this configuration brings a dramatic and damaging level of severity. Pluto/Mars conjunct in the 8th illustrates that her natural drive, her sense of power and perhaps even her sexuality has been severely injured. Mars and Pluto being in Virgo suggest that she has internalized messages of subservience, like she has done something wrong.

The Moon is also square Venus in Taurus in the 5th House. Having successful attachments (Moon) in relationships (Venus) has been problematical. Her Moon profile suggests that Diana has been so acutely wounded and emotionally ravaged by encounters with intimate others that joy (5th House Venus) has become impossible. Her heart is in a state of distress and shock. Healing the Moon/Venus square brings her comfort and peace.

In this particular chart, the Moon is conjunct the South Node. Her past has been defined by lunar qualities (being nurturing and receptive) so she is naturally comfortable being a mother with a humanitarian (Aquarius) outlook. The Aquarian South Node indicates a pattern of removal or marginality, and its placement in the 2nd shows a vigilance and focus on bolstering a sense of worth and potency.

Uranus, the ruler of the South Node, resides in the 8th House—a pattern of relying on an intimate partner to feel secure is a dynamic she is attempting to change. Uranus opposes the South Node, indicating that she is inextricably connected to the very sources that cause her trauma—in a sense, dependent on them. Naturally aligned with the Moon, Diana's end of the deal was to be supportive and nurturing, and in a sense, powerless. The Moon conjunct a 2nd House South Node shows identification with traditionally feminine roles such as mothering or caretaking of some variety.

The North Node is in the 8th House in Leo. The soul is interested in experiencing joy, grandeur (Leo) and meaningful intimacy with others (8th House). The North Node is conjunct Uranus, Mars and Pluto—she is reclaiming her individuation, sexuality and power. The goal is to have complete authority over her choices (Mars, Pluto) and enter the psychological arena of intimacy (8th House) to work through (Virgo planets) issues in a healthy manner. She is evolving (North Node, Uranus) into a dynamic and engaged (Leo) seeker of truth and authenticity (8th House). Leo also has connotations of royalty.

The ruler of the North Node is the Sun itself, which is located in the 7th House and in Cancer. The 7th House is about equality, peaceful connection and diplomacy. Cancer shows a soul intention to get in touch with her heart, and learn how to share it openly with others (7th House). With a soul history riddled with power struggles, achieving a sense of equality is a healing method. Also, there is a history of emotional trauma and detachment, so recognizing her vulnerability and trusting others (7th House) is necessary for her growth.

The Sun is also trine Neptune in the 10th House. Her soul intends to sink deep into herself (Cancer) and to sustain a public role (10th) of a compassionate (Neptune) and healing (Scorpio) nature. She has already developed a humanitarian outlook (Moon, South Node in Aquarius) and now is the time to emotionalize (Neptune trine Sun) and take action (10th House) in support of her benevolent intentions. The Sun is conjunct Mercury indicating that being a spokesperson for emotional (Cancer) truths is necessary in both interpersonal (7th) and worldly (10th) arenas.

The lunar phase is the waning quincunx, which corresponds to the sign of Scorpio. This describes a visible Moon interested in conflict resolution. Although the Moon will always be in Aquarius, the lunar phase suggests that the action needed in the present lifetime is to charge the Moon with a more daring presence. The waning quality is about finishing emotional matters to eventually arrive at a place of completion and integration.

Dr. Martin Luther King Jr.

Reverend and civil rights leader Dr. King has his Pisces Moon in the 11th House. The feeling nature is soft, sensitive and wants to make the world a better place. There is a palpable sense of longing (Pisces) and maybe even sadness that the state of the world (11th) does not reflect what it possibly could be. An 11th House Moon has a public orientation, and the aspects to the Moon illustrate the conditions surrounding this public need.

First, the Moon is conjunct Venus in Pisces, also in the 11th. This Venus is social and active—interested in networking and building bridges within a community or society. There is an openness and intention to dissolve (Pisces) barriers among peoples. This relational nature (Venus) seeks to reach an idealized spiritual goal (Pisces). Together with the Moon we have a soul capable of beautiful, compassionate love for humanity. There is sweetness here—a dream (Pisces) that is uplifting and inspiring to those he meets.

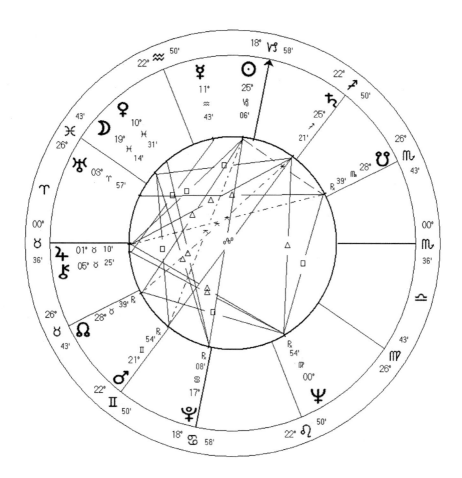

The Moon is a focal point of a T-square. Saturn in Sagittarius and Mars in Gemini oppose each other, and both square this sensitive Moon. The 9th House Saturn in Sagittarius alludes to claiming the mantle of authority (Saturn) on religious matters (Sagittarius, 9th), but this position is also a burden to his heart (Saturn square Moon). The religious work and role he assumes (Saturn) are emotionally resisted by this soul. The Piscean sensitivity would rather bask in love than be challenged.

The Moon's square to Mars (3rd House cusp) also points to resistance. The drive (Mars) is eager to pursue intellectual endeavors (Gemini, 3rd) but this too is in conflict with the more fluid Piscean nature—integration has been elusive in the karmic history. In fact, challenging aspects between the Moon and Mars often equate to unresolved issues of anger. There is a feeling of being thwarted and upset about directing the will. This is greatly emphasized by the Mars/Saturn opposition which shows an embattled and frustrated dynamic between assertion and restriction—self-determination (Mars) and obligation (Saturn) are at odds.

The Moon, however, is bolstered by a trine from Pluto in Cancer, late in the 3rd House. This gives the emotional temperament a perspective on collective change, rooted in a powerful deep-seated conviction (Pluto in Cancer). This soul is in touch with its own emotional drama involving tribe (Cancer) participation which is funneled into the collective humanitarian need for progress (Moon in 11th House).

King's Pluto is the ruler of the Scorpio South Node residing in the 8th House—an unambiguous statement about karmic familiarity with dramatic and volatile situations. He has seen his share of death, carnage and brutality and knows of the transformative power in such experiences. Considering that Pluto (ruler of the South Node) is trine the Moon, he has somehow been able to use this experience to garner emotional strength. In short, this soul has wisdom, the kind accrued only through involvement with the dark.

Neptune in Virgo in the 5th House squares the Nodal axis. One of the major lessons is to further develop the pristine (Virgo) spiritual (Neptune) impulse. The 5th House is frankly the house of having fun. The placement of such a key planet in this spontaneous and egocentric house may indicate shame (Virgo) about weak boundaries (Neptune) with his social desires (5th). Indeed, adultery is a well-known part of his biography—and impulses of this variety could also contribute to the dramatic and wounding nature of the South Node profile. King is learning humility (Virgo) and the ability to share (5th) his developed awareness of Spirit (Neptune) in the most proactive ways, instead of behaving selfishly, thereby alienating (Neptune) and hurting (Scorpio South Node) loved ones (in the 8th House).

Uranus in the 12th House in Aries forms a trine to the South Node. This suggests that his personal (Aries) connection with Spirit (12th) has been a source of awakening and growth (Uranus) for him in previous incarnations. He is aligned with Spirit like a warrior (Aries) for truth (Uranus). He is willing to sacrifice (12th) his free will (Aries) for a greater cause (Uranus)— which is exactly how he met his end (12th).

The North Node is in Taurus, located in the 2nd House. His soul wants a more comfortable and serene disposition. However, the route there runs through the public sphere since Venus, the North Node's ruler, is situated in the 11th and conjunct the Pisces Moon. This connects back to the resistance he has in fulfilling and acting in accordance with his public responsibilities, as indicated by the tension of the Saturn/Moon/Mars T-square. The soul is eager to use its interpersonal gifts (Venus) to inspire (Pisces) crowds (11th), which leads to societal change, thereby satisfying the need for greater calmness (Taurus North Node).

With a 10th House Capricorn Sun, King is being called in the present life to once and for all put aside any reservations and hold a highly visible leadership position (10th House)—one of strength and integrity (Capricorn). The Sun opposes the powerful Pluto, further linking his life force with a sense of mission and destiny rooted in the deep reservoir of soul experience. This opposition is a clear indication that he is to make a pronounced impact by channeling psychological truths through his very presence.

The Sun is also square Jupiter, positioned right on the Ascendant conjunct Chiron. The soul intent is to behave (1st) as a philosopher, teacher or spiritual/religious leader (Jupiter) in a solid, hands-on and practical (Taurus) manner, thereby attaining the need for peace. The conjunction with Chiron suggests that this truth-seeking and inspirational persona (Jupiter) will be connected to a weakened and beleaguered position struggling to find solace (Chiron in Taurus). Remarkably, Jupiter is in a Grand Trine configuration with Saturn and Neptune, bringing several components of his spirituality into direct behavioral manifestation (Jupiter in the 1st House). The Sun also forms a trine to the North Node, providing a smooth energy flow between the present life force and the prime lessons.

The lunar phase is a waxing crescent which provides the energetic boost to use the 11th House Piscean nature in grounded, unwavering ways (Taurus association). The mounting energy of the Moon is filled with its compassionate longings, thereby channeling an inner dream (Pisces) into something tangible to work on. This is a chart showing an incredible sense of mission— the story of a soul who chose to come to this Earth school to be a presence that would inspire and change the planet.

Shirley MacLaine

Actress and spiritual advocate Shirley MacLaine has a Virgo Moon in the 12th House conjunct Neptune. This combination speaks strongly about an emotional disposition of service, humility and surrender to Spirit. Virgo often feels small and strives for greater perfection, and here it's towards a spiritual ideal (12th House). This is a soul with a strong attachment to contemplative (12th, Neptune) practices (Virgo) and requires moments of retreat. This lunar profile also suggests possible loss, banishment or sadness underneath the inclinations to contact Spirit. Loneliness, upset or somehow feeling marginalized may be evident.

The Moon is square Chiron in Gemini in the 9th. This Chiron relates to her thinking (Gemini) about world views (9th). Shirley's heart (Moon) has been injured (Chiron) in relation to what she stands for (9th), which quite likely resulted in the 12th House sense of loss. She is learning to find ways to heal (Chiron) within religious settings (9th) and try to connect the contemplative need (12th House Moon) back to a more active and far-reaching scope (9th House).

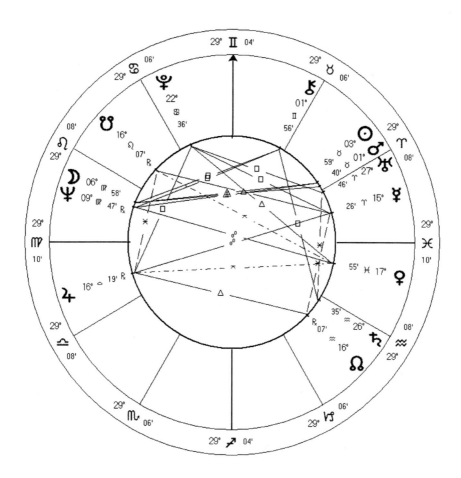

The South Node is in Leo in the 11th House indicating a celebrated (Leo) role and self-preoccupation within communal networks. Her soul has identified with a particular group of people (11th) which resulted in validation and reward (Leo). "I get my vitality (Leo) by being one of them (11th)," is part of the pattern.

Ruling the South Node is the Sun in Taurus in the 8th House conjunct Mars (Taurus) and Uranus (late Aries). This is quite a story! Shirley has been determined and obstinate (Taurus Sun) in the face of horrific consequences, possibly including death (8th). The Sun is aligned with Mars the warrior, also in Taurus, suggesting the same headstrong willingness to fight.

Violence is suggested by the attendance of Mars configured in the Nodal story, and clinched by Uranus (sudden) in Aries (battle, aggression) next to it.

Uranus orbits outside the perimeter of Saturn, the status quo. It represents something difficult to integrate, often introducing a shock to the system. It is beyond the immediate grasp of control and presents a "break" of some kind. It is my reading of this chart that her soul died in a shocking way by her own refusal to comply with the authorities that opposed her.

Indeed, Saturn in Aquarius opposes the South Node. Saturn, aligned with expectation, difficulty, control and authority, can be limiting, if not oppressive. This Saturn's residence in Aquarius suggests this tyrannical force lacked tolerance for individuation, unconventionality and non-conformity (Aquarius). Residing in the 5th House indicates that Shirley's soul was simply forbidden to express its uniqueness as it was a threat to the conventions of the day. As discussed, she chose not to comply with this and paid a heavy price. We can also understand the Moon/Neptune conjunction in the 12th, with its associations with removal, secretiveness and being in a downtrodden position (Virgo), in light of this information.

Jupiter in Libra in the 1st forms a sextile to the South Node. Her soul stood for and behaved (1st) according to a philosophy (Jupiter) of peace and harmony (Libra). In lieu of what appears to be formidable pressure, she held to a belief system that advocates mercy and fairness. Mercury in Aries trines the South Node and opposes Jupiter. One asset she has well-developed is the ability to speak (Mercury) for herself in a direct (Aries) manner to others (7th). Or said more bluntly, she's good at fighting with words. This ability may sometimes be at odds with her peaceful philosophy, and thus the opposition between Mercury and Jupiter. Shirley might say, "I just had to speak my truth, I couldn't bite my tongue! I hope they go easy on me because I'm a pacifist." She may have had a hand in her own troubles through a liberal usage of pointed quips.

Venus in Pisces in the 6th House tightly makes a quincunx to the South Node and is brought into the story. The 6th is a relational house, but pertains to connections of an unequal sort such as guru/disciple or mentor/apprentice. Venus is about connections of all varieties, including romantic, but also friends, acquaintances and associations. Pisces in the 6th equates to spiritual work and practices. One strong possibility is that Shirley's soul was involved in spiritual mentorship—considering the South Node is in Leo, she was likely a leader or star of the group (11th). Venus is opposed to the 12th House Neptune, further emphasizing the spiritual nature of such training. To connect it to the other pieces discussed, this training was surely frowned upon by the powers that be and was part of her battles.

The North Node is in Aquarius in the 5th House conjunct Saturn. The intention is to freely express (5th) individuality (Aquarius) and to become an expert (Saturn) on such matters. Instead of being defeated by authority, it's time to now be a progressive (Aquarius) leader (Saturn). Rising to the power and visibility of the North Node helps reconcile the more secretive or sheltered disposition of the 12th House Virgo Moon.

Uranus rules the North Node—its residence in Aries conjunct the 8th House Mars and Sun emphasizes the themes of aligning with power and becoming a formidable force. Interestingly, Uranus is tightly sextile Saturn, which links back to themes of assuming authority. Uranus is also square Pluto in Cancer in the 10th House. This brings the Uranian leadership (Aries) squarely into making a profound (Pluto) and heartfelt (Cancer) impact in a most public way (10th). Those with Pluto in the 10th tend to be agents of great change and evoke extreme reactions. The frictional aspect from Pluto to Uranus exponentially drives this home.

As the ruler of the South Node, the Sun is an integral part of the karmic story. It illustrates that her life force (Sun) was involved in conflict (conjunct Mars) in psychologically difficult arenas (8th) which likely resulted in death or major disturbance. The Sun is also about presence, and striving to embody its gifts is a major undertaking for the present lifetime. So Shirley is learning to become more comfortable and secure (Taurus) aligning with her strength (Mars) and individuality (Uranus). The main focus of this energy is in search of greater reserves of power, to explore the taboo and forbidden, and to engage passionately with other souls (8th). In a sense, she is picking up where she left off and now she is to find greater peace and tranquility (Taurus) as her karma is quite tumultuous.

The Sun forms a trine to the Moon. This soul clearly wants to strengthen and solidify spiritual proficiencies and to assume leadership intentions. The lunar phase is the waxing trine (Leo association) adding further spirited vitality and a playful quality. With such a heavy karmic profile, this phase stimulates the lively and outgoing qualities of Leo. This is observed most compellingly in Shirley's acting career as well as her often entertaining persona.

Dick Cheney

Vice President Cheney has a Pisces Moon situated in the 7th House revealing an emotional need to merge in joint purpose with others. Always with Pisces there is a tendency for selflessness—to be part of larger causes without the need for personal advantage. There may be confusion around understanding, or being in touch with, personal emotional concerns.

This Moon makes numerous aspects. Most compelling is the square to Mars in Sagittarius in the 4th House. This Mars speaks of a home life and/or psychic roots involved with fighting (Mars) for particular belief systems and global perceptions (Sagittarius). Moon/Mars hard aspects suggest unresolved anger or highly charged motivations. With Sagittarius involved, there is an emotional need to further a deep-seated (4th House) agenda.

The Moon makes quite a snug sextile to Uranus in Taurus in the 9th House. The emotional need is connected to a desire to find liberation (Uranus) through durable and fixed (Taurus) understandings of the world (9th House). Finding safety (Taurus) in some form of philosophical or religious system (9th House) has historically brought emotional (Moon) advancement (Uranus).

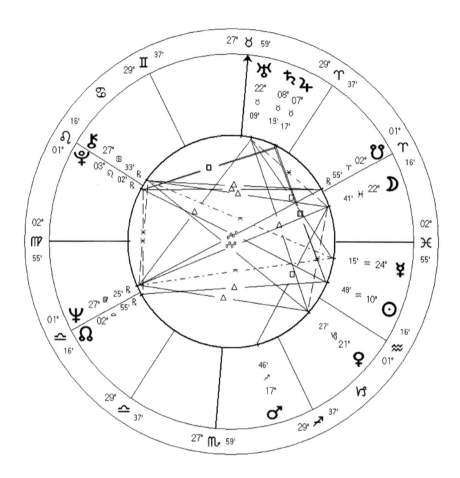

The Moon is also tightly sextile Venus in Capricorn in the 5th House repeating the need to join with others in conservative and work-related functions. Putting forth conventional or traditional (Capricorn) ideas of human interaction (Venus) is linked to this lunar need for partnership. The Moon is also opposed to Neptune in Virgo in the 1st House—a tendency to act (1st) with a degree of unconsciousness (Neptune) with his service intentions (Virgo).

The Moon's trine to Chiron in Cancer in the 11th rounds out the lunar profile. This aspect conveys an affiliation with emotionally nurturing (Cancer) groups and alliances (11th) that

263

support and accept (trine) any feelings of inadequacy (Chiron). Chiron in Cancer in the 11th House may also suggest emotional rejection from the world—perhaps by those who are not in his group.

The Moon is also in the neighborhood of the South Node which is positioned in Aries in the 8th House. Although we will interpret the South Node independently, the proximity to the Moon is noted. The emotional disposition is linked to the spiritual lessons being addressed. Another linkage of the lunar profile with the South Node is Mars, which squares the Moon, and serves as the ruler of the South Node.

The Aries South Node suggests lessons regarding volatility—possibly with roles in fighting (Aries) to the finish (8th). There is a willingness to courageously stand his ground within severe and psychologically charged scenarios. This profile can either suggest a soul responsible for brutality, or caught up in such circumstances. Mars in Sagittarius (described above) rules this South Node adding the storyline of deep-rooted (4th) religious/philosophical/political zeal (Sagittarius) contributing to conflict.

Pluto in Leo in the 12th House forms a close trine with the South Node. There is collaboration with this Pluto and how it contributed to his soul lessons. A 12th House Pluto concerns the absolute destruction (Pluto) of joy (Leo) within realms of loss, undoing and dissolution (12th). Themes of obliteration, power and irascible force emerge when connected to the bloody South Node. This Pluto conveys terror on a global scale (12th House). Furthermore, it's conjunct Chiron in Cancer in the 11th, emphasizing severe emotional wounding—noticeable on the world stage.

Neptune opposes the South Node, bringing a fascinating vector to consider. A 1st House Neptune in Virgo portrays a humble, selfless, thoughtful do-gooder. Cheney is moving *toward* this, once the South Node familiarity with violent or other disturbing settings is reconciled. This Neptune adds an element of grief—a plea for atonement and forgiveness. He is learning how to act (1st House) with humility (Neptune in Virgo).

The North Node resides in the 2nd House in the sign of Libra. Cheney's soul is learning how to ground the self (2nd) with peace, diplomacy and consideration (Libra). He is discovering the merits of tranquility and self-assurance—to develop the self-esteem (2nd House) to be friendly and courteous (Libra).

Ruling the North Node is Venus (Capricorn, 5th House). Here we see the intention to form connections based on trust and uprightness. This Venus is in aspect to the Moon and Uranus, so evolving this planet circles back to emotional healing (Moon) and finding a new (Uranus) way to understand life (9th House). Venus is also trine Neptune, linking these two peaceful and benevolent functions. In short, Cheney is softening—healing from the violent karma the South Node indicates.

Pluto makes a sextile to the North Node. The higher version of this Pluto is to transform power (Pluto) into surrender (12th) through an open-hearted (Leo) approach and temperament. Finding the joys of Spirit and feeling a part of the universal oneness (12th House), brings cleansing and soul advancement. Connecting this to the tranquil and secure Libra North Node is very much the idea. Also, Pluto conjuncts Chiron—making amends in regards to his role in the wider network (11th) and finding softness (Cancer) and healing (Chiron) through collaboration.

Finally, we arrive at the Sun. The present lifetime involves progressive (Aquarius) training (6th House). The intention is to humbly take concerted measures in learning how to care for the world family, our environment and all things that connect us all together. Having an eye toward future potentials, to envision how we can all contribute to evolution (Aquarius) is indicated. Cheney is to be on the front lines—to do his share in getting involved in humanitarian (Aquarius) projects (6th House). Growing into his Sun, he undoubtedly would be more liberal, maybe even radical (Aquarius).

The Sun is square both Jupiter and Saturn in Taurus in the 9th House. Connecting this charitable life force with religious, educational or political settings augments its scope and impact. Jupiter and Saturn are cautious, practical and somewhat conservative in Taurus. The square from the Aquarius Sun ideally electrifies and awakens the stultifying and material tendencies of the pairing. Without a *progressive* bolt from the Sun, the connection would simply give intellectually obstinate (Aquarius) energy to business (Taurus) and political/religious agendas (9th House).

In addition, the Sun opposes the 12th House Pluto. Getting in touch with transformative spiritual joy and sustenance is of major importance. A sub-optimal response to this aspect would renew power and manipulative (Pluto) tendencies within realms of secrecy (12th), thereby renewing the karmic struggle. Cheney is here to become more aware (Sun) of the wounding (Pluto) his soul has inflicted on the collective (12th). Without this awareness, the chances of replicating such brutality are quite substantial and horrifying.

The lunar phase corresponds to the waxing crescent, associated with Taurus. The Pisces Moon is given a burst of accelerating energy to connect with others (7th) in compassionate and collaborative ways (Pisces) ideally fueled by the progressive solar intention. The struggle would be to attain security through financial means (Taurus association) and to become headstrong about emotional growth.

Linda Lovelace (Linda Sue Boreman)

Adult movie star Linda Lovelace has a Taurus Moon in the 5th House. She has a need to feel comfortable and sensuous (Taurus) in sharing herself (5th) with others. This need becomes infused by the powerful, even dark, qualities of her 8th House Pluto which squares it. Having her Pluto in the sign of Leo brings in performance or playful connotations, but Pluto suggests a wound or disturbance in these processes. Her soul is learning to integrate the need for sensuality in reconciliation of psychosexual disturbance (Taurus Moon square 8th House Pluto). The potential to act out unconsciously is highly likely.

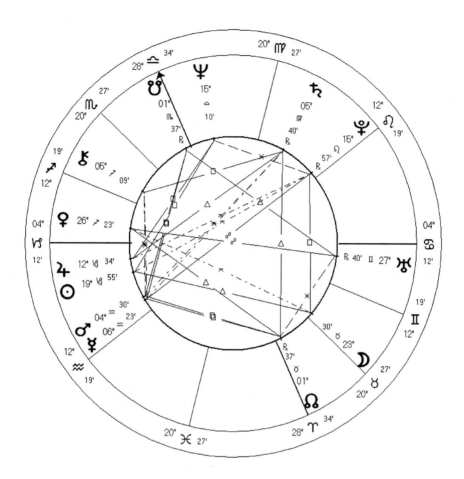

The South Node in Scorpio in the 10th House tells a shocking story of public illustration of the Pluto wounding. The soul is familiar with being seen, or having some kind of role and reputation (10th) with taboo subjects (Scorpio). Pluto of course rules the South Node from the 8th House, bringing her gravest soul wounds into plain view.

The Nodes are squared by the Mars/Mercury conjunction in Aquarius in the 1st House. A central lesson to integrate involves the communication (Mercury) of passions (Mars) of an unconventional (Aquarius) nature. Linda's sexual or driven (Mars) behavior (1st House) has tendencies to be detached or involving many partners (Aquarius), and her soul seeks to work on this. She was involved in spreading a message (Mercury) of this variety, which contributed to her karmic troubles. Messages of free love are not inherently evil, but if the behavior is an extension of unprocessed wounding material (8th House Pluto square Moon), one can see how the messages distanced (Aquarius) her from addressing underlying issues.

The North Node is in Taurus in the 4th House. Further growth is attained by becoming more comfortable and secure (Taurus) in moving inward (4th) and behaving in a more private way. Venus in Sagittarius in the 12th House rules the North Node. Part of the program is to find meaningful (Sagittarius) relationships (Venus) that are more contemplative (12th). This Venus is tightly opposed Uranus in Gemini in the 6th—indicating the soul desire to find a new way of relating (Uranus) based on humility, modesty (6th House) and proactive communication (Gemini). A less than optimal response to this Venus equates to having a variety of partners. Indeed, Uranus (opposed Venus) is trine the South Node and its rule-breaking relationship behavior is part of the karma to heal.

Saturn in Virgo in the 8th forms a trine to the North Node. If she can ardently work (Saturn) on psychologically difficult matters (8th) in a conscientious and thorough manner (Virgo), her growth is accelerated and given greater meaning. The flip side is a career (Saturn) being subservient and of service (Virgo) in intimate and taboo realms (8th House). This Saturn is closely quincunx her Mars, bringing her sexual behavior clearly into the mix.

The Sun is in Capricorn in the 1st House. The energy of the present incarnation involves taking personal responsibility (Capricorn) for behaving (1st House) with integrity. Linda's soul would like to embody a more conservative approach. Furthermore, the Sun is conjunct Jupiter, also in Capricorn. Finding a sense of spiritual purpose (Jupiter) rooted to more traditional modes of behavior (Capricorn) would be appropriate.

The Sun is also square Neptune in Libra in the 9th House—learning to find a spiritual (Neptune) relationship (Libra) path (9th) has reached a crisis point (square). The struggle of such a configuration is to have poor boundaries and identity confusion (Neptune) regarding partnering (Libra) and view them as sources of adventure and exploration (9th).

There is a trine between Sun and Moon. Bringing serious or more restrained (Capricorn) awareness into the lunar unconscious is part of her spiritual growth. The lesson may be that she doesn't have to display (5th) her sensuality (Taurus) so openly—her needs can ultimately become satisfied in more moderate or conventional (Capricorn) ways. Interestingly, the Sun makes a quincunx to Pluto, tying in the energy of presence directly with the gravest wound in her soul. This ideally fosters greater awareness of her Pluto and would lessen the proclivity to act out so unconsciously.

The lunar phase is the waxing trine, associated with Leo. This is quite an extraverted and playful Moon as it naturally resides in the 5th House. Considering that her soul is quite wounded (Pluto square Moon), getting back to a place of contentment about life (Leo association) is necessary. Linda's soul ultimately wants her to have peaceful (Taurus) and loving (Moon) connections but to incorporate the Capricorn sense of integrity and boundaries. It seems that Linda had some difficulty rising to the promise of her Sun and seemed to behave in accordance with her instinctual disposition (Moon square Pluto). As a result, the Leo association of the lunar phase injected more of a playful (even performance) quality to her innate disposition.

Dane Rudhyar

Finally, we explore the chart of 20th Century pioneering astrologer Dane Rudhyar, whose influence on modern astrology is enormous. Rudhyar has an Aquarius Moon in the 2nd House. The emotional disposition is troubled, out of touch, free-spirited with a need to be different. The Moon's residence in the 2nd indicates a lack of confidence in and security to exercise the freedom impulse—perhaps he does not feel grounded to a solid foundation.

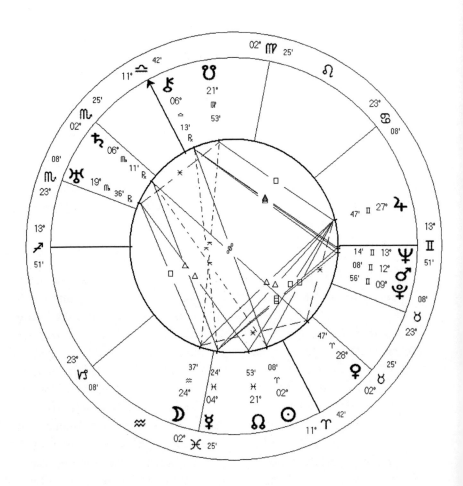

The dominant aspect to the Moon is a square from Uranus in Scorpio in the 11th House, which also rules it. This emphasizes turbulence or emotional shock to the system from outside sources (11th) that left psychic hurt (Scorpio). The 11th is a house of reception, of being appreciated by the larger world. Rudhyar's soul may not feel emotionally cared for by those he affiliates with. The work is to find new ways to relate (Aquarius) and a group (11th) where he can assert his individuality (Uranus) in powerful (Scorpio) ways.

The Moon is trine Jupiter in Gemini in the 7th, describing a considerable social need to communicate and exchange ideas with others. This is somebody who loves company and likely seeks many friends for intellectual stimulation.

The Moon makes a rather tight quincunx to the Virgo South Node in the 9th. This South Node describes apprenticeships or positions of subservience—industriousness and dedication (Virgo) within contexts of theological or philosophical speculation (9th House). Following some form of doctrine is likely. The emotional need for freedom (Aquarius Moon) has been frustrated. The belief system (9th) he learned may not have been emotionally nurturing for him and led to the paradoxes and disturbances in his Moon.

Nevertheless, the sextile from Uranus to the South Node suggests that his group membership brought a certain degree of support for his growth, albeit the square to the Moon (from Uranus) tells us it wasn't an emotionally easy association. Viewed in bright light, Uranus speaks of deep investigative questioning (Scorpio) within systematic and transpersonal frameworks (11th). There was likely a rigid code to follow (Virgo South Node in the 9th) that could have contributed to his sense of being controlled or manipulated (Scorpio) by his group (11th).

Jupiter is square the Nodal axis. This philosophical energy (Jupiter) asks lots of questions (Gemini) and is prone to follow the lead of others (7th House) to arrive at a belief system (Jupiter). The internal need for individuation (Aquarius Moon) did not have the confidence (2nd) to deviate. Reclaiming philosophical authority (Jupiter) is in the evolutionary crossroads (square the Nodes).

Ruling the South Node is Mercury in Pisces in the 3rd House. Rudhyar's mind was far more spacious, non-linear and contemplative than those of his contemporaries and teachers. The mind of a mystic was trapped in service to a narrower religious ideal (Virgo in the 9th). Mercury is square Pluto in the 6th House further emphasizing wounding (Pluto) around intellectual pursuits (Gemini) from positions of apprenticeship (6th House). How frustrating to be more advanced spiritually, but operating from positions of less power! Pluto is conjunct both Mars and Neptune in Gemini further adding angst (Mars) and disillusionment (Neptune) with available learning processes (Gemini).

Furthermore, Mercury is quincunx Chiron in Libra in the 9th House. His mind was unable to integrate peacefully (Libra) in a religious setting (9th) thus a nagging wound (Chiron). The task here is to arrive at a more cooperative (Libra) relationship and ultimately heal the intellectual upset. Rudhyar was bolstered by a studious and disciplined approached to his studies as witnessed by the trine from Saturn in Scorpio to Mercury.

Although Mercury is in free-flowing Pisces, this trine from Saturn not only grounds, but deepens (Scorpio) the intellect. Positioned in the 11th, it illustrates a determination to find the truth (Scorpio) of the underlying laws of the universe (11th). The relatively loose trine from Mercury to Jupiter further emphasizes the expansive thinking and perhaps an inclination toward verbosity.

The North Node is in Pisces in the 3rd House—a clear intention to continue developing the contemplative (Pisces) mindset (3rd) on his own terms. He is moving away from the stuffiness of the South Node and into the limitless fascination and speculation of the North.

The ruler of the North Node gives more information about how the soul wants to advance. Ruling the Pisces North Node is Neptune in Gemini, right on the 7th House cusp. Rudhyar needs to connect with (7th) and learn from (Gemini) more mystically-minded (Neptune) allies. We can never do the 7th House alone—it is incumbent upon him to discover the right people who can assist him. Furthermore, Neptune is conjunct Mars and Pluto (both in Gemini) in the 6th House. This involves the need to participate actively (Mars) and transform (Pluto) intellectual wounding (Gemini) by a concerted program (6th) toward that goal. He then becomes a powerful (Pluto) spiritual (Neptune) leader (Mars) and mentor (6th).

The proximity of Neptune to Pluto (which is square Mercury) further emphasizes the necessity to heal an intellectual wound. With this chart, it would be easy for Rudhyar to have an enormous chip on his shoulder, which would stifle growth. The possibilities of the Neptune/Pluto conjunction are considerable. Rudhyar has access to far-reaching intellectual realms the rest of us can only dream of. Adding Mars to the mix brings power and determination to reap the benefits. Also of note is the trine of the (Mars, Pluto, Neptune) stellium to the 9th House Chiron—by accessing his spiritual power he makes amends with organized religion or whatever 9th House setting the South Node represents for him.

The Sun is in Aries in the 3rd House confirming themes of intellectual leadership. Rudhyar is perfectly positioned to bring awareness and energy into developing his intellect on his terms, rather than following (South Node in Virgo) the program of an institution or religion (9th). The aspects to the Sun are most interesting.

The Aries Sun is square Jupiter, stating the intention to become a philosopher (Jupiter) who teaches (Gemini) others (7th). Whereas the South Node pointed to subservience and adherence to a doctrine, this aspect shows maturation into a leader and teacher. The Sun is quincunx Saturn, further supporting a desire to become a powerful (Scorpio) authority (Saturn) in a community (11th). The Sun is also opposed Chiron, connecting the life force back to religious settings to integrate the wound into his very essence. Rudhyar's work may potentially bring philosophical peace, not only to himself, but to others with similar wounds. (It's also worth noting that the Sun is not too far away from the Nodal axis, though including further analysis of this would be repetitious).

The lunar phase is the waning sextile, associated with Aquarius. The Moon is gradually dissolving and conceiving a vision of a new day. The emotional trauma is ready to let go, and through that process, maintain and strengthen its progressive need. This phase concerns the future, the alternative, the bravado to conceive of the impossible. Of course Rudhyar chose astrology, the pinnacle of Aquarian systematic thinking, to become a leader (Aries) in intellectual pursuits (3rd House).

Afterward

The development of consciousness is the central act of evolution. In everything we may encounter, there is a continuum of possibilities dependent on how energetically attuned and mindful we are. Our Suns have unlimited available wattage, incredible potential to be fully present.

The Moon grounds us to incarnated life as imperfect beings, vulnerable and beautiful, constantly absorbing life. Like flowers that sprout from seeds, we evolve from the base of our spiritual experiences, integrating awareness and vitality into the soul, transforming doubt into wonder.

The eternal lunar cycle reminds us of the interplay of darkness and light, the ebb and flow of life. As the Moon waxes toward fullness, cycles back and diminishes—we are born with eagerness, only to eventually perish. Are we resigned to an alarming fate, or emboldened to grow and maximize our potential? As the waning crescent Moon sheds its final tear, a ready new one is being born. As creations of this universe who reflect its design—we too are born yet again.

Located on this spherical wonder of a planet in this most hospitable solar system, it is the Sun, the eternal life force, that gives our spiritual journeys perspective. Everything encircles this brilliant sustainer of life. All of us are warmed and given light by which to see. Its power is obvious but mysterious; catch a glance, but only fools stare too long. Use its gifts, but do not sit idly, for time is a most impatient companion.

Stepping onward through the day and night, clarity gradually sharpens. All is changing, adapting, transforming. Life is evolving, reaching up to this source of radiance in a continual process of photosynthesis. A crescendo builds to spiritual realization.

And the flower absorbs the benevolent sunshine and feels a shift. The roots that connect to ancient memories maintain their strength, but adapt to the freshness of a new day. In every splendid and fragile moment the alchemy continues. With resistance or acceptance, we are pulled forward. Through acceptance and informed motion, we realize our true essence. We live to narrow the gap between past and presence, contemplating the lights in the reflection of sky. Traveling through starfields straight to the heart of the Sun, all of our yearning...returns home.

Regarding charts used:

Birth information for all charts used is consistent with Astrodatabank, except in the following instances:

Oprah Winfrey: Astrodatabank's 4:30 a.m. time is "from memory," not the birth record. On Oprah's talk-show, a "life-clock" that illustrates the exact amount of time a person has before reaching 80 years old was demonstrated. From the programming of the "life-clock" on a particular show, a birth time of 7:50 p.m. was later calculated by several mathematicians.

Tom Cruise: www.Astrotheme.com lists 12:05 p.m. Astrodatabank lists 12 p.m. (unknown).

Saddam Hussein: www.Astrotheme.com lists 7:05 a.m. Astrodatabank lists 12 p.m. (unknown).

Dr. Martin Luther King: His precise birth time is unknown. Sources from his family state, "about noon," and 12 p.m. is the time most frequently used. Jim Lewis performed a rectification and arrived at 11:21 a.m., which is used here.

All charts are cast using Porphyry house system.

Acknowledgements

I had the privilege of doing intensive *soul-work* with Josh Levin during the writing of this book. Shining awareness and being present to my dimly-lit lunar crevices was the perfect complement to this writing—not to mention transforming my life! Thank you.

Thanks to my editor, Judith Crawford, for your skill and wit. To Evelyn Terranova: you did a superb job with the cover art—thank you "big sis!" Thanks to Steven Forrest for being an incredible mentor and for providing such a nice "blurb." I also greatly appreciate Demetra George and Rick Levine for their kind and thoughtful words for the cover. Bill Streett, thank you so much for website design/support and friendship.

I also want to acknowledge the support I've received from others in the astrology community including: Robert Blaschke, Kelly Lee Phipps, Jeff Jawer, Mary Plumb, Laura Gerking, Donna Van Toen, Maurice Fernandez, Moses Siregar, Greg Bogart, Annie Banks, Robin Manteris, Phillip Sedgwick, Jane Martin, Danielle England, Stephanie Clement, Rocky Mountain Astrologers, The Association of Young Astrologers, members of the Steven Forrest Apprenticeship Program, The Mountain Astrologer, Dell Horoscope and Considerations.

Thanks to Lisa Lawless for graphic design, Sarah Myers and Barbara Edwardson for assistance with the final production, and Maria Jekic for Aquarian inspiration. Many thanks to all the clients and students I've worked with—you have made me the astrologer I am. Finally, thanks to my family and friends for your love and support.

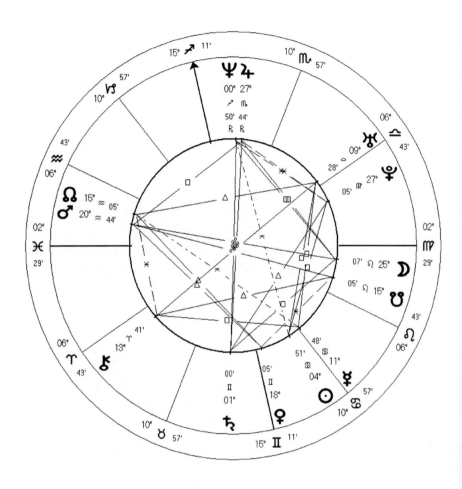

Eric Meyers
June 26, 1971
11:29 p.m.
New Haven, CT

CPSIA information can be obtained at www.ICGtesting.com
Printed in the USA
LVOW081922071011

249618LV00001B/85/A